KU-784-376

CONTENTS

Author

Patrick Keatinge is Jean Monnet Professor of European Integration at Trinity College Dublin. He is a Member of the Royal Irish Academy, and was a founder-member of the Academy's National Committee for the Study of International Affairs, the Irish Committee for Contemporary European Studies and the Institute of European Affairs (IEA). He was Senior Research Fellow at the IEA from 1993 to 1996. His academic interests include international relations, European security and Irish foreign policy. He edited *Studies in European Union 1: Political Union* (1991) and *Maastricht and Ireland: What the Treaty Means* (1992) for the IEA, and wrote the IEA interim report *Towards a Safer Europe — Small State Security Policies and the European Union: Implications for Ireland* (1995). Professor Keatinge has written, edited and contributed to a number of books on Irish foreign policy and European affairs.

■ PREFACE

The pace of change in public affairs has increased in many ways since Ireland joined the European Community nearly twenty-five years ago, but in no respect has this been more evident than in the extraordinary series of events following the collapse of communism in Europe at the beginning of this decade. No European country, and few outside Europe, has remained untouched by the sudden disappearance of what had seemed an immutable fact of political life; in conjunction with other facets of rapid change, especially those arising from the globalisation of economic forces, the end of the Cold War has faced governments with a major challenge of adaptation.

One aspect of this adaptation involves a return to an old problem, that of European security. For the third time this century we have returned to the drawing board, to devise ways in which European states can coexist without the threat of resort to force in their dealings with each other. On this occasion, the prognosis is more encouraging than it was in 1919 or 1945, largely because some of the lessons so painfully learned in two world wars have been applied over forty years of a deliberate strategy of political and economic integration between states in western Europe. It would be foolhardy to claim, however, that successful adaptation is assured. On the contrary, the current debate about "Europe" suggests there are considerable difficulties in finding our bearings in this more complex and uncertain world.

This book has two broad aims. The first is to identify the main challenges to the international security of European countries, and to examine how the process of European integration, through the agency of the European Union, is itself being adapted to meet these challenges. The focus here is on the way in which security policy is being reassessed in the Union's Intergovernmental Conference, and on the different positions being pursued by the member states.

The second aim is to analyse the position of a particular member state, Ireland, and to explore the issues its government and people face in adapting to a changing security environment. Ireland's balance of advantage as a member state has hitherto been quite clear in terms of economic and social policy, but it has been outside the mainstream of policy debates on European security. One effect of its experience as a neutral state — which, unlike the other neutrals, was marginal to the Cold War confrontation — has been a neglect in the public domain of some of the questions which now arise in the context of policy adaptation.

The preparation of the book was assisted by discussions in the Institute of European Affairs' working group on security policy, chaired by Mr. Peter Barry TD. I am very grateful for the support, and often detailed comments on draft chapters, by members of the group, who were extremely generous with their time and expertise. As might be expected on a subject of this nature, their interpretations and opinions varied, and the book does not attempt to be a statement of consensus. I remain wholly responsible for its conclusions and for any errors of fact.

Much of the research for this project took the form of discussions and interviews held over the past three years with officials from foreign and defence ministries, politicians, journalists and academic colleagues from most European countries. Their embassies in Dublin have always been helpful in providing information and access to their own governments. I am especially indebted to those officials in the Department of Foreign Affairs who, in spite of long hours at the "coal face" of adaptation, have always been most generous with their time.

Finally I must thank my colleagues at the Institute of European Affairs. Brendan Halligan has been a constant motivator and active participant in this project, and I have received every encouragement from Brian Farrell and Terry Stuart. Odran Reid and his staff have sustained the impetus of the working group, Myles Geiran and Sheila O'Sullivan have been assiduous researchers and Iain MacAulay, Finbarr O'Shea and Helen Litton have brought the text to publication.

Patrick Keatinge

August, 1996.

■ INTRODUCTION

The question of international security, together with its military component "defence policy", is one of the main concerns of the European Union's Intergovernmental Conference (IGC) which was launched on 29 March 1996 in Turin. Ten years ago such an item would have evoked images of the antagonism between two incompatible worlds, condemned to an uneasy relationship which varied between the threat of nuclear annihilation and a grudging coexistence. A different situation confronts the participants in the IGC. The duel between the superpowers has been called off, yet it cannot be said that Europe is secure. The police states of the former communist empire have been replaced by the uncertainties of fundamental political and economic transition; where political violence has erupted, in the Balkans and the Caucasus, it has claimed a greater loss of life in five years than was experienced during four decades of Cold War partition in Europe; organised crime and environmental degradation show scant regard for more open borders.

The Treaty on European Union (TEU), agreed at Maastricht in 1991, includes among its objectives a determination to "strengthen the security of the Union and its Member States in all ways" and to "preserve peace and strengthen international security, in accordance with the principles of the United Nations Charter as well as the principles of the Helsinki Final Act and the Paris Charter" (TEU, Article J 1.2). Yet what do these aspirations mean in practice in the post-Cold War world, with its profusion of new challenges?

In particular, European governments and peoples are faced with a question of fundamental moral and political significance. Where does the responsibility to meet these challenges lie — with the European Union as such, with its individual member states, or indeed with the many other European states which are associated with the Union? When one of the effects of increased transnational crime is the scourge of drugs on the streets of Dublin, the relevance of collective action is clear enough for the citizens of Ireland, but what is the extent of Ireland's responsibility for supporting economic transition in Poland, or keeping a precarious peace in Bosnia?

THE IEA PROJECT ON EUROPEAN SECURITY

In 1993 the Institute of European Affairs (IEA) established a project on European security, with the aim of improving the level of information on these matters and clarifying the strategic choices facing the Irish government in the IGC. During the Cold War the security debate, which was predominantly influenced by military considerations, lay outside the political scope of both the European Community and neutral Ireland. Hence many of the debates about security policy — and indeed the language in which they were conducted — were unfamiliar to both politicians and public in a country accustomed to seeing EC membership primarily in economic terms. But the changing security agenda since 1989 emphasised the need to come to grips with this neglected dimension of public policy.

An interim report was published early in 1995 (Keatinge, 1995). In order to provide a comparative context in which Ireland's predicament might be more clearly understood, it analysed the positions and policies of other small European states as they attempted to adapt to a more open but much less stable European order. It concluded that, for Ireland, the 1996 IGC was an opportunity to clarify positions on the new challenges of European security. However, it would thereby raise the awkward question of defence in a more politically visible, and hence unavoidable, way than at any previous stage of the country's involvement in European integration. Whatever course was followed by the Irish government and people with regard to military commitments, on the broader question of security, particularly in central and eastern Europe, there would be no cost-free choices. Ireland, like other relatively secure states, would be expected to contribute to the stability of Europe as a whole.

This book represents the IEA's final report on European security, carrying the analysis forward to the opening phase of the Intergovernmental Conference. It covers three broad themes:

* the continuing changes in the unstable security environment

* the proposals for changes in the EU's role in international security policy, covering the existing procedures for a common foreign policy and the development of a common defence policy

* the questions arising from the IGC for the Irish government and people.

THE NATURE OF SECURITY POLICY

The book is based on the usage of the term "security policy" which was adopted in the IEA's interim report, and is presented here in summarised form. Readers interested in a more detailed discussion should turn to Appendix I.

The concept of security is seen as going beyond the classical threat to the state's sovereignty and territorial integrity arising from military intervention by another state. That contingency has not disappeared, but lies at one end of a broad policy spectrum. The increasing complexity of relations between states, including the blurring of traditional distinctions between the international and the internal dimensions of politics, requires a more comprehensive analysis which potentially includes almost the whole range of governmental activity. However, in order to establish a manageable focus on this extensive subject-matter, the book concentrates on the international security policy of the relevant political authorities. Security policy, then, is defined as *measures taken by governments and international organisations to promote political stability and to avoid, or at least mitigate the effects of, political violence.*

Three broad functional dimensions of security policy are used throughout — *prevention, protection* and *crisis management.*

Figure 1: Functional Dimensions of Security Policy

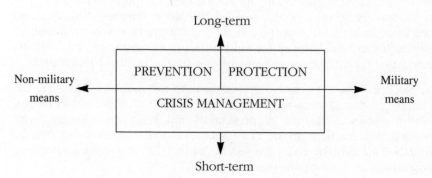

3

The first approach, *prevention*, recognises that stability, once achieved, cannot be taken for granted. It must allow for the existence of latent conflicts, but aims for a process of peaceful change in which, over time, the interests and even the identities of the contending groups may become compatible. It emphasises measures to prevent potential conflicts arising. Prevention implies policies of reassurance, confidence-building and inclusiveness; the policy instruments to be employed are those of persuasion rather than coercion. The preventive approach is often encapsulated in the notion of "civilian power". In the long term, it is hoped that the patient pursuit of preventive measures may establish the basis for a more ambitious collective security system.

The second approach, *protection*, is also a long-term strategy. Assuming the eventual success of preventive security cannot always be guaranteed, provision must be made to deal with military threats of a traditional kind. Given the increasing costs of military policy instruments, collective defence measures may be agreed among groups of like-minded states in order to deter potential adversaries.

Crisis management, on the other hand, concerns immediate responses to actual challenges. In the short term, preventive measures may prove inadequate. Where violent conflict occurs the goal is to intervene in order to bring collective resources to bear on settling disputes if possible, but if not at least containing them and mitigating their negative effects. International crisis management may involve almost the whole spectrum of policy instruments, from persuasion to coercion, available to states and international organisations.

Deciding the appropriate mix of policies for crisis management, and ensuring their implementation, are among the most problematic aspects of contemporary security policy. Conflict resolution requires mediation and economic inducement, but agreements may have to be enforced by military means. It can be as difficult for third parties to agree on the compatibility, extent and timing of these measures as it is for disputants to accept them.

In practice these three broad approaches are not mutually exclusive; the critical question is what weight to accord to each. The present European system shows a balance of prevention and crisis management, with protection in the background as an insurance policy of last resort. It is far from being a genuine collective security system, but may be described as a *cooperative security regime* (see chapter 2).

INTERNATIONAL AND INTERNAL SECURITY

It is often remarked that traditional distinctions between "international security" (involving conflicts between states) and "internal security" (to do with conflicts within states) have become blurred. Thus most of the conflicts of the post-Cold War era have been primarily internal in their origins (the Gulf crisis of 1990–91 being a notable exception), though their effects have rarely been contained within the boundaries of one state. Security policy, as seen in this book, has to do with both the relations between states and the internal politics of, in particular, the most insecure of European states. The effects of insecurity in one context are all too easily felt in the other. However, the ways in which the European Union and its member states deal with *their* internal security (both collectively and nationally) is not examined in detail here; that will be the subject of a separate IEA report on the "third pillar" of the Treaty on European Union, covering justice and home affairs.

PLAN OF THE BOOK

Part I revisits the complex and still rapidly changing *security environment* which succeeded the certainties of the Cold War at the beginning of the 1990s. At the risk of oversimplification this was described as a "tentative cooperative security regime" in the IEA's interim report, reflecting the situation at the end of 1994.

Since then, much has happened. Chapter 1 describes the continuing instability of the international system. Attempts to stabilise post-communist Europe continue uneasily, between the competing claims of a resentful Russia and its former satellites in central and eastern Europe. The beginnings of a more concerted approach to security in the Mediterranean region have been made, against the background of violent challenges to the Arab–Israeli peace process. Global developments vary between the hopeful (such as further steps towards nuclear non-proliferation), the disturbing (tensions arising from China's role as an Asian power) and despair (the threat of further genocide in central Africa). Above all, the immediate test for European security is the crisis in Bosnia, which has been transformed from an intractable and vicious armed conflict to a precarious peace process.

In trying to assess the significance of these events, chapter 2 asks to what extent a "cooperative security regime" has been established. The analysis focuses on the strengths and weaknesses of political leadership by the major states. This, it is argued, depends to a large extent on their domestic political base. Neither in the case of the United States, nor with regard to the EU "triumvirate" of large member states (Germany, France and the United Kingdom), is it possible to be wholly confident of the prospects of consolidating the overall security regime in a significant way. Thus the multilateral security organisations through which they channel their collective efforts, while experiencing continuing evolution in their roles, still fall short of representing a credible "international community". Of three alternative scenarios outlined in this chapter, the current position approximates that of a "tentative cooperative security regime".

Part II looks in detail at the *security policy of the European Union*. Although it is not exclusively a security organisation, the EU, following the example of the European Community in western Europe, arguably has the potential for a central role in the creation of a more satisfactory security regime. Whether this potential is realised will depend in part on the outcome of the Intergovernmental Conference, in conjunction with the success or otherwise of its actual policies.

Chapter 3 identifies the range of proposed changes which have already emerged in the IGC. These concern the existing procedures of the EU's Common Foreign and Security Policy (CFSP), in which maximalist positions envisage some form of majority voting. They also include the more general commitment in the Maastricht Treaty to devise "a common defence policy, which might in time lead to a common defence" (TEU, Article J 4.1), and which would involve the Western European Union (WEU). The range of options for an EU–WEU relationship vary from one of minimal change, through forms of differentiated commitment in which member states are not required to become full members of the WEU, to an eventual merger of the two bodies. However, decision-making in this field will remain the prerogative of national governments.

The examination of this "blueprinting process" also includes an assessment of the preliminary national positions of the member states. For this purpose, three categories of member states are treated separately. Chapter 4 covers the group of larger countries — France, Germany, Italy, Spain and the United Kingdom — from which the most influential proposals may be expected. Germany is the major source of proposals for maximalist reform, supported by Italy and Spain but less clearly by France in a joint Franco-German approach. The British position is at the other end of the spectrum.

So far as security policy is concerned, the remaining ten smaller member states fall into two subdivisions — those which are full members of the WEU (Belgium, Greece, Luxembourg, the Netherlands and Portugal) and those which are WEU observers (Austria, Denmark, Finland, Ireland and Sweden). Chapter 5 summarises the positions of the first group, in which the Benelux countries especially favour maximalist changes. Chapter 6 demonstrates the reservations still held by the WEU observer countries about full membership of that body, and their generally cautious approach to reform of the procedures of the CFSP. However, there is also a willingness to develop the

WEU as a framework for their participation in international crisis management, on a case-by-case basis; this is seen particularly in a joint Finnish–Swedish proposal.

Given the range of national positions at the beginning of the IGC, it is argued in chapter 7 that it is difficult to envisage an outcome leading to radical procedural or institutional change. However, this conclusion must be seen in the context of the possible linkages and bargains to do with other aspects of the IGC; the possibility of new forms of "differentiated" or flexible integration cannot be ruled out.

Part III concentrates on the issues and options in the *debate on European security in Ireland*. In chapter 8 current attitudes towards security policy are evaluated in the context of the government's White Paper on Foreign Policy, published in March 1996. The emphasis in public debate on "neutrality" reflects concern about several dimensions of security policy, and future decisions about Ireland's commitment to both the Common Foreign and Security Policy and a common defence policy will depend on how these issues are interpreted, possibly in a referendum after the Intergovernmental Conference.

Chapters 9–11 expose these questions to further examination. The protective dimension of security policy, though less salient now, is covered in chapter 9. While NATO and the WEU retain their classical purpose of collective defence, they are adapting to a new role in crisis management, and the future role of nuclear weapons is uncertain. In the IGC context what pressure exists for non-alliance states to make full alliance commitments comes from the demands of political solidarity rather than for specific security reasons, and is unlikely to be a determining factor in the negotiations.

The continuing debate on the theory and practice of international crisis management, dealt with in chapter 10, is arguably more pertinent to current needs of security policy. Practice is driving theory, and traditional assumptions about the appropriate political and military conditions for the engagement of contributing states require careful reassessment. For countries which have previously acted as UN peacekeepers this includes the question of operating under the aegis of coalitions led by military alliances, as the UN itself relies increasingly on regional organisations.

Chapter 11 looks at the questions arising from the new opportunities to develop a long-term preventive approach to European security. Here, the EU's Common Foreign and Security Policy offers possibilities of developing common policies to control the proliferation of armaments, though there can

LIBRARY, LETTERKENNY

be no realistic expectations of dramatic or swift success. But perhaps the single most important preventive element of the EU's security policy is the Union's further enlargement to the east, and thus the costs it entails should be assessed in this light.

Finally, chapter 12 recapitulates the broad parameters within which the Intergovernmental Conference is taking place, and reviews the major options facing the Irish government. The choices made by the government, and — if there is a referendum — by the people, will determine whether Ireland assumes a relatively passive stance with regard to the changing European security environment or engages more fully in the emerging cooperative regime.

CHANGE AND ADAPTATION

The pace of change in the modern world is such that it is often difficult to distinguish the transient from the fundamental, or to relate what governments do on our behalf to forces which seem either remote or uncontrollable. This is no less true of European security than of other facets of public life. Repeated claims in recent years that we live in the midst of "historic" change sit uneasily beside an awareness that for most people, at least in western Europe, life seems to go on much as before. For those in eastern Europe, historic change may simply mean greater uncertainty.

Yet to describe the 1990s as a time of historic change in Europe is not empty rhetoric. For the third time this century governments are trying to agree on ways in which European states can coexist without the threat of resorting to force against each other. The first attempt, the creation of the League of Nations in 1919, was an evident failure well before its twentieth anniversary and the resumption of war in Europe. The second occasion produced a universal security organisation, the United Nations, but the Cold War soon limited its scope and partitioned the European continent. Now we have a third chance to reconstruct an ordered and equitable system of states in Europe — what is the prospect of success?

In one respect the prognosis is more encouraging than it was on either of the previous occasions, in which reconstruction followed widespread total war with an appalling human cost. But the advantage deriving from this fact — and the extraordinary opportunity which this generation has to reconstruct by collective agreement and not diktat — must be qualified by two observations. The first is that the old problem of resort to force has not been eliminated altogether. Most European states feel a residual need for military protection, and several are directly or indirectly affected by actual political violence. The second point is, paradoxically, that the generally benign situation in which we find ourselves may dull the incentives which governments feel to adapt their policies with the necessary urgency or commitment.

The European Union is at the centre of the process of adapting security policy. Political integration in western Europe was always about security, especially as a means to organise and sustain Franco-German reconciliation as the only acceptable alternative to Europe's most damaging rivalry. Now the challenge is to replicate this approach on a continental scale, and the Intergovernmental Conference, by adapting the European Union, is an essential means to this end. The details of treaty revision and institutional reform may appear obscure when taken out of context, but in the long term they will be a vital part of the future context of security policy, for they express the willingness of governments, and ultimately of their peoples, to adapt to the new situation.

But European security will also depend on the parallel adaptation of other international organisations with a more exclusive vocation in the field of international security. All the ingredients in what has been referred to as the "alphabet soup" of multilateral diplomacy — the UN, OSCE, NATO, NACC, PFP and WEU — are also being reassessed, and sometimes changed in significant ways. Probably the most important adaptation here is that of NATO, since it is the primary framework for the engagement of the United States — a country which has been a critical variable in European security since the First World War.

One of the main conclusions of the following chapters is that the adaptation of both the EU and NATO is not likely to result in a radical alteration in the broad division of labour between the two institutions. Nonetheless, each is changing in important ways. In addition to its classical role of military protection, NATO is becoming an increasingly important element in international crisis management, in conjunction with the other security organisations. The European Union may develop its comparative advantage as a "civilian power" in preventive security policy, and in conjunction with the WEU it may acquire a "gendarmerie", or armed police, role in crisis management. The questions to be resolved in the IGC and in parallel discussions in NATO and the WEU have to do with the refinement of this division of labour.

As a participant in the IGC Ireland, too, faces the question of adapting to the changed security environment. In what ways, and to what extent, should the state's policies be altered to bring them into line with the requirements of a cooperative security regime? In the past geography has insulated Ireland from many of the worst effects of European insecurity, and the difficult choices imposed on most other European states have often been avoided. So too has much of the political debate which elsewhere has determined security policy.

The analysis of the Irish debate, in Part III of the book, indicates a slow and incomplete adaptation, when compared with the great majority of European states. Traditional attitudes to neutrality, a concept which is much broader in public perception than in state policy, retain considerable influence. Particularly where the issue of force in international relations is concerned, it is not clear that the changes of the 1990s have been fully absorbed in public debate. For many politicians the military alliances, NATO and the WEU, are seen in terms of their Cold War role as elements of a nuclear collective defence rather than as the basis for new modes of crisis management. In short, the distinction between these two dimensions of security policy is not acknowledged.

Even with regard to the non-military aspects of European security, the full engagement of Ireland cannot be taken for granted. Although there has long been a definite awareness of the country's economic interests in participation in European integration, the very idea that it might involve a security interest — either for Ireland or for Europe as a whole — has not been so evident. It may be all too easy, for example, to regard the further enlargement of the European Union as a medium-term economic cost to existing member states rather than as a long-term security benefit for all. The more long-sighted view, that if Europe becomes less secure so too will Ireland's economic interests, may be difficult to sustain in the short-term context of democratic politics. Yet when all is said and done, adaptation to a changing environment is no more than enlightened self-interest.

PART I

THE SECURITY ENVIRONMENT
REVISITED

CHAPTER 1
ELEMENTS OF CHANGE: RECENT TRENDS

The pace of events since the collapse of the Soviet empire in 1989–91 has often made it difficult to judge the significance of the many changes to what had for so long seemed an almost immutable division of Europe into competing blocs. In this chapter the main elements of change are described, with particular emphasis on developments which have taken place since the beginning of 1995, when the IEA interim report on security was published (Keatinge, 1995). The following chapter then poses the question of whether the security environment is becoming either more or less benign in character.

A CONTINENT IN FLUX

Before commenting on recent trends, it is worth recalling the principal characteristics of European security during the 1990s. These include the following themes:

* *a greater diversity of risk:* general political instability within and between the countries of the former eastern bloc; disputes arising from ethnic tensions; a range of low-level risks associated with transnational crime and environmental degradation

* *a new balance between prevention and protection:* the Cold War emphasis on collective defence is now less salient than attempts to develop a preventive approach drawing on a wide range of policy instruments, including economic assistance, support for democratisation, and the promotion of individual and minority rights

* *the perception of a need for protection nevertheless persists:* the demands for military security guarantees by the countries of central and eastern Europe combine with the durability of NATO as the framework both for American engagement in European security and for its members' military restructuring

* *the greater complexity of crisis management:* the record of post-Cold War crisis management has been mixed, and in particular the wars of the Yugoslav succession have seriously damaged the credibility of the European Union, the principal multilateral security organisations and their leading members

* *an abrupt change in the distribution of power:* the clear loser is Russia, yet the United States has been an "intermittent superpower" in Europe; the major states in the EU have lost domestic political authority, while Germany has been distracted by the strain of unification, with a consequent failure to influence events decisively

* *a complex multilateralism:* a gradual reappraisal of international legal norms is taking place, amidst difficult and as yet incomplete attempts to adapt "the institutional architecture" — the array of international organisations which were established in the very different circumstances of the Cold War era.

STABILISATION TO THE EAST?

Russia

The attempted transition of the Russian Federation to pluralist democracy and a market economy remains the great imponderable of European security. On both counts the transition has started: a constitutional framework, institutions for representative government and a degree of economic privatisation testify to that. But the implementation of reform has been uneven, the material circumstances of most Russians have declined and the legitimacy of the whole process hangs in the balance.

Moreover, the fact that Russia is a federation incorporating non-Russian nationalities, and hence subject to internal tension, was demonstrated in a negative manner in the government's handling of the rebellion in Chechnya. President Yeltsin's decision to intervene with military force in December 1994 flew in the face of his claim to respect minority and human rights, and thereby impeded the development of Russia's application for membership of the Council of Europe and the finalisation of its partnership agreement with the European Union.

There was some compensation in the fact that this exercise in blunt coercion did not work, and was clearly seen not to have worked. The Russian public seemed to view it as an irresponsible adventure, and eventually President Yeltsin himself acknowledged its failure. The ineffectiveness, and sometimes evident reluctance, of the military forces involved were also widely noted (IISS, 1995, pp. 82–3).

All of this, together with the persistent difficulty in moving away from a sterile military confrontation, testified to the weakness rather than the strength of the new Russian state. Such political authority as existed was concentrated on the person of the president and his unaccountable entourage, and President Yeltsin's two periods of hospitalisation in 1995 did little to restore confidence in the government's direction of public policy. Nevertheless, the economy seemed less prone to crisis, with a significant decline in inflation and a steadier exchange rate.

The problem for the Russian government was, of course, that such progress as was made hardly weighed in the balance against the immediate experience of reduced standards of living for the great majority of the electorate. The results of the parliamentary elections in December 1995 thus registered an unequivocal protest against the reform process. The most successful parties in what is still an incoherent party system were the (largely unreconstructed) communist party led by Gennadi Zyuganov, followed by Vladimir Zhirinovsky's extreme nationalists, which between them won 33 per cent of the vote; the main supporters of democratic transition trailed with close to 17 per cent. Boris Yeltsin's comeback in the subsequent presidential election in the summer of 1996 kept the reform process alive, but both the margin and the manner of his victory demonstrated its fragility. Speculation about the president's health continued to underline the uncertainties attached to the country's leadership.

An inescapable feature of Russian political debate, right across the political spectrum, is an assertive nationalist rhetoric so far as foreign policy is concerned. This varies from an unashamedly imperialist revanchism to a more diffuse regret for the superpower status of the former Soviet Union. This is bound to make Russia a difficult partner for neighbouring countries so recently ruled from Moscow, irrespective of the actual capacity of Russian governments to restore former influence.

The significance of the formal framework in which eleven of the ex-Soviet republics join with Russia, the Commonwealth of Independent States (CIS), remains unclear (Appendix II). In some cases, such as Belarus, Russian influence appears to have been largely regained almost by default; with others, such as Ukraine, an uneasy *modus vivendi* remains. In the Caucasus and central Asia several conflicts are unresolved and there remains abundant material for future crises involving Russian interests.

Central and eastern Europe

The prospects for post-communist transition are brighter among the countries collectively referred to as "CEECs" (central and east European countries). This category now includes three former Soviet republics

(Estonia, Latvia and Lithuania) as well as former members of the Warsaw Pact. Economic reform has been more coherent than in Russia, and especially in the cases of the Czech Republic, Estonia, Hungary, Poland, Slovakia and Slovenia is starting to show positive results. The experience which some of these states have already had with a democratically legitimate change of power to former communists has been a significant indicator of political stabilisation rather than a regression to former practice.

In Poland the electoral victory in November 1995 of a former communist, Alexander Kwasniewski, against the hero of the anti-communist revolution, President Lech Walesa, was an example of this phenomenon. The more dubious behaviour in Slovakia, in the struggle between the premier, Vladimir Meciar, and the president, Michel Kovac, appears untypical against this background.

A detailed assessment of the security environment in central Europe concludes on a more optimistic note than is generally found in relation to the CIS region: "these states are within reach of the levels of domestic stability enjoyed in Western Europe, and are pursuing policies geared to attaining the same level of pacification and cooperation in inter-state relations. Geopolitically, they are more vulnerable, and it will take time to build the level of west–central European solidarity needed to shore up the expansion of the security-community" (Gambles, 1995, pp. 107–8).

A success for the preventive approach?
The solidarity referred to in the above evaluation is still being developed. Some credit at least for the greater extent of stabilisation among the CEECs than in Russia must be given to the deliberate long-term strategy of preventive measures applied by the EU to these countries. Nine of them (Bulgaria, the Czech Republic, Estonia, Hungary, Latvia, Lithuania, Poland, Romania and Slovakia) have Europe Agreements with the EU, are Associate Partners in the WEU and participate in NATO's Partnership for Peace (PFP). In the summer of 1996 they were joined by Slovenia, the only former Yugoslav republic to have achieved this status. In short, these countries are accepted as prospective members of the European Union, enjoying a "western" identity which is not readily available to Russia.

A more specific manifestation of the preventive approach is the European Stability Pact, which was signed in Paris on 20 March 1995. When it was first proposed by the French government in 1993 this initiative met with a sceptical response, but in revised form as a "joint action" of the EU it served as a framework for the encouragement and consolidation of bilateral agreements to resolve actual or potential minority problems (Hardeman and

Benoit-Rohmer, 1994). Negotiations in two '"round tables", incorporating states in the Baltic region and east central Europe, led to the establishment of the overall pact, which is monitored under the auspices of the Organisation for Security and Cooperation in Europe (OSCE).

However, the Stability Pact will have to be judged more as a process encouraging negotiation than as a substantive agreement. The early results have been mixed. On the eve of the Paris conference it seemed that the Hungarian and Slovak governments had been persuaded to agree on the treatment of the Hungarian minority in Slovakia, but subsequent Slovak legislation restricting minority language rights suggested that implementation of the pact would be a long haul. A Hungarian–Romanian treaty dealing with the contentious issue of the large Hungarian minority in Romania was signed only in September 1996. The merit of the Stability Pact is to keep such issues on the agenda.

On a pan-European level, the preventive approach comes under the aegis of the OSCE, as the former Conference on Security and Cooperation in Europe (CSCE) became known from January 1995. As is sometimes the case with international organisations, the change in title reflects evolutionary changes in structure rather than a radical change in its role. The OSCE did manage to establish a presence in Chechnya, serving with mixed results as a framework for negotiations between the Chechen rebels and the Russian authorities.

The Russian initiative to launch a major discussion in the OSCE on a "security model for the twenty-first century", with the aim of rationalising the organisation of European security cooperation, was launched by seminars in Moscow and Vienna. This project is motivated by both Russian fears of exclusion from "the west" and Moscow's desire to play a leading role in the "new security architecture" in Europe. However, it is likely to be a gradual process, reflecting rather than determining developments on the ground.

The dilemma of reassurance: the question of NATO enlargement

Russia's original objective of an overarching role for the OSCE has been diluted in the security model initiative, but both policies can be seen as counterweights to the proposed enlargement of NATO, to include Moscow's former allies in the old Warsaw Pact. The demands for a formal military security guarantee have been an integral part of the overall reorientation of these countries and of the Baltic states towards "western" international structures since the collapse of the Soviet empire. That has posed a dilemma for NATO governments: by thus contributing to the stabilisation of the new regimes in central and eastern Europe, does the eastwards expansion of NATO run the risk of destabilising a humiliated Russia, thereby decreasing rather than increasing security overall?

The NATO response (which also reflects anxieties about the technical and financial feasibility of enlargement) has been to accept enlargement in principle, to reject the proposition that the reassurance of Russia is necessarily at risk, and to pursue a parallel policy of developing a special relationship, over and above that with other non-NATO countries, to mark Russia's key role (van Eekelen, 1995, pp. 31–8). So far as the implementation of NATO enlargement is concerned, the policy seems to be to hasten slowly. It may be that the issue has as much to do with the domestic politics of the major actors as with their security interests (Zelikow, 1996).

The involvement of all the states concerned, including Russia, was a central feature of the establishment of the North Atlantic Cooperation Council (NACC) in 1991, and in the development of NATO's Partnership for Peace (PFP) programme from the beginning of 1994. The PFP arrangement allows for substantive military cooperation between NATO and the individual partner, largely in terms of the latter's preferences; it could thus be presented as *both* a preparation for NATO membership *and* the framework for a cooperative relationship with Russia which would not involve membership.

However, full membership of NATO is still pressed in central and eastern Europe and claimed to be divisive in Moscow. In September 1995, an official *Study on NATO Enlargement* was published, clarifying the rights and obligations expected of any new members. The focus in this document is on the "why and how" of enlargement, rather than the "who and when"; the process is seen as gradual and on a case-by-case basis, indicating only general criteria and lacking a defined timetable. This is likely to be the last word, so far as official NATO is concerned, until after the American presidential election is resolved in November 1996. The routine NATO Council meeting in December, or perhaps a special summit meeting in the spring of 1997, could see agreement on what is expected to be a small number of candidates for membership. Meanwhile, the debate within NATO as to the implications, feasibility and wisdom of the territorial expansion of the alliance continues (Allin, 1995; Asmus, Kugler and Larrabee, 1995; Michael E. Brown, 1995; Plesch, 1995).

One important aspect underlying the uneasy relationship between Russia and NATO is the actual and potential distribution of military capabilities on the European continent. The most positive legacy of the Cold War relationship between NATO and the Warsaw Pact, the Treaty on Conventional Armed Forces in Europe (CFE) signed in 1990, agreed much reduced overall and regional ceilings for conventional weapons, to be implemented by November 1995. Russia claimed it could not meet the requirements in the "southern flank" region, because of commitments arising out of serious instability in the Caucasus (on both sides of the Russian border), and urged a renegotiation of the treaty (Rogov, 1995).

In principle, this position was not unreasonable since the treaty was originally negotiated in very different circumstances; however, in practice renegotiation on the basis of national defence interests could easily lead to the unravelling of Europe's most successful arms control measure. The review of the CFE thus risked being linked in a negative way with the NATO enlargement question. That this did not happen (modifications were agreed at the review conference in June 1996) was an encouraging sign that the tactics and nationalist rhetoric of the Russian presidential election would not damage an important arms control agreement. But the long-term future of the CFE, as well as other agreements such as the START II treaty on nuclear forces reductions and the Open Skies treaty allowing for verification, cannot be taken for granted.

STABILISATION TO THE SOUTH?

The security challenges to the south of Europe are more diverse than those arising from the dissolution of the Soviet empire. Attempts to view them through a single lens — such as oil dependency or, more recently, Islamic fundamentalism — are not wholly convincing. A broad geographical survey, running from the north-east of the Mediterranean basin to the west, reveals a variety of risks for European security.

Turkey's attempt to develop a more substantial relationship with western Europe made progress in 1995 with the negotiation of an agreement for a customs union with the EU. Assent by the European Parliament, achieved in December 1995, was not, however, a foregone conclusion. Both the Kurdish rebellion in south-eastern Turkey and the partition of Cyprus remained on the foreign policy agenda, casting familiar shadows over the general human rights credentials of the Turkish regime. The separate Turkish–Greek dispute over territorial rights in the Aegean recurred with a naval and air confrontation at the end of January 1996, which came close to provoking a serious crisis for the Greek government.

The Israeli–Palestinian peace process survived continuing violence in the immediate aftermath of the assassination of the Israeli prime minister, Yitzhak Rabin, by a Zionist extremist in November 1995. At this stage the extension of Palestinian self-rule and the explicit incorporation of Jordan in the process were items on the positive side of the ledger, but the inclusion of Syria seemed to be the key to ending the "dirty war" on the Lebanese–Israeli border. Yet if protracted negotiations, accompanied by

400123388

19

intensive American encouragement, seemed the best hope to achieve some sort of settlement, they were more likely to ensure the displacement rather than elimination of radical Islamic opposition to Israel. Negotiations remained hostage to events. Israel's disproportionate retaliation against Hizbullah attacks in April 1996 was a major setback to the peace process, and the victory of the Likud leader, Benjamin Netanyahu, in the Israeli elections six weeks later threatened to unravel it altogether.

Most of the governments on the southern coast of the Mediterranean are faced with rapidly expanding populations, ineffective economies and a greater or lesser degree of political radicalism. Violent dissent has so far been contained in Egypt, at the cost of increasing repression, but the civil war in Algeria has persisted, in spite of attempts to initiate negotiations between the government and the Front Islamique de Salut. In this case, the spillover from a non-European war into Europe has been direct, including several fatal bomb attacks in Paris.

However, the fear of political radicalism inducing large-scale migration from north Africa to Europe in the longer term has not been confined to France. Pressure from the southern member states of the EU to devise a collective preventive strategy has resulted in an attempt to create for the Mediterranean region a cooperative security regime broadly on the lines which are familiar in the east–west context. In November 1995 a multilateral framework — the Euro-Mediterranean Partnership (E-MP) — was established in Barcelona (Barcelona Declaration, 1995). The signatories included the governments of the fifteen EU countries, eleven others (Algeria, Cyprus, Egypt, Israel, Jordan, Lebanon, Malta, Morocco, Syria, Tunisia and Turkey) and the Palestinian Authority. The scope of the agreement ranges from military confidence and security-building measures to economic, financial and cultural cooperation, but only time will tell whether the "Barcelona process" can contribute to the stabilisation of international relations in Europe's southern neighbourhood.

GLOBAL PERSPECTIVES

The tendency to concentrate on Europe's all-too-obvious "arc of insecurity", from Murmansk to Morocco, should not disguise the fact that Europe does not exist in a political vacuum. Historical ties and universalist values frequently combine to involve European governments in security politics elsewhere in the world.

Even in Asia, where European interests and influence are primarily economic, security issues may assume greater importance in the medium to long term. The proposition that the twenty-first century will see the dominance of Asian economies is a familiar cliché, but the implications for international security are not so clear-cut. Asia is not a region well served by cooperative security structures, and has yet to come to terms with the possible rise of China as a dominant regional power, without the culture of military restraint associated with post-1945 Japan. The ambiguous status of Taiwan is contested by military threats of the crudest sort; the nuclear ambitions of North Korea are matched only by its government's primitive rationality and growing incapacity. In an evolving balance of power, it should not be forgotten that the OSCE region — the broadest institutional expression of "Europe" — stretches from Vancouver to Vladivostok. Russia is an Asian as well as a European power, and the United States is still (much of the time) a "super" — i.e. global — power.

More immediate challenges can be found closer to Europe, particularly where the development cooperation policies of European states and of the European Union are undermined by political violence. Central Africa is a case in point. Following the genocide in Rwanda in the summer of 1994, the return of refugees and their political rehabilitation have been fraught with difficulties, while there also remains the possibility of a similar episode in neighbouring Burundi. The question of effective military intervention under UN auspices — avoided until it was too late in 1994 — could well arise again, in either country.

The proliferation of weapons of mass destruction may seem to be at the other extreme of anarchical violence, but it, too, requires the attention of European governments. At the review conference of the Nuclear Non-Proliferation Treaty (NPT) in New York the spring of 1995 the fifteen EU member states negotiated successfully on the basis of a "joint action" aimed at promoting an indefinite extension of the treaty, rather than extending it for specified periods (Simpson, 1995). The implications of this position are examined below in more detail (chapter 9), but one consequence may be that a Comprehensive Test Ban Treaty (CTBT) may be more realisable.

However, an immediate consequence of the end of the NPT conference was the resumption of nuclear testing by China and shortly afterwards by one of the two European nuclear powers, France. This became a visibly divisive issue among the EU member states, not merely as might be expected between France and the four countries which have never subscribed to nuclear guarantees (Austria, Finland, Ireland and Sweden), but also between France and some of its NATO partners. Subsequent French claims that France's nuclear deterrent was a necessary element of a future European defence if anything served to fuel the controversy. The short-term effect of the nuclear testing issue may prove different from that envisaged by the

French government; the programme of tests was curtailed and a firmer position on the CTBT was promised. Nevertheless, the nuclear issue is likely to recur in some form so long as nuclear forces exist.

The institutional expression of global security, the United Nations Organisation, has experienced very mixed fortunes since the end of the Cold War. The early 1990s saw the UN expand its scope, particularly in the field of peacekeeping, under what seemed to be an activist Security Council. Unfortunately, when the fiftieth anniversary of the organisation was celebrated in 1995 it was only too clear that the activism of the Security Council had not been matched by its willingness to commit the necessary resources, or to follow through on threats to meet force with force. Nowhere was this more cruelly demonstrated than in Europe.

BOSNIA: THE TEST FOR CRISIS MANAGEMENT

Humiliation for the UN?

The violent disintegration of the former Yugoslavia since 1991 has shown the limitations of crisis management by "the international community". These limitations are serious enough in the context of particular crises, but they have a broader significance in so far as they all too easily bring the whole process of cooperative security into disrepute. In Bosnia few reputations — of individuals, political groups, governments or international organisations — have been enhanced. Arguably, the basic reason for this failure lies in the differing agendas of the major states, but as the principal framework for collective policy from the beginning of 1992, the UN has not for the first time served as a convenient scapegoat.

The war in Bosnia (the focus of this complex conflict since the spring of 1992) thus merits the closest attention as a benchmark of the condition of European security. Up to the autumn of 1995, international crisis management combined four elements: mediation by UN and EU personalities; humanitarian aid protected by lightly armed troops in traditional peacekeeping mode (UNPROFOR); the enforcement of UN sanctions by NATO and the WEU; a tentative measure of enforcement by air power, jointly authorised but very rarely used, by NATO and the UN. For three years this intervention contained the war and negotiated transitory ceasefires but failed to influence its conduct or outcome in a significant way.

On 26 May 1995, after the erosion of yet another ceasefire had coincided with a new campaigning season, the Bosnian-Serbs responded to a limited air strike by seizing more than 300 UN troops as hostages, the last of whom was not released until 18 June 1995. The promise of reinforcement of their UN contingents by the British and French governments failed to dissuade the Bosnian-Serbs from taking the enclaves of Zepa and Srebrenica in July. The collapse of these supposed "safe areas" was the nadir of the UN intervention; at Srebrenica an isolated and inadequately supported Dutch unit appeared unable to prevent the deliberate massacre of large numbers of prisoners.

The changing balance of force

The response of the UN contributing countries, at a conference in London on 21 July 1995, took the form of a "last chance" warning that more powerful military capabilities would be used, though the increased determination of the French was in contrast to the continued reluctance of the Russians. The first decisive use of force, however, came from another quarter. Two weeks later, with surprising ease, the Croatian army recovered the whole of the Krajina region, originally lost in 1991. As with a much smaller scale success in Western Slavonia at the beginning of May, the Serb government remained aloof. The balance of military advantage had changed significantly.

The second decisive use of force was the implementation of the warning issued at the London conference, formally triggered by a mortar attack on Sarajevo market on 28 August 1995. During the next two weeks this took the form of wide-scale NATO air attacks ("Operation Deliberate Force") on the Bosnian-Serb military infrastructure which, in conjunction with continuing Bosnian government and Croat gains on the ground, created the conditions for a general ceasefire on 11 October 1995 and subsequent diplomatic negotiations which took the Bosnian crisis into a qualitatively different phase.

In all of this, although the UN remained the source of legitimation for collective action, the role of individual states became more significant (Roberts, 1995–96, p. 24). In particular, that of the United States came to the fore. Long-standing policies, such as encouraging both the rebuilding of Croatian military capabilities and the alliance between Croats and Muslims in Bosnia, bore fruit. Long-standing inhibitions against deploying American troops on the ground meant that NATO air capabilities, not UNPROFOR, would be the preferred instrument of military leverage. The sudden opportunity for intensive mediation on the basis of a new military balance led to a final round of top-level negotiations in Dayton, Ohio, from 1 to 21 November 1995. With some foresight, one of the main negotiators, the American diplomat, Richard Holbrooke, had earlier in the year written an article entitled "America, a European Power" (Holbrooke, 1995).

A Balkans peace process?

The Dayton Agreement, which was formally signed in Paris on 14 December 1995, provided for a loosely constructed Bosnian state, within its pre-war borders but subdivided into a Bosnian-Serb republic and a federation of Croats and Muslims. The division of territory inevitably bears all the marks of more than three years of deliberate "ethnic cleansing" by the use of force and intimidation.

Military support takes the form of a UN-authorised but NATO-led Implementation Force (IFOR) of over 50,000 troops, contributed by all the NATO member states (including a medical team from Iceland, which has no army) and by a wide range of non-NATO countries, including three neutrals (Austria, Finland and Sweden) (Appendix III). The presence of more than 15,000 American troops and about 1,500 Russians (with their own "command" relationship with the NATO commander) marks a significant change from UNPROFOR; so too does the greater combat military capability of the force, which operates under rules of engagement significantly less circumscribed than those of its predecessor. Thus it was able to establish its freedom of movement and separate the disputants from the moment of its deployment.

Responsibility for coordination of the civilian aspects of the peace process was assigned by the peace implementation conference in London on 8 December 1995 to a "High Representative", the former Swedish premier and special EU envoy, Carl Bildt. It involves economic reconstruction, in which the EU is the principal source of funds, and measures of political reconstruction, such as holding elections, establishing the new organs of government, decommissioning arms and resolving minority issues. Here the OSCE plays a leading role.

In short, the whole array of security institutions is deployed in this peace-building phase of the Bosnian crisis, which if successful should go some way to restoring the credibility of cooperative security. It is worth underlining the basic and in many respects novel conditions of this important experiment in international crisis management:

* the need for US leadership, and its acknowledgement by most European countries

* Russia's participation in a NATO-led force

* France's deepening involvement in NATO

* the participation of many non-NATO countries, including several traditionally seen as neutrals

* the background role of Partnership for Peace as a framework which had facilitated this cooperation

* the involvement of the major multilateral organisations, in which the capacity of the UN, the OSCE, NATO, the WEU and the European Union to act together will be tested.

However, success in Bosnia is far from assured. The American commitment to IFOR was originally limited to twelve months, and the general commitment of both the United States and Russia has been vulnerable to the vagaries of their respective domestic politics during what was for both of them an election year. The warring parties in former Yugoslavia have a dismal record in keeping to agreements, and progress on establishing the conditions for free elections and the apprehension of suspected war criminals has been very slow.

Moreover, the acquiescence of the different factions depends not merely on what occurs in Bosnia; the ambitions of the Croat and Serb governments, and their treatment of ethnic minorities within their own borders, will also influence the outcome. The repression of the Albanian majority in Serb-ruled Kosovo, for example, is the sort of issue which could disrupt the Bosnian settlement. All in all there is much to be said for the view that the reconstruction of the Balkans remains the immediate challenge for European security.

IRISH LESSONS FOR EUROPEAN SECURITY

Like many of the actual and potential conflicts throughout the European continent, the conflict in Northern Ireland has roots which go back much further than the Cold War. Like them it has often been influenced by external forces and events on a continental scale, and in that respect is part of the European security environment.

Unlike the conflicts in post-communist Europe, however, that in Northern Ireland was not significantly affected by the rise and fall of east–west rivalry between 1945 and 1989, largely because of Ireland's irrelevance in broader geopolitical terms. The end of the Cold War had little direct effect in Northern Ireland, where the course of the conflict was determined mainly by the interplay of internal factors.

Nevertheless, the Northern Ireland conflict does suggest some broad lessons for European security policy in the post-Cold War era. It demonstrates the difficulties even relatively well-established democratic states have in containing or resolving conflict. The localised nature of the antagonism, between communities with different national identities or allegiances, eludes the straightforward majoritarian principle of representative democracy. "Low-intensity" violence in the form of paramilitary terrorism can be organised by small minorities with relative ease, and can hold at bay the much greater coercive capability of the state.

The difficulty in bringing the resources of the international community to bear once violence has broken out is also evident in this case. Even when, after a quarter of a century, an "armed struggle" was transformed into a "peace process" in the summer of 1994, with very considerable encouragement by outside forces such as the United States and the European Union, the peace process was hostage to disruption by a very small minority less than eighteen months later.

The costs of having to resort to crisis management in Northern Ireland, as in Bosnia, have already been high and will be paid for many years to come. The incentive to search for more effective preventive strategies in security policy is only too obvious.

CONCLUSIONS

Even a superficial survey of recent events in the security environment suggests several general conclusions:

* the post-Cold War international system is still unstable, and characterised by rapid change

* to the east, Russia is the major source of uncertainty

* western governments face a serious dilemma in trying to reassure both Russia and the countries of central and eastern Europe that force will not again be a factor in the former Soviet sphere of influence

* attempts to build a cooperative security regime in the Mediterranean are at a very early stage

* crises may be expected elsewhere in the world, and there is no quick solution to the proliferation of weapons of mass destruction

* the implementation of the peace process in Bosnia is the immediate priority for European security.

In order to meet these challenges governments have been developing a cooperative security regime to replace the adversarial arrangements associated with the Cold War. The next chapter examines their efforts in more detail and assesses their success to date.

CHAPTER 2
A CO-OPERATIVE SECURITY REGIME?

Given the pace and extent of change in international politics during the past seven years, it is difficult to assess the overall shape of the post-Cold war system. Much has been promised, but real achievements have been accompanied by uncertainty and, in some places, war. This chapter moves away from this inevitably confusing narrative of events in order to evaluate the current security environment, by asking to what extent a "co-operative security regime" has been established.

The analysis proceeds through the following stages:

* an outline of the characteristics of a co-operative security regime, to provide a benchmark against which the actual situation may be measured

* an assessment of one of these factors, political leadership by the larger states

* an assessment of the multilateral institutions which are a prominent feature of this type of international politics

* a summary of the current situation as one of three alternative scenarios.

CHARACTERISTICS OF A CO-OPERATIVE SECURITY REGIME

The concept of a co-operative security regime is most readily grasped in terms of the three dimensions of security policy referred to in the Introduction — prevention, protection and crisis management. The long-term preventive approach is its hallmark, with an emphasis on reassurance, confidence-building and inclusiveness. Influence is expressed in terms of "civilian power" rather than coercion. The other long-term strategy, protection, which relies on defence against or deterrence of military threat, is very much in the background as a measure of last resort. Where conflicts do nevertheless flare up in the short term, the structures and procedures of co-operative security are deployed to manage and eventually resolve the crisis.

The world in which such an arrangement exists is still a world of sovereign states, that is to say an anarchical political system without a central political authority. It is, however, a rather benign anarchy, whose members — the states — do not always stand on their formal sovereignty, and are usually reluctant to coerce each other. Where coercion is thought to be necessary, it will be undertaken collectively, within a framework of generally accepted rules.

Co-operative security nonetheless falls short of the idea of true "collective security", which is embodied in the UN Charter (though not applied in practice). Collective security implies unconditional deference to a central authority and strong centralised instruments of enforcement. The co-operative security concept is a much looser arrangement and involves "institutional consent rather than ... threats of material or physical coercion" (Nolan, 1994, pp. 4–5).

One of the principal factors in the development of a co-operative security regime is the leadership of the major states amongst its membership. At the very least it suggests — in the classical language of international politics — a concert of the great powers. But co-operative security goes further than the replication of an exclusive club of latterday Castlereaghs and Metternichs. It operates through complex networks of multilateral institutions, the development of which has been such a striking feature of the late twentieth century.

Multilateral security organisations, such as the UN, the OSCE, NATO and the WEU — and also the EU with regard to its security dimension — perform several functions in the overall regime:

* they provide an ordered, rule-bound setting which may mitigate the power rivalries of the major states, and hence cement their solidarity

* they include all members of the system, and thus maximise the opportunity for smaller states to exert some influence

* they allow for economies of scale in trying to deploy policy instruments (diplomacy, aid, economic or military sanctions)

* they encourage the creation and promotion of international norms, which over time may contribute to an international rule of law.

It is arguable that much of what has occurred in the security environment since the end of the Cold War can indeed be understood as an important stage in the development of a co-operative security regime. There has been a concert among the major states, together with an adaptation and amplification of multilateral institutions. What is not so clear, however, is how soundly based the regime is at present, or how durable it may prove to be. Several broad scenarios can be envisaged: the continuation of a *tentative* regime; movement towards a *consolidated* regime; regression to a malign scenario, *adversarial Europe* (Keatinge, 1995, pp. 95–7).

In order to examine the present condition of the co-operative security regime, its main elements — political leadership and multilateral organisation — will now be examined in more detail.

POLITICAL LEADERSHIP: CONCERT OR CACOPHONY?

The recent activism in the UN Security Council, so long largely blocked by east–west rivalry, indicates the existence of a concert of sorts. Even *China* — still the odd man out of the five permanent members, and not so directly concerned with European security as the others — generally prefers abstention to the veto. However, a closer look at the domestic constraints on these countries' foreign policies suggests serious limitations to both the degree of harmony which may be expected and the durability of the concert itself.

The uncertainties surrounding *Russia* have already been described in chapter 1 as one of the principal challenges to a secure Europe. Given the stress of remaking both political system and economy, against a background of nostalgia for a past of apparent supremacy, it should not be surprising if Russia is an unpredictable partner and striker of discordant notes.

The United States of America, on the other hand, is a long-standing partner of west European countries and the European Union. The latter relationship has been changing considerably since 1989, the US–EU summit meeting in December 1995 endorsing a broad range of common goals and activities (US and EU, 1995). The United States is still the only superpower, and nowhere more so than in the manner of its leadership of the international community in the Bosnian conflict from the early autumn of 1995. Here was determined and intensive diplomacy, backed by credible military strength, and a readiness to take risks.

Yet it must be remembered that in the first instance the risks pertained to American domestic politics, where a beleaguered president faced a hostile and in some respects isolationist congress within eighteen months of a presidential election. Six months previously, the United States had not looked so much in control; President Clinton was at odds both with his congress and with his European allies, precisely over the situation in Bosnia which seemed intractable. And if 15,000 American troops are at last on the ground in Bosnia, it is within a tightly defined time-scale of twelve months (or earlier, in the event of a breakdown of the peace process). Although this commitment may survive electoral pressures, and perhaps even be extended, in general the United States can be seen as a "reluctant superpower" (Cox, 1995, p. 125).

Foreign policy leadership by the European triumvirate of Germany, France and the United Kingdom does not look any more soundly based, either on shared strategies between the three states or on the domestic consensus within each of them. The extent to which they share common approaches to security policy is examined more fully below (chapter 4). However, the domestic constraints on their foreign and security policies can be quite striking, and in some cases acute, for example with regard to the early stages of the Yugoslav conflict in 1991.

Germany is probably the least constrained, in that the government of Chancellor Kohl is not obliged to face a federal election until 1998 and the main element in his coalition, the CDU/CSU party group, does not have the problems of leadership or credibility with the public which seem to affect all its rivals. However, a slender parliamentary majority and a weak coalition partner could alter electoral calculations. Perhaps a more serious difficulty lies in the government's struggle to convince the German electorate that the major plank of the chancellor's European policy, Economic and Monetary Union (EMU), is either feasible or desirable. So far as security policy is concerned, in spite of recent changes, the long-standing "culture of restraint" is still a strong influence (Meiers, 1995).

France is a less predictable element. The victory of the Gaullist candidate in the presidential elections in the spring of 1995 was soon followed by mixed signals. With regard to security policy, President Chirac made a personal contribution to the more determined approach followed by the international community in Bosnia, but his insistence on resuming nuclear tests proved to be more controversial than anticipated, both inside and outside France. The general economic policy of the new government was also erratic. The unexpectedly severe public service strikes in November–December 1995, the harvest of an election won on contradictory promises, may increase the difficulty of adhering to a joint European policy with Germany.

French defence policy is also on the threshold of radical reform. Proposals to restructure the armed forces, including the end of conscription and a readiness to participate more fully within a reformed NATO, look like moving France away from its long-standing Gaullist exceptionalism. However, neither the internal implementation of these reforms nor their consequences for France's partners can be foreseen at this stage.

The United Kingdom is on the rack of internal divisions which have focused on European policy. It is hardly any compensation to the prime minister, John Major, to realise that the fault line in his own party — and perhaps in the country as a whole — runs deeper than "Europe". The consequences of this continued "civil war" absorb much of his efforts. A preemptive strike against his rivals in the mid-summer of 1995 brought him time, but an increasingly thin parliamentary majority has narrowed his policy options to such an extent that few expect a less nervous approach before a general election. Although this may be delayed to the last possible moment in May 1997, an earlier dissolution cannot be discounted.

For some observers of international politics, these instances of serious domestic constraints and weak national leadership are not random cases, but rather symptoms of the changing nature of the nation-state, leading to a general "crisis of governance" (IISS 1995, pp. 5–7). If this is so, the prospects for consolidating co-operative security are not encouraging. If the major actors are unable to provide continuity and resolve in the long term, the smaller states in the system are even less well placed to sustain a coherent strategy.

MULTILATERALISM: INTERLOCKING INSTITUTIONS?

If political leadership has been muted since the end of the Cold War, has the adaptation of multilateral institutions served to take up some of the slack, or do they also reflect the drift in the policies of their leading member states? After all, "especially in the security arena, great powers choose whether to use a given institution, not the other way round" (Zelikow, 1996, p. 8). On one hand, it is true that even a simple description of these institutions demonstrates a considerable degree of adaptation in recent years (see Appendix II); in particular, the overlap in their memberships bears witness to their inclusiveness (see Appendix IV). On the other hand, a brief evaluation of the recent performance of security organisations reveals a mixed balance sheet.

The dilemmas facing the *United Nations* in Bosnia, leading to recurrent humiliation, have already been referred to in chapter 1. Of course, it is not fair to judge the UN on the basis of one operation, and in any case its weaknesses derive more from its members' failures of commitment than from its own organisational deficiencies. That said, the mood at the various occasions during 1995 celebrating the fiftieth anniversary of the organisation was distinctly more sceptical than three years previously, when the secretary general's *Agenda for Peace* was published (Boutros-Ghali, 1992, 1995). The UN is at the same time overburdened with demands for action and deliberately underresourced, often by some of the larger members. However, it remains the focus of the promotion and reshaping of international norms, and the major source of international legitimacy. Member states may treat the UN in a cavalier fashion but they do not leave it.

The *OSCE* performs a similar norm-setting function with respect to its more restricted regional membership. Nevertheless, a membership of fifty-three states, including Canada, the United States and the former Soviet republics in central Asia as well as the conventionally "European" countries, contains a great diversity of views and interests. This militates against the OSCE becoming a dominant security organisation, covering all facets of security policy with equal authority. Its strengths lie mainly in the field of prevention; its process of routine political dialogue and more specialised missions, particularly with respect to quiet diplomacy on minority and human rights, represent a confidence-building ethos the effect of which is difficult to measure precisely because it is undramatic. Its primary political significance lies in the extent to which it can incorporate Russia into a common security framework (van Eekelen, 1995, p. 25).

On the other hand, with regard to crisis management the OSCE's contribution is more marginal. It is not that the organisation does not possess procedures and mechanisms to develop a more central role, but rather that there is no clear consensus among its members for moving in this direction (Kooijmans, 1995). It remains to be seen whether the OSCE's part in the Bosnian peace process evolves in a more favourable way.

NATO faces two major questions concerning its adaptation to the co-operative security regime. The first is the determination of its overall political profile: is it to become the principal military organisation of a broader "western" group of states — sustaining the engagement of the United States, reintegrating its prodigal son, France, and expanding its membership into central and eastern Europe? Whether such a role is compatible with the maintenance and further development of co-operative security is still open to debate (see chapter 1). The association of Russia (and in the longer term, other major actors in world politics) with an enlarged NATO is a critical issue for the future of European security.

The second question for NATO is less about what it looks like to others than what functions it performs as an organiser of multinational military capability. Its comparative advantage lies in an integrated command structure and, more broadly, a collective military culture which is not replicated in any other organisation. But NATO's response to the change in emphasis from collective self-defence — in which it achieved unprecedented significance — to the more diffuse and in many ways more challenging demands of international crisis management has yet to be fully tested.

NATO foreign ministers signalled a further stage of the adaptation of the alliance in response to both these questions at a meeting in Berlin in June 1996. However, the performance of IFOR in Bosnia may prove to be equally important. This is a NATO operation because a reluctant US congress and probably most other parties involved believe that only NATO's integrated command structure and military assets, including large-scale American deployment of ground troops, possess the necessary credibility with the disputants to sustain the peace process. If this assumption should be proved wrong, the future of NATO could be quite uncertain.

The adaptation of the *European Union* and its associated military organisation, the *Western European Union,* are examined in much greater detail in Part II of this book. Suffice it to say here that the reputation of neither organisation as an element in multilateral security is unquestioned. The EU's comparative advantage as the major coordinator of economic support in the strategy of long-term prevention is clear, though inevitably it is impossible to judge whether its efforts will prove to be sufficient.

With regard to crisis management, however, the record has been poor. The EU (and its predecessor, the European Community) suffered as much if not more humiliation in the former Yugoslavia as the UN. The WEU's role, as part-coordinator of sanctions enforcement measures and policing in Mostar, has been marginal. The WEU is to a large extent still a "paper organisation" and its future is as dependent on the reform of NATO as on reform of the EU. Although many see its vocation in the field of military crisis management, it is no accident that at present it is NATO, not the WEU, which is the main actor in Bosnia.

Are these different organisations "mutually reinforcing" or "interlocking", as diplomatic parlance puts it? It is true that a broad complementarity can be discerned, particularly with respect to long-term prevention. The UN and the OSCE develop international norms, provide frequent occasions for political dialogue and in general legitimate action by the "international community". The EU coordinates economic support, up to the significant inducement of future membership in many cases.

But where crisis management is concerned, the ad hoc often prevails. In two important crises of the post-Cold War era (German unification and Yugoslavia) the major actors sooner or later chose ad hoc diplomatic channels (the "2 plus 2 group" and the "contact group" respectively) to coordinate positions, rather than go through the more cumbersome orthodox institutions (Stark, 1995). Moreover, a recent study of the effects of multilateralism in former Yugoslavia argues that while it has been a significant factor in sustaining the concert between the major actors (a basic prerequisite for co-operative security), it has also sometimes had a perverse effect on the management of the actual crisis, by becoming an excuse for inaction (Jakobsen, 1995).

The Bosnian peace process offers a final comment on the condition of the current security regime. When decisive action was eventually taken in the autumn of 1995 there was a cruel irony in a heavily armed NATO-led force being assigned to keep the peace, thereby replacing a lightly armed UN operation which never had a peace to keep. If there had been a coherent and decisively led regime, that order would have been reversed.

ALTERNATIVE SCENARIOS

The above analysis suggests that the current situation at best only approximates a co-operative security regime. This conclusion may be reinforced by a comparison between three alternative scenarios. These should be seen neither as descriptions of existing reality nor as predictions of the future, but as representing contrasting expectations of the broad directions in which the security environment may evolve (Wessels, 1995, p. 390).

The scenarios are summarised in Table 1. The first, called *consolidated co-operative security*, is relatively optimistic. It assumes a world in which the forces of economic globalisation are both positive and manageable — a world of sustainable growth. The foreign policies of the major states outside Europe reflect a broadly co-operative orientation; the United States is actively engaged in a transatlantic partnership, and with the larger Asian countries. Among the latter, China is increasingly incorporated in regional and global interdependencies.

Table 1: Three Scenarios

	Consolidated Co-operative Security	Tentative Co-operative Security	Adversarial Europe
Global conditions	*moves to sustainable growth *USA engaged *China incorporated in regional security	*ad hoc management of economic globalisation *USA reluctant superpower *China's succession problems	*protectionist regional blocs *USA withdraws from European engagement *China's expansionist nationalism
Characteristics of European Security	*Russia's comprehensive democratisation *EU triumvirate in concert *strengthening co-ordination within and between multilateral institutions	*Russia's transition problems *EU triumvirate uncertain *competition or incoherence between multilateral institutions	*Russia's revanchist nationalism *EU triumvirate fragments *optional recourse to weak multilateral institutions
Security Policies	*preventive policies expanded, routinised *military protection as last resort, re risks outside Europe *agreed multilateral mechanisms for responses to crises	*preventive policies agreed but implementation weak *slow adaptation of military from protection to crisis management *ad hoc responses to crises within loose multilateral framework	*preventive policies seen as futile *military protection, especially nuclear deterrence, on top of agenda *mostly unilateral responses to crises by major actors

The European security architecture, in this scenario, involves strong evidence of the comprehensive democratisation of Russia, the implementation of a concerted strategy by the major states in the EU and the strengthening of coordination within and between multilateral institutions. So far as security policies are concerned, the preventive approach is expanded and routinised, and protective policies are limited to measures of last resort, mainly in relation to risks from outside Europe. There are agreed multilateral mechanisms and operational capabilities for swift responses to international crises.

This first scenario comes close to the creation of a west European style "security community" extended throughout the continent. Clearly it does not fit the circumstances of the 1990s. These might more accurately be seen in terms of the second scenario, *tentative co-operative security*. There can be little confidence that global economic forces are effectively managed by governments or international organisations, or that markets move unerringly towards social or political harmony. The United States is more often than not a reluctant superpower, and the strains of political succession in China suggest more than a hint of national assertiveness.

In Europe, Russia's transition to democracy is not assured, and the cohesion of the EU triumvirate is often maintained only by agreement at the lowest possible level of action. Multilateral institutions continue to be affected by bureaucratic competition and incoherence. Although the preventive approach to security policy prevails in principle, and is expressed in many political and even legal commitments, policy implementation is often weak. The protective approach is reduced in importance, but national military establishments and alliances are slow to adapt. International crisis management more often than not is ad hoc.

A third scenario, *adversarial Europe*, is based on more pessimistic assumptions. The global economy degenerates into protectionist regional blocs, the United States limits its global liabilities wherever possible, but an expansionist China has few scruples in pursuing regional hegemony in Asia.

Russia in effect abandons any serious pretence to democratisation, and follows a revanchist strategy where it can. The European Union no longer represents a concentration of potential political influence, and the major states in western Europe have occasional and uncoordinated recourse to what they see as the option of multilateral diplomacy.

In this scenario, preventive policies are seen as futile, and there is a regression to the salience of policies of military threat and counter-threat.

Nuclear deterrence, and the associated tendency to arms racing of all sorts, is at the top of the security agenda. International crisis management mostly consists of unilateral responses by the larger states.

This scenario is not altogether a replay of the Cold War. The element of global ideological rivalry would be missing, and although Russia still possesses more than enough nuclear capability to be a central player, the reconstruction of its conventional military capabilty would be difficult. Indeed, Russia — as a threatened Asian power — might have an interest in forming alliances with western states. But such alliances would hardly be stable, and no-one shoud be under any illusion that this would be other than a regression to a form of power politics in which smaller states would be increasingly marginalised.

In comparing the three scenarios, that of tentative co-operative security best encapsulates the present condition of the security environment. Arguably, it will only be possible to judge whether there is significant movement towards a consolidated regime after some considerable lapse of time. On the other hand, a regression to adversarial Europe could be much more abrupt.

CONCLUSIONS

The security environment is seen in terms of a tentative co-operative security regime, marked by institutional trial and error, as well as the underlying weakness of the governments of the major states. It faces two critical tests in the near future: sustaining the engagement of Russia after the presidential elections, and implementing the peace agreement in Bosnia.

That the outcome of these tests is in no way predictable is itself a measure of how tentative co-operative security remains. A negative result in either could unravel much of what has been achieved since the end of the Cold War, perhaps inducing a return to an adversarial pattern of security politics. It will take a successful outcome in both before the regime could be said to be consolidated.

PART II

THE EU INTERGOVERNMENTAL CONFERENCE

CHAPTER 3
BLUEPRINTING FOR SECURITY AND DEFENCE

The European Union and its predecessor the European Community are generally thought of as "economic and social" organisations, to do with the creation of a common market and, more recently, an economic and monetary union. In their impact on member state economic policies and on the everyday life of their citizens this perception is understandable, but it understates a central achievement — the creation of a "security community", a group of countries among which war was no longer conceivable.

During the Cold War, national sensitivities and military dependence on the United States precluded the development of a direct role for the EC as such with regard to security against external threat — that was seen largely in terms of collective defence, and therefore the business of NATO. However, since 1989 the member states of the EC/EU have been faced by the question of how best to adapt the institution to the new challenges of European security. This part of the book examines the issues involved, as they appear on the agenda of the Intergovernmental Conference which has been called to review the Treaty on European Union.

This focus on the IGC is appropriate in that the European Union represents the most cohesive and dynamic group of European states, and its policies include the main elements of "civilian power". The reform of its policy-making framework in the IGC, through a review of and amendments to its legal base, the Treaty on European Union, is therefore a matter of great significance for European security. However, it should be remembered that the issues of institutional reform discussed in the following chapters do not exist in a vacuum. The untidy complexities of the security environment always have the potential to change the political agenda, while outside the IGC other security organisations, such as the UN, the OSCE and particularly NATO, are also being adapted.

The Intergovernmental Conference can be seen in very broad terms as a "blueprinting process". It is not that it has the task of designing the EU's policy-making system from scratch — the original blueprints are there already, in the form of the series of treaties which culminated in the Treaty on European Union in 1992. But it does require a return to that blueprint, and raises questions about whether a redesign is necessary. And, even in its preparatory stages, the IGC has already spawned a series of suggestions from member state governments and the Union's institutions for changes to the blueprint.

In this chapter the "blueprinting process" is analysed under the following headings:

* the existing basis of the EU's foreign and security policy, including its links with the WEU

* the extensive preparations which (together with the context of the security environment) have shaped the agenda of the IGC

* the range of proposals to reform the decision-making procedures and institutional capacity of the EU's Common Foreign and Security Policy

* the range of proposals to define a common defence policy, including changes to the relationship between the EU and the WEU.

Succeeding chapters will comment on the attitudes towards these proposals of the EU's member states, whether they are major actors, small alliance states or the WEU observers.

THE EUROPEAN UNION'S EXISTING SECURITY POLICY

Security as a primary goal
It is worth recalling the emphasis on security as one of the fundamental reasons for creating a system of European integration. The treaty establishing the European Coal and Steel Community, signed in Paris on 18 April 1951 by the original six EC states (Belgium, France, Germany, Italy, Luxembourg and the Netherlands), expresses its purpose thus: "to substitute for age-old rivalries the merging of . . . essential interests; to create by establishing an economic community, the basis for a broader and deeper community among peoples long divided by bloody conflicts . . ." (Paris Treaty, 1951).

During the Cold War this goal was focused mainly on security among the integrating countries themselves. Given the military dimension of east–west relations, in which NATO was the principal forum for western interests, the evolution of an EC security policy with regard to third parties was slow and indirect. From the early 1970s, with the establishment of systematic foreign policy consultations — the process of European Political Co-operation (EPC) — and the parallel growth of a policy of development co-operation in north–south relations, the basis of a broader concept of security policy was being laid. By the time the Single European Act was being negotiated in 1985, the "political and economic aspects of security" were an explicit item on the agenda of European integration.

The Treaty on European Union brought this development a stage further by making the assertion of the EU's "international identity", particularly through a "common foreign and security policy", one of its primary goals, referred to in Article B of the treaty. The objectives of this policy are defined in Article J 1.2.

They are as follows:

* to safeguard the common values, fundamental interests and independence of the Union

* to strengthen the security of the Union and its member states in all ways

* to preserve peace and strengthen international security, in accordance with the principles of the United Nations Charter as well as the principles of the Helsinki Final Act and the objectives of the Paris Charter

* to promote international cooperation

* to develop and consolidate democracy and the rule of law, and respect for human rights and fundamental freedoms.

In addition to these general aims relating to security policy, the Treaty on European Union, in the context of development cooperation, includes the objective of "the sustainable economic and social development of the developing countries, and more particularly the most disadvantaged among them" (TEU, Article 130u). This is generally regarded as an integral part of the broad concept of international security to which the EU is committed.

The core of the policy framework: the Common Foreign and Security Policy
The Common Foreign and Security Policy provided for in the treaty "shall include all questions related to the security of the Union, including the eventual framing of a common defence policy, which might in time lead to a common defence". The main legal basis of the CFSP is Article J (Appendix V). Although the European Court of Justice has no role in this part of the treaty, this article is a more legally binding evolution of previous practice in European Political Cooperation.

Decision-making in the CFSP remains intergovernmental, that is it requires the consensus of all member states. This is in contrast to the supranational method (allowing a majority to prevail) which is used for nearly all matters of economic integration. To reflect the existence of this difference within a single institutional framework, the treaty is considered to have three "pillars", with separate legislative and consultative procedures. The CFSP is thus sometimes referred to as "the second pillar", the first covering economic and social matters on a supranational basis, and the third dealing with internal order and judicial cooperation on intergovernmental lines.

One of the main complications in the treaty lies in the fact that measures dealing with economic integration and internal security which are also relevant to the conduct of the CFSP are dealt with in the other pillars. In particular, the first pillar, containing the activities of the old European Community, includes foreign trade and development cooperation policy — two of the principal elements of civilian power. The effective coordination of policies, for example to do with economic sanctions or humanitarian aid, can be difficult because of the different procedures employed in the two pillars.

The inclusion of "defence" (i.e. the military dimension of security policy) is tentative in the Maastricht Treaty. It is recognised as an objective of the Union, but the inclusion of words like "eventual" and "might in time" reflect an aspirational quality in the commitment. In the short term defence is delegated to the WEU at "the request" of the Union, but the manner of this delegation is ambiguous and leaves the WEU with a considerable degree of autonomy (Appendix V). The elaboration of a medium- to long-term relationship between the two bodies is a major task for the IGC.

The Western European Union
Based on the Brussels Treaty of 1948, which was largely superseded by NATO, the WEU was the channel through which Germany assumed collective defence responsibilities alongside the Benelux countries, France, Italy and the United Kingdom in 1954, after the plan for a European Defence Community (EDC) failed. This virtually redundant military alliance was "reactivated" in 1984, mainly at the instigation of France, which wished to strengthen west European influence within NATO. In order to reassure the United States that this did not undercut NATO's primacy in the defence field, in 1987 the WEU states reaffirmed their adherence to NATO's policy of deterrence, with an emphasis on its nuclear element (van Eekelen, 1995, pp. 42–3).

At the Maastricht IGC in 1991 the WEU's position between the EU and NATO reflected differences between supporters of a European as against an

Atlantic alliance. The concept of a "European security and defence identity" — a term which appeared in the WEU's declaration at Maastricht — was hotly contested. This controversy became less acute with the arrival of the Clinton administration in the United States. At the NATO summit meeting in January 1994 the European Security and Defence Identity (ESDI) appeared in a more prominent place, and the possibility of NATO resources being made available to the WEU was raised. This idea — in the form of the concept of Combined Joint Task Forces (CJTF) — came closer to realisation at a NATO foreign ministers' meeting in Berlin in June 1996. However, it has not been easy to reach agreement in NATO on this and other reforms of that organisation, and it is still unclear just how the WEU will mesh in practice with the transatlantic alliance (see chapters 9 and 10). This question is likely to be one of the determining influences on the IGC.

Since 1991 the WEU has developed a modest operational role, and has experienced institutional rationalisation and expansion. It now involves twenty-eight states, from full members and associates to observers, and includes six former Warsaw Pact members and three former republics of the Soviet Union. Up to the opening of the IGC it was the forum in which a future European common defence policy was discussed.

Two potential components of a European common defence — a number of multinational military units known as "forces answerable to the WEU" (FAWEU), and the British and French nuclear forces — remain outside the scope of EU policy. The designation of FAWEU includes the original Franco-German innovation, the joint "Eurocorps", to which Belgium, Luxembourg and Spain also contribute. Although conceived as an experiment in military integration with implications for deeper political integration, the Eurocorps is in practice still far from being a putative European army. As is the case with other FAWEUs, the deployment of individual national units rests with national governments. Nuclear forces are not even within the notional WEU framework, being the national prerogatives of two large states, France and the United Kingdom. The full members of the WEU still subscribe to the concept of nuclear deterrence, but in practice the significant nuclear guarantee is that of the United States, in the context of NATO.

The EU's security policy: an evaluation
The current impression of the institutional arrangements of the EU's security policy is of a confusing and incomplete jigsaw puzzle, without a very clear sense of the final design, or of the determination of the member states to achieve it. The implementation of the CFSP in the field of security has been low-key, and the public perception of the EU's performance has been negative more often than not. Positive achievements of a preventive nature, such as the Stability Pact, the evolving partnership with Russia and the

beginnings of a Euro-Mediterranean security network by their nature take time to make an impact on the public, and they have failed to compensate for weakness with regard to crisis management. In many member states the experince in Bosnia has exerted an especially negative influence on public attitudes towards the CFSP as a whole.

PREPARING FOR THE IGC

The Treaty on European Union, agreed at Maastricht in December 1991, explicitly provided for its own revision by "a conference of representatives of the governments of the Member States . . . to be convened in 1996" (TEU, Article N). Article J 4 of the treaty, which covers security and defence, was among those articles specifically designated for inclusion on the agenda (TEU, Article J 4.6).

This is the sixth such conference, designed to create or reform the fundamental legal base of European integration. The first three dealt with the creation of the European Coal and Steel Community (1950–51), the European Economic Community and Euratom (1955–57), and the first comprehensive overhaul of the treaties, the Single European Act (1985). The fourth and fifth took place simultaneously (1990–91), with two separate negotiations on economic and monetary union and political union only being brought together in the final stage prior to agreement by the European Council at Maastricht.

Normally these important negotiations, formally conducted at foreign minister level, have been preceded by a preparatory phase including a report, in order to shape the agenda of the actual negotiations. The exception to the rule was the political union IGC in 1990–91; this was hastily added to the prepared negotiations on economic and monetary union as a result of the turmoil which attended the sudden unification of Germany in 1990. In effect, it reflected the need (felt most acutely by the German government) for Germany to reassure its partners that it was a European Germany rather than a German Europe that was in the making.

There were, nonetheless, two negative consequences of this hasty improvisation. First, the implications of "political union" remained ambiguous throughout the negotiations and beyond; arguably this lack of transparency was an important factor in increasing scepticism among public opinion during the traumatic and damaging ratification of the Maastricht Treaty, which dragged on to the autumn of 1993.

The second problem concerned security policy more directly. The relevant provisions in the treaty were drawn up at a time of extraordinary confusion in the security environment: the UN-authorised war against Iraq, the breakdown of Yugoslavia and the dissolution of the Soviet Union. International negotiations are difficult enough at the best of times, but diverging interpretations of interests and events were hardly surprising at that juncture. The consequent compromises resulted in treaty terms which were both ambiguous and incomplete. Indeed, Article J 4.6 testifies to a recognition of the need for early revision.

As a response to these deficiencies, preparations for the current IGC have been more intensive. In the first half of 1995 a series of reports on the functioning of the Treaty on European Union was produced by the main institutions. The Council's report, being itself the outcome of intergovernmental consensus, is the least ambitious in scope (Council, 1995). It reflects quite different expectations about what the CFSP might achieve, irrespective of the political will of the member states. The prescriptive elements are quite narrowly focused, and the report offers few hostages to fortune on the broad issues of security and defence.

The Commission approach is more wide-ranging and critical (Commission, 1995 a). It points to unnecessarily cumbersome procedures, especially between the three pillars of the treaty, and a lack of preparation and continuity in the overall political direction of the CFSP, and it argues the case for qualifed majority voting. It considers the development of the security and defence arrangements to have made very little progress.

The European Parliament's input (European Parliament, 1995a, 1995b) not surprisingly emphasises the question of democratic control of the CFSP. The Parliament prescribes a greater role for the Commission in the planning and implementation of policy, and the eventual absorption of the WEU by the European Union; it also suggests the creation of a European Peace Corps for conflict prevention.

In June 1995 all of these reports, in addition to similar documentation from member state governments, were presented to an ad hoc committee of representatives of all the foreign ministers and of the president of the Commission plus two members of the European Parliament. This body — the Reflection Group — was chaired by the Spanish minister, Carlos Westendorp; it produced an interim report in August and a final report in December (Reflection Group, 1995). Meanwhile in November the WEU Council of Ministers published its own range of options for the relationship between the EU and the WEU (WEU, 1995a).

The contrast with the very sketchy preparation for the previous IGC could hardly be greater. However, the better preparation on this occasion has revealed the complexity of the issues and a considerable diversity of approaches by the member states. The political context is still one of a continent in flux, with the enormous challenge of the further enlargement of the EU, already agreed in principle at the European Council in Copenhagen in 1993. Indeed, when the IGC opened in the spring of 1996 the prevailing mood about the prospects for reform of the second pillar was sceptical, even among those who favoured change.

The first phase of the IGC, up to the European Council in Florence on 21–22 June 1996, was mainly confined to a formal presentation of the participants' positions, with only a general discussion of the major themes, but no real negotiation. The report of the Italian presidency identified what it saw as the main trends emerging at that point, but did not attempt to formulate possible compromises (European Council, 1996a).

BLUEPRINTING: THE MAIN ISSUES AND OPTIONS

The work of the IGC, including its preparatory stage, is about the design of an institutional framework, with its associated rules and procedures, in order to make policy. It is not about the content or substance of specific policies, though of course the negotiating governments will have these in mind when they try to shape the policy framework. The subject-matter of the IGC will thus inevitably tend to be abstract, and couched in legal language, but the outcome of the whole process will determine the political character of the Union, for better or worse, for some time to come.

Before introducing the second pillar issues, it is necessary to identify the range of overall *options* which is in theory open to the negotiators at the IGC. These options relate to the general strategic direction for the EU as a whole, not just for the second pillar. They are presented here in ascending order of political integration.

A first broad option is a *renationalised Europe*, in which there would be a regression to at most the situation in the early years of the European Political Cooperation process, involving consultations between foreign ministries but nothing further.

Maintaining the status quo would be a second option. This *minimalist Union* might involve some technical tidying-up of the existing treaty, or even its reordering in a coherent and simplified way, but would not include significant changes of substance.

A third general option would be to try to exploit the desire of a large majority of member states to make substantial changes in at least some of the more important activities, in order to increase the effectiveness of an enlarged Union. Those which did not feel willing or able to commit themselves would have limited derogations or more definitive opt-outs; this would be a *differentiated Union*. In its extreme form, this option would become a two-tier entity with quite different rights and obligations for a "core group" and the others.

The most ambitious option for the IGC would be a *pre-federal Union*. In moving towards the creation of a federal Union, this maximalist option would involve decisive moves towards majority voting in foreign policy, and the creation of a comprehensive common defence policy.

While all these options (and a multitude of variants) are available in principle, the first is unlikely to be explicit and the fourth seems unlikely to last the course of the IGC. A renationalised Europe is not far from the minds of the increasing number of "Eurosceptics" in many of the member states, but governments may find it is neither politically correct nor wise to negotiate in these terms. A pre-federal approach does not suffer that disadvantage — indeed, it is the classical orthodoxy of European integration — and will retain its advocates around the table. However, the public mood since Maastricht has not been noticeably federalist, and for this IGC — for the first time — the public mood has been a serious constraint from the outset. Thus the greater part of the debate is likely to range between the minimalist option and a differentiated Europe, which may contain some elements, perhaps only partially realised, of the maximalist approach.

There is a basic puzzle underlying these often arcane debates about institutions and procedures. It concerns the relationship between the collective will to act and the institutions through which action is decided and implemented. For minimalists,"where there's a will there's a way"; by the same token, though, no amount of institutional reform can by itself create the necessary will. On the other hand, maximalists see institutions as determinants of political will in the long term, and as a necessary condition for the effective expression of political will in the short term. The outcome of the Intergovernmental Conference will reflect the tension between these two different political temperaments.

So far as the second pillar is concerned, the IGC covers two sets of *issues*: the way in which the common foreign policy is made at present, and the way in which the military dimension of security policy ("defence") might be incorporated in the future.

Under the first heading, the *common foreign policy*, the major issues may be summarised as follows:

* the legal status of the Union, and its legal structure which emphasises the need for consistency between the three pillars

* whether the decision-making procedure should expand the very limited provisions for majority voting

* the institutional capacity of the Union in the preparation of the CFSP

* the implementation of policy, involving the external function of the rotating presidency of the Council

* the method of financing the CFSP

* its democratic accountability.

When it comes to the second set of issues, concerning *security and defence*, the IGC is entering much less familiar territory. Three closely interrelated issues are likely to be on the agenda:

* the definition of "defence policy", with a possible distinction between collective self-defence of the Union's territory and military involvement in international crisis management

* the decision-making procedure relating to defence questions

* the future relationship between the European Union itself and the WEU.

THE COMMON FOREIGN AND SECURITY POLICY

Objectives
The aims of the CFSP, listed above, are placed within the broader framework of UN legitimacy and the principal pan-European agreements at Helsinki in 1975 and Paris in 1990. This formulation provides a general and unexceptionable description of best democratic practice in late-twentieth-century diplomacy. To attempt to define it in more detail might encroach on the question of means rather than ends, and the conservative view is that, as well as leading to divergent views on specific policies, this would be inappropriate in the basic legal document of the European Union.

On the other hand, there is a strong case for making the purpose of the CFSP more concrete and explicit, in order to emphasise its relevance. One proposal, for example, suggests references to: the aim of stability in central and eastern Europe; the need to reassure Russia; the development of partnerships with neighbouring countries in the Mediterranean basin; support for multilateralism; the reform of the UN; and relations of partnership rather than dependence with developing countries (Federal Trust, 1995). Wording to that effect might give a more regional specificity to what is at present a rather banal list of universal goals.

Legal aspects

The legal structure of the treaty, divided into three pillars with different policy-making rules, is often seen as a source of delay and ineffective policies. The separation of the first and second pillars is artificial; both are aspects of the "external action of the Union". The first pillar uses the "Community method" of qualified majority voting in conjunction with an active role for the Commission to decide on development cooperation policy and external commercial policy, both of which can be used as foreign policy instruments, to grant aid or impose economic sanctions. In the second pillar decisions are more easily blocked and the Commission's position is less prominent. Harnessing both sets of parallel procedures to a single policy action can be a cumbersome business.

It can also be confusing for the external actor involved, whether it be another international organisation or a state. The Union as such (unlike the European Community) does not even have a formal legal existence for the outside world, and the Reflection Group Report, for instance, raises the possibility of revising the treaty to give it the advantage of international legal personality. This question is on the table at the IGC. There appears to be a willingness to remedy the evident anomaly, though there may be difficulties with regard to some member states' constitutional procedures.

Changing the internal legal structure is a more controversial matter. Doing away with the separate pillars is generally seen as a maximalist reform, involving a move to qualified majority voting, and may be resisted on that score alone. Yet the difficulty of ensuring consistency between the pillars is seen as central, particularly by the Commission. It even argues that in some respects the Maastricht Treaty has made matters worse; for example, the new Article 228a on economic sanctions, designed as a formal codification of existing practice, "has served to make procedures more unwieldy" (Commission, 1995a, p. 68). The report on the first phase of the IGC, while referring to the need to improve consistency between the CFSP and external economic relations, assumes the persistence of the pillar structure.

Decision-making procedures

The persistence of the requirement of unanimity for CFSP decisions is generally seen as the hallmark of the second pillar. In fact the Treaty on European Union already includes potential modifications of this principle. Of the two types of policy instruments referred to in the treaty, "common positions" and "joint actions", the former can only be decided by consensus of all member states and is thus subject to the veto of any one of them. This is a strictly intergovernmental procedure. However, that for joint actions is more complex. The initial decision to undertake a joint action is decided by unanimity, but the member states may decide that further specified decisions within that framework may be taken by qualified majority vote (TEU, Article J 3.2). In effect this is an attempt to distinguish between "primary" decisions of principle and "secondary" decisions of implementation.

In practice, however, the majority vote possibility has not been used and the procedure has remained a dead letter. One reason for this state of affairs is confusion as to which instrument, the common position or joint action, is appropriate in any given circumstances. The original intention seems to have been to make joint actions the jewel in the CFSP crown, given what seemed to be opportunities to develop more streamlined procedures which did not have to revert to the test of consensus for even the most trivial consequential decision. In practice, though, this was to miss the point that it is often impossible to be sure in advance which decisions are only secondary or implementing decisions. The particular value of common positions, which acquire weight precisely because they do represent the complete membership of the Union, may also have been underestimated. The clarification of the scope of these policy instruments is being discussed at the IGC.

Another softening of the hard edge of unanimity which is already in the treaty, in one of the declarations attached to it, is an agreement "that, with regard to Council decisions requiring unanimity [in the CFSP], Member States will, to the extent possible, avoid preventing a unanimous decision where a qualified majority exists in favour of that decision" (TEU, Declaration 27). But declarations are not binding obligations, and so far this particular one has had no identifiable effect.

It is likely that the IGC will consider ways of either resuscitating these existing provisions or using them as a basis for more substantial change. Maximalists will promote a less constrained move towards qualified majority voting, perhaps returning to the attempt made during the 1991 IGC to identify categories of common interests which could be handled in this way. Alternatively, they might seek a restrictive definition of a state's "vital interests" which would be necessary to prevent a common decision.

Advocates of the maximalist position argue that the existence of majority voting is important, not to bully doubters into submission, but to discourage member states from resorting too easily to the veto on trivial grounds without having to justify their opposition to their partners.

There has also been an emphasis on developing the intermediate option of some form of abstention, as suggested by Declaration 27. The Reflection Group Report refers to several ad hoc arrangements: "positive or constructive abstention", "consensus minus one" and "super-qualified majority" are among the variants listed (Reflection Group, 1995, Annotated agenda, para. 154). These procedures are not, however, spelled out in treaty language, but they all seek a degree of flexibility which would prevent action by the Union being blocked by a small minority, and are thus significant in the overall IGC perspective of developng a form of differentiated integration.

Procedures for flexibility beg some important questions. The first is how large the minority (and small the majority) can be without straining the notion that the policy adopted is that of the Union as a whole. In order to sustain the principle that all members subscribe to the basic objectives of the Union, it is sometimes argued that such measures would involve the political solidarity of all member states, and perhaps even financial solidarity with respect to the particular decision. This implies that the opposition of the state or states in the minority is not so acute that they cannot acquiesce in silence. In practice this may be difficult, since the reason for abstention in the first place may derive from a visible domestic controversy; in these circumstances pressing the claims of solidarity may compel the abstaining member state towards an outright veto.

The minimalist position on decision-making regards this search for procedural flexibility as being largely misconceived. If there is no unanimity in the first place, it is argued, there is no point in trying to pretend that the Union can act effectively. In this view, Article J might be tidied up by eliminating the (so far redundant) possibility of qualified majority voting in Article J 3.2, and leaving Declaration 27 where it is, as an exhortation to good behaviour.

The preparation of policy
In contrast to the diversity of views already apparent on the issue of decision-making, there seems to be wide agreement that improvements can be made to the preparatory stage of policy formulation. At present, the resources available are divided between the Council secretariat, which has a small unit devoted to the CFSP and is mainly responsible for servicing the

rotating presidency, the Commission's geographically divided directorates and the member states' foreign ministries.

The degree of decentralisation in this arrangement is such that, particularly in responding to crises, the policy of the Union is based on hasty improvisation, with the larger foreign ministries often being the only source of specialised information or expertise. The near-vacuum at the centre means that there is no effective "institutional memory" for the Union as a whole; much has to be reinvented on each occasion a decision is called for. In these circumstances it is hardly surprising if the Council has to base its decisions on inadequate information and improvised policy positions. This is in marked contrast to the first pillar, where the Commission is the focus of a painstaking process of preparing policy positions which have a realistic chance of being agreed by all the interests concerned, and ultimately by the Council.

The Reflection Group Report refers to the establishment of an "analysis, forecasting, early warning system and planning unit" to meet this need (Reflection Group, 1995, Annotated agenda, para. 153). The questions for the IGC mainly concern its location and composition; the Council secretariat appears to be generally favoured for the former, while the inclusion of officials from the Commission, national foreign ministries and (for some) the WEU secretariat is seen as a way of maintaining links between the relevant institutions.

The creation of such an analysis unit in that way might not even require amendment of the treaty. However, a group of experts, reporting to the Commission, argues that this unit should be independent of the Council secretariat because the latter is too beholden to the member states. In its view, it should be staffed by personnel from all the relevant institutions but headed by a specifically designated senior CFSP official (Experts Group on the CFSP, 1995). This idea of giving the CFSP a stronger personal leadership has also been raised in the context of a reform of the presidency of the Council.

Presiding over the CFSP
The presidency of the Council, which rotates every six months between the member states, has the responsibility for ensuring the implementation of common measures and representing the CFSP in the outside world (TEU, Articles J 5.1, J 5.2). In these tasks it is assisted by the Council secretariat and by its immediate predecessor and successor in the office of presidency — the "troika" system.

The effectiveness of this arrangement has been criticised, especially by the Commission, because of varying commitment by specific member states and the disruption associated with a lack of continuity. It is also argued (mainly by the larger member state governments) that the smaller states, no matter how effective their internal management of the presidency, simply do not possess the diplomatic profile to represent the Union externally.

Whatever the merits of these arguments, the IGC is considering whether the presidency's role with respect to the CFSP should be reinforced or even replaced by the appointment of a senior figurehead. Indeed, the Reflection Group devoted considerable attention to "the personification" of the CFSP (Reflection Group, 1995, Annotated agenda, paras. 157–62). It refers to several options: the designation of a member of the Commission; the appointment of a "high representative" by the European Council; or the appointment of a CFSP secretary-general within the council secretariat.

The eventual choice of any (or none) of these options could be a controversial issue at the IGC. The higher the political profile of the post (for example, a senior political personality appointed by the European Council), the more it is likely to cut across the prerogatives of the presidency and to rival the other existing personification of the Union in general, that is the President of the Commission. Also, from the point of view of outside governments or organisations it could complicate rather than simplify the answer to the question — who represents the EU? A more modest variant also suggested in the Reflection Group Report is for a secretary-general to both head the new analysis unit and assist the presidency with CFSP matters. All of these ideas are on the table at the IGC, together with changes to the troika system and the appointment of special envoys.

Financing
The question of financing the CFSP becomes more important as the EU moves from the previous emphasis on declaratory policy to common actions involving relatively large expenditure. The Treaty on European Union allows for operational as well as administrative expenditures to be charged to the Community budget, rather than relying on national contributions. According to the Reflection Group Report, a broad majority of member states favours this practice.

However, establishing satisfactory procedures to implement the provision has proved much more difficult than anticipated. For example, the question of how specific the oversight of the European Parliament should be has been a bone of contention. Given the latitude normally allowed in the conduct of national foreign policy (where specific expenditure often cannot be identified in advance), it is argued that a similar approach is appropriate for the CFSP. Whether the issue can be resolved without treaty revision remains to be seen.

Democratic accountability

The financing issue is part of the broader question of the accountability of the CFSP. In the post-Maastricht context, with its emphasis on "transparency" and "openness" in policy-making, accountability may loom larger than it has in previous IGCs.

At present, the European Parliament has general rights to be "informed" and "consulted" about the CFSP, but it seeks a tighter definition of its position in this regard, including arrangements to allow for the subjects of Council decisions to be treated confidentially (European Parliament, 1995a, A., 3 (iii)). However, the Parliament's overall position with regard to the IGC remains rather weak; it is not a participant in the negotiations, and has to rely on complex consultative arrangements to make its views known. The progress report on the initial phase of the IGC has very little to say about the European Parliament's role in the second pillar beyond suggesting that the general wish is to keep the treaty base as it is (European Council, 1996a, p. 44).

To the extent that the second pillar is still characterised by intergovernmental procedures, accountability is not the sole prerogative of the European Parliament, but must be shared with national parliaments. Indeed, several governments are concerned lest the European Parliament acquire greater rights of policy oversight than those possessed by their national legislatures. Of course, the IGC cannot come to decisions as to how national parliaments conduct their business, but it would be surprising nonetheless if the attitudes and perhaps even the procedures of national parliaments, and their relevant standing committees, were not influenced to some extent by this issue.

SECURITY AND DEFENCE

In the 1991 IGC, the negotiations on security and defence were focused on two broad options: a "Europeanisation" of defence cooperation which would develop the WEU as the military branch of the European Union, or the maintenance of the "Atlanticist" status quo which depended mainly on NATO. Following American warnings that the first option would threaten the survival of the transatlantic alliance (a view energetically pursued by the British and Dutch delegations at the IGC), the outcome was ambiguous.

The WEU was recognised as "an integral part of the development of the Union, to elaborate and implement actions of the Union which have defence implications" (TEU, Article J 4.2), but it was made clear that it was also "a means to strengthen the European pillar of the Atlantic Alliance" (TEU,

Declaration on Western European Union, para. 2). The basic commitment in the Treaty on European Union to include defence, as part of the totality of "questions related to the security of the Union", did so in a future-oriented and almost apologetic way: "the eventual framing of a common defence policy, which might in time lead to a common defence" (TEU, Article J 4.1).

The Commission argued in 1995 that this dimension of EU policy "has yet to take effective shape" (Commission, 1995a, para. 161). Thus the current IGC involves a consideration of what the language of the treaty means, and what further commitments it might lead to. Although on this occasion the American attitude to the very idea of "European defence" is less negative than it was in 1991, the transatlantic dimension, in the shape of NATO reform, is still the ghost at the feast.

Treaty language: what is "defence"?
At first sight, defence seems to be an activity implying the existence of an aggressor, but usage of the word in the context of public policy has long held broader connotations. Thus defence has to do with all things military, and defence policy is policy "towards contingencies in which armed force might be used and towards how that use should be managed" (Martin and Roper, 1995, p. 1).

These contingencies may indeed include the classical image of defence against aggression — the protective dimension of security policy — but they also include the military aspects of international crisis management. This distinction has become more evident since the end of the Cold War, during which the classical usage tended to predominate in policy debates. Unfortunately both types of activity now tend to be lumped together under the same label, thus often obscuring precisely what is at issue — "the use of our military capabilities" (van Eekelen, 1995, p. 73).

In the context of military cooperation, the two broad categories are sometimes referred to as the "article five" commitments and the "Petersberg tasks". The former covers the collective self-defence of the cooperating states' territory, on the basis of mutual security guarantees in legal form — Article 5 of the North Atlantic Treaty of 1949 (the "Washington Treaty"), and Article V of the WEU Treaty of 1948 (amended in 1954 as the "Modified Brussels Treaty") (see Appendix VI). These commitments are those of an orthodox military alliance — if one member is attacked, the others are obliged to come to its aid.

On the other hand, the possibility of using armed forces where there was no external aggression was recognised in a WEU declaration in June 1992 (the Petersberg Declaration), which referred to "humanitarian and rescue tasks;

peacekeeping tasks; tasks of combat forces in crisis management, including peacemaking" (Appendix VI). This formulation begs questions as to precisely what sort of commitment may be involved, which will be examined below (see chapter 10), but it does not require membership of a military alliance.

A further source of confusion in the text of the Treaty on European Union is the distinction between a "common defence policy" and a "common defence". For some the wording suggests a two-stage evolution (with a very hazy time-scale), in which the Union moves from a relatively low level of ambition to a higher one. Thus, for example, an official Swedish report suggests that a common defence policy would include cooperation on specific military matters, but would not necessarily be comprehensive in its scope or fully integrated prior to the agreement on a common defence (Astrom and Leifland, 1994, p. 38). On the other hand, this idea of a gradual, sequential development has been rejected as unworkable by those who see the concurrent development of both common defence policy and common defence as logical and desirable (Martin and Roper, 1995, p. 2).

The respective importance of article five commitments and the Petersberg tasks is not self-evident in either model. If it does nothing else, the IGC might try to clarify the existing terminology of the treaty.

Decision-making procedures
Article J 4.3 of the Treaty on European Union makes it clear that decisions with "defence implications" will be taken in a strictly intergovernmental way, by excluding them from the joint action procedures, which allow for a very circumscribed measure of qualified majority voting. Such decisions must be taken by unanimity, and the WEU will be brought into play only on the "request" of the Union.

Before examining the issue of the relationship between the two institutions, it is necessary to underline the more restricted parameters of the discussion on decision-making in the field of defence than those pertaining to the CFSP as a whole. These are summarised in the two principal preparatory documents for the IGC as follows:

* "Participation in military operations in the framework of the Petersberg tasks will remain a matter for national decision" (Reflection Group, 1995, para. 172).

* "Whatever the outcome of the IGC, participation in the new tasks defined at Petersberg will remain a matter for national decision" (WEU, 1995a, para. 98).

In short, there is no automaticity in such commitments. It follows from this that flexibility or differentiation is the name of the game in the context of a common defence policy. In order to ensure that action is not blocked by a small minority (how small being a subsidiary question), the procedures for "constructive abstention" and the like, referred to above, may be particularly relevant here. Of course, the same difficulty arises; these procedures may not cover the case where opposition to the majority takes the form of a claim to vital national interests.

The relationship between the EU and the WEU

There is a strong overlap in the composition of the EU and the WEU, but it is not complete and the difficulty in establishing the relationship between the two stems from this. One problem, which has not received much attention in the preparatory stages of the IGC, lies in the basic conditions of membership of the WEU. In 1991, in the second of two WEU declarations attached to the Maastricht Treaty, the WEU member states invited EU member states not in the WEU to become either full members or observers. It might be inferred from this that membership of the WEU is a corollary of EU membership as of right; however, this is to discount the implications of the WEU's parallel position as the European element in NATO. With regard to the article five commitments of both alliances, the bottom line of the mutual assistance guarantee is still seen as the American commitment, and the United States and some European members of the WEU are understandably reluctant to see countries join the WEU without at the same time subscribing to NATO.

In practice the potential confusion arising from the 1991 WEU invitation has not been realised, since the new EU member states chose to be observers and not to apply for full membership. But the question might be posed in the context of further EU enlargement. If, for example, Estonia joins the EU can it claim entry to NATO by the "back door" of the WEU? That would match Estonian aspirations, but does not fit current NATO thinking, given the sensitivities involved in reconciling NATO enlargement with the reassurance of Russia (Asmus and Nurick, 1996).

Clarification of this issue is a matter for NATO rather than the WEU or the European Union's IGC. The latter is concentrating on the overall pattern for future relations between the WEU and the EU, based on options formulated in the Reflection Group and by the WEU itself. These represent a range of choices from minimum to maximum change and incorporate a variety of intermediate positions.

The *minimalist* option is described as a "reinforced partnership between an autonomous WEU and the EU". The partnership already exists; the

C. LIBRARY, LETTERKENNY

59

reinforcement consists of developing closer political and administrative links between the two institutions. Thus, for example, regular WEU summit meetings would follow those of the European Council, with decisions taken by full consensus, and there would be more intensive coordination of the respective secretariats. So far as military matters at the operational level were concerned, the focus would be on improving the development of collaboration in crisis management, including the possibility of using NATO assets in cases where NATO (in effect the United States and Canada) was not willing or able to be involved.

Another aspect of collaboration that would continue under this and the more ambitious options would be the protracted and hitherto not very successful search for a rationalisation of the European defence industry. The Western European Armaments Group (WEAG), established under the aegis of the WEU in 1992, is the main forum for this task. Significant change to what is in effect the protection of national arms industries under Article 223 of the EEC Treaty might require amendment of that article. The framing of arms export controls, which already takes place in the CFSP, would not necessarily be precluded by such a development (see chapter 11).

Reinforced partnership would not, however, lead to any significant legal or institutional change. The WEU treaty, due to be reviewed in 1998, could simply be extended. The WEU itself would remain an autonomous body, presumably able to act at the behest of its own full members as well as at the request of the EU. The status of the five EU member states which are WEU observers would allow those countries to contribute to WEU operations should they so wish (WEU, 1995 a, Option A; Reflection Group, 1995, Annotated agenda, para. 175).

The *maximalist* option is the integration or merger of the WEU into the European Union, described most fully as "Option C" in the WEU document. This clearly would require major legal changes, including the disappearance of the WEU treaty and the incorporation of its provisions in a revised European Union treaty. This could be realised in one of two ways. First, all aspects of defence, including the collective defence commitment, would be commitments of the CFSP; in this case, states unwilling or unable to subscribe to mutual security guarantees (the current position of the WEU observers) would opt out of that commitment. Alternatively, the crisis management aspects of defence would be written into the CFSP, to which all member states would subscribe; the collective defence agreement would be contained in a defence protocol attached to the main treaty, to which those member states which were willing would opt in.

The *intermediate* options are more complex. That there are intermediate options, of course, testifies to the modest expectations of the IGC outcome currently held by many governments, in contrast to the mood preceding the 1991 IGC. Even maximalists recognise that their objectives may only be realisable in the medium to long term.

One intermediate position seeks to differentiate the EU and WEU in terms of the military functions to be ascribed to each. The European Union would concentrate on the Petersberg tasks, either by being able to direct, not merely "request", the WEU to act on its behalf, or by taking them over and leaving the WEU purely as a collective defence organisation (Reflection Group, 1995, Annotated agenda, para. 176).

The other formulations concentrate their differentiation more on the extent of authority the European Union might exercise over the WEU, and the legal and institutional implications this might have for treaty revision. Three variants have been suggested, in ascending order of authority exercised by the EU (Reflection Group, 1995, Annotated agenda, para. 177; WEU, 1995a, Options B 1–3). The first envisages the European Council issuing general guidelines to the WEU, as it does for CFSP joint actions; the second allows the EU to give concrete instructions to the WEU; the third would involve a legally binding EU–WEU agreement in which the latter would be obliged to implement the former's decisions.

All of these options, whether minimalist or maximalist, are framed in a permissive way which leaves many circles to be squared in the actual IGC. Thus, for example, the WEU document states "whatever form European defence arrangements take in the future, the collective security guarantee currently embodied in Article V of the modified Brussels Treaty must be preserved". But not necessarily, it would seem, by all EU member states. The WEU's list of "principles and guidelines to assist the IGC" (WEU, 1995a, para. 98) concludes with the following statement: "the sovereign decisions of WEU observers regarding their defence arrangements will be respected. The IGC should promote European arrangements that enable all WEU and EU countries to contribute to the fulfilment of Petersberg tasks. European defence arrangements should encourage equitable burden-sharing between nations." The defence arrangements of WEU observers, with the exception of Denmark (as a member of NATO), do not include Article V commitments.

The transatlantic dimension
The point has already been made that the question of European defence has long been a function of the engagement of the United States in European security, through the NATO alliance. The evolution of the WEU, or the broader idea of a European Security and Defence Identity, is bound up with the evolution of NATO just as much as with that of the European Union.

One of the main ways in which that relationship is being developed is through the concept of Combined Joint Task Forces, introduced at the NATO summit meeting in 1994 and affirmed at a NATO foreign ministers' meeting in June 1996. This represents an arrangement whereby NATO assets (for example, integrated commands or logistic capabilities) could be made available to the WEU, even when the United States does not itself wish to be involved. More precise indications of how it is to be implemented are as likely to be shaped by the operational experience of crisis management in the field as in diplomatic discussions. Thus the fate of the NATO-led operation in Bosnia, and the attitudes of the major actors in it, will remain significant influences on the IGC debate on security and defence.

CONCLUSIONS

The European Union, like the other multilateral institutions involved in European security, is still adapting its policies and its policy framework to the post-Cold War international system. The establishment of a Common Foreign and Security Policy in the Treaty on European Union in 1991 left many questions unanswered, particularly so far as defence was concerned.

There has been a more intensive preparatory phase for the 1996 Intergovernmental Conference, leading to a wide range of suggestions for reform, though even those who advocate maximalist proposals do not envisage radical changes in the IGC. The issues regarding the CFSP itself include the question of whether the unanimity requirement in its decision-making procedure should be relaxed in some way, and various ways of strengthening its institutional capacity.

The fleshing out of the very sketchy provisions on defence is more problematic. Decision-making in this field is likely to remain the prerogative of national governments, but a variety of suggestions have been advanced for the relationship between the European Union and the WEU. These fit mainly within the broad integration options defined earlier in this chapter as the minimalist Union and the differentiated Union. The extent to which national positions on these questions diverge is explored in more detail in the next three chapters.

CHAPTER 4
THE MAJOR ACTORS IN THE IGC

The proposals which have already emerged during the preparatory stage of the Intergovernmental Conference, in the various reports referred to in chapter 3, are not the product of some disembodied "spirit of Europe". Although those deriving from the Commission and the European Parliament are shaped to a considerable extent by those bodies' role as articulators of a common interest, national proposals vary in motivation. They can be "integrationist" in form, but are primarily expressions of largely national visions of what common European interests ought to be; of national interests more narrowly conceived; and of the idiosyncratic compromises of national domestic politics.

The role of the European Union as part of the multilateral security framework can hardly be understood without an appreciation of the common or diverging views of its member states, the subject of the next three chapters. An analysis of the national input to the blueprinting process often provides more focused arguments for specific proposals and some indication of their likely success, as well as an insight into the various national positions at the outset of the actual IGC negotiations.

This chapter looks at the security policies of the major actors. It deals with the following themes:

* the general profile of a "major actor"

* the maximalist role of Germany

* the contrasting position of the United Kingdom

* the enigmatic policy of France

* the extent to which this "triumvirate" combines its security policies

* the security policies of the other major actors, Italy and Spain

* the option of a large state directorate for foreign and security policy.

MAJOR ACTORS: THE PROFILE OF POLITICAL LEADERSHIP

The sovereign equality of states — the formal legal principle on which international relations are conducted — is often contrasted with the Orwellian reality that, where power and influence are concerned, some are more equal than others. The status of the "great powers" has been an important determinant of international politics for centuries.

If the term "major actor" is preferred in this book, it is partly to indicate that in a world of global markets and sceptical but influential public opinions even the larger states are often neither as great nor as powerful as in previous periods. This is particularly evident with regard to the larger states in the European Union, both because their historical fortunes have waned and because of the internal disciplines of European political integration.

Nevertheless, size still matters. The possession of a relatively large population — and the corresponding economic significance of a large domestic market — by itself gives a country great influence in the determination of collective policies in the Union. Its government may assume the "responsibility" to lead the other member states in what it considers the appropriate direction, and it may well be that there is an acceptance on the part of the smaller states that at least some element of leadership is both desirable and necessary.

The legitimacy of leadership by the major actors is reinforced by the principle of democratic representation. They have a right to some expression of the fact that they represent the interests of a large number of the Union's citizens. Thus in the arrangements for qualified majority voting in the Council, France, Germany, Italy and the United Kingdom have ten votes each, and Spain has eight. There is a significant gap to the next in line, the Netherlands, with five votes.

This criterion provides a preliminary group of five major actors in the EU, corresponding with populations ranging from 38.9 million in Spain to 80.5 million in Germany (Appendix VII). Of course, that range in population itself suggests that counting heads is a very crude indicator of political influence. The analysis will have to deal with intangible factors such as historical experience and reputation, together with the degree of domestic consensus regarding the country's European policies. Thus in assessing these major actors' positions on security policy in the IGC, attention will be paid to the following:

* the government's general policy approach to European integration

* its specific attitude towards the CFSP

* the state's overall profile on military policy

* specific attitudes to a future common defence policy.

GERMANY: THE MAXIMALIST CHAMPION

For nearly half a century European integration has been a central constant in German policy. It has been seen as the essential framework for the country's political rehabilitation, its economic success and, more recently, its reunification. This tradition was explicitly acknowledged in the agreement of the Christian Democratic Union/Christian Social Union/Free Democratic Party coalition which continued in government under Chancellor Helmut Kohl after the general elections of October 1994. Chancellor Kohl has repeatedly argued that integration is essential in order to compensate for Germany's natural predominance (arising from its size and central location) and in order to exorcise the demons of the past.

The main element of German strategy is the projected single currency envisaged in Economic and Monetary Union. Political union, implying some form of greater centralisation of political authority, is viewed as a necessary corollary of EMU in what is the most overtly federal approach to integration of any of the major actors. However, the German public has yet to be convinced of the merits of the single currency, and a considerable part of the government parties' arguments in favour of the scheduled change has to do with security, as well as the more specific consequences for economic policy.

The further enlargement of the EU to the east is a prominent theme in this argument. It is assumed that the stabilisation of Germany's eastern neighbours is a basic prerequisite for the security not just of Germany but of the EU, and that enlargement is the best means to that end. Given the obvious long-term problems associated with this approach, in the interim the CFSP will be a vital channel of influence.

Thus in the opening round of the pre-IGC debate, it was not surprising to see these themes in a paper produced by the CDU/CSU parliamentary group under the names of Karl Lamers and Wolfgang Schauble (CDU/CSU, 1994). Both enlargement and the CFSP — the latter with a particular emphasis on the urgency of creating a common European defence — were among the five main proposals, together with the argument that a "hard core" of those member states willing and able to proceed with what is in effect a pre-federal agenda should do so.

A second CDU/CSU paper, published in June 1995, deals with the second pillar in more detail (CDU/CSU, 1995). Although neither paper is a statement of official government positions, they may be taken as reflecting the government's preferences quite closely; the more recent document (which drops the controversial hard core concept) is a reasonable guide to German thinking on the reform of the second pillar.

It refers to four "prerequisites" for a successful CFSP. The first is a change to the decision-making procedure, which for decisions without military implications should be by qualified majority (possibly using a system of "double majorities", taking account of a majority of the EU population as well as that of its states). Decisions with military implications must be taken in such a way that a minority of member states cannot block joint action by a majority, but neither can any country be obliged to participate in such a joint action against its will. These objectives are justified on the grounds that the way in which common political will is formed is "the decisive institutional issue", and that current (intergovernmental) procedure has been the main reason for the deficiencies of the CFSP.

The second prerequisite is an improvement in the institutional capacity of the CFSP; it recommends the common analysis unit which found such widespread favour in the Reflection Group (though the second CDU/CSU paper has less to say on how this might be achieved than its predecessor did). The third prerequisite is stated even more succinctly; that secure funding must be available through the Union's budget.

Before turning to the final CDU/CSU prerequisite, a common defence policy, an additional emphasis in the document must be acknowledged. Following the logic of majority voting in the second pillar (and consequent restriction in democratic control by national parliaments), the European Parliament's rights must be broadened. Thus consultation before the adoption of European Council guidelines should be mandatory, and the President should be informed on every occasion a decision is taken by qualified majority voting.

Since the Second World War defence policy has always raised problems of both external and internal legitimacy for German governments; the solution has always been found in an international rather than national context. German rearmament was conducted within NATO (and according to arms control limitations in the WEU context); the renunciation of a German nuclear capability was reaffirmed as recently as 1990 in the reunification treaty.

It was not until a ruling of the Constitutional Court in July 1994 that it was altogether clear that German troops could participate in international crisis management operations outside the NATO treaty area under UN authorisation. Thus although there is now a German contribution to the IFOR operation, the long-standing "culture of restraint" regarding military policy is likely to persist for some time (Meiers, 1995).

Against that background, the CDU/CSU paper's strong emphasis on a common European defence policy is as much an expression of traditional German policy as it is of innovation. It also rests on the proposition that a federal union is incomplete without encompassing all the basic attributes of a state-like international actor, including its own defence.

However, German policy is still firmly predicated on the primacy of NATO in the field of defence. The CDU/CSU paper also acknowledges that in practical terms the objective of a common European defence policy is unlikely to be reached at the current IGC. If the merger of the EU and WEU cannot be achieved in the short term, a fixed timetable for this process must nevertheless be agreed, so that it is achieved in "the medium term". Meanwhile the full members of the WEU should give that organisation the necessary operational capabilities to carry out the Petersberg tasks, and closer organisational links should be developed between the new CFSP analysis unit and the WEU secretariat.

German opposition parties, and indeed the mass public, are less firmly committed to this maximalist conception of the future second pillar. In particular, the Social Democratic Party and the Green Party are divided on the question of moving away from the culture of military restraint. However, the issues of enlargement and of the international community's weakness in Bosnia have already had direct impact on German society, for example in the form of legal and illegal immigration and asylum-seeking. Whatever position is pursued by the German government at the IGC, security is at or near the top of the agenda.

THE UNITED KINGDOM: PRINCIPLED MINIMALISM

British policy towards European integration has generally been as modest, if not actually hostile, as Germany's has been ambitious. A reluctance to undertake novel forms of political engagement, particularly when expressed in the quasi-constitutional language and grandiloquent rhetoric associated with the "construction of Europe", were hallmarks of this attitude even before British politics became more overtly nationalist in tone in the 1980s.

Since the end of the Cold War the United Kingdom's membership of the EU has become a central and divisive issue in domestic politics, not so much between the two large parties as within the governing Conservative Party, led by John Major. The prime minister's attempts to cope with the stridently Europhobe tendency on his backbenches and the increasingly Eurosceptic response within his own government have served only to emphasise the more negative aspects of what might otherwise be a pragmatic critique of the issues facing the IGC. With a barely perceptible parliamentary majority, the British government's policy now tends to advocate pragmatism with ideological fervour.

So far as the second pillar is concerned, the United Kingdom's position is that fundamental treaty revision is unnecessary (Hurd, 1994). In particular, it opposes the argument that the lack of majority voting has anything to do with the success or failure of the CFSP. Common political will, and the enhanced influence that derives from it, cannot be forced by outvoting minorities; only patient consultation and debate can arrive at a consensus which will be durable enough to ensure the implementation of any decision. The idea that non-military decisions be taken by majority and military decisions by unanimity is seen as impracticable in a situation which may well include both sorts of decisions (Hurd, 1995).

The question of whether these arguments about the CFSP should be presented in a schematic way, on the lines of the CDU/CSU papers, seems to have been determined as much by internal Tory party divisions as by any other consideration. The White Paper on the subject made a relatively late appearance in the IGC debate (UK, 1996). However, it was a different matter where defence policy was concerned. Here the British government exploits the comparative advantage of a long reputation as a major military power, its status as one of the five permanent members of the UN Security Council, and its possession of nuclear forces and a relatively large conventional military capability. Next to the United States, the British contribution to IFOR is the second largest, with 10,482 troops deployed in Bosnia and Croatia at mid-summer 1996 (Appendix VII).

Hence it is not surprising that the most detailed British input to the IGC debate on the second pillar takes the form of a memorandum on defence issues, published in March 1995 (UK, 1995).

In effect, this is the basis of the "reinforced partnership" proposal for future relations between the EU and a still autonomous WEU (see chapter 3). Its rationale is based on four "key considerations":

* EU member states may have defence interests which remain exclusively in the national domain (such as the Falkland Islands)

* the nation-state remains the "basic building block" in the international order, and "it is a national Government's duty to answer to national Parliaments when troops are sent into action"; hence intergovernmental decision-making in the context of European cooperation is essential

* "differing rights and responsibilities" of all member states, including abstention from mutual security guarantees, must be respected

* most future missions will involve different coalitions, decided on a case-by-case basis, hence the need for flexibility in institutional structures and procedures.

Throughout this document and subsequent official statements the emphasis is on improving operational measures as opposed to allowing defence to be "a plaything in the game of European construction" (Portillo, 1995). The British position rejects a clear-cut division of labour between NATO (collective defence) and the WEU (crisis management). Above all, it rejects the proposition that European defence is an integral part of the European Union; the WEU may be the framework for the formation of ad hoc military coalitions but it is not seen as a subordinate branch of the EU. British spokesmen argue that procedural reforms such as "constructive abstention" are neither workable nor necessary (Rifkind, 1996).

Two final points about the United Kingdom's approach merit attention. First, there is an explicit argumentation which seems designed to accommodate the defence reservations of the neutral member states. Second, there is little evidence that a Labour Party in government would adopt a significantly different position on the second pillar, irrespective of a more positive style and perhaps even substance on other aspects of the IGC agenda. The Labour Party's approach lays more emphasis on conflict prevention and multilateralism, but the CFSP remains firmly intergovernmental and there is no support for a merger of the WEU with the European Union, which remains without a military competence (British Labour Party, 1995, pp. 14–15).

FRANCE: AN UNFOLDING ENIGMA

Unlike the United Kingdom, France was a founder-member of the European Community and throughout the history of west European integration its commitment has been crucial. That is not to say it has always been forthcoming. The assertive nationalist tradition, associated especially but not exclusively with the Gaullist movement, has often been an uneasy bedfellow with federalist conceptions of supranational policy-making.

The election of Jacques Chirac as president in the spring of 1995 served to accentuate this underlying tension. President Chirac's campaign had been based (among many other things) on the notion that "Europe" is a "necessary ambition" for France, but his political base includes leading opponents of the Treaty on European Union, such as Philippe Seguin. The initial performance of his government, particularly with regard to economic policy, was erratic. The attempt to introduce sweeping reforms, on the grounds of preparing the economy for EMU, led to unexpectedly widespread public sector strikes in November and December 1995. The immediate consequence was a challenge to the credibility of France's commitment to EMU, and indeed to the viability of the whole project.

Against that background, the new French government was not surprisingly slow to promote its position on the IGC in any detail. However, two points seem clear so far as the second pillar is concerned. First, it remains the second pillar, based on the existing intergovernmental form of decision-making. France may be closer to the British than to the German position on that score.

Second, there is considerable interest in the creation of a high-profile secretary-general for the CFSP. Indeed, the personification of the CFSP — "a voice and a face" for the Union's diplomatic persona — is seen as the major French proposal in this field. This post is presented not merely as the administrative head of a future CFSP secretariat or analysis unit (and possibly as head of the WEU secretariat as well); reporting directly to the European Council and the General Affairs Council, it is a position almost on a par with that of the president of the Commission. For some maximalist supporters of integration this seemed to be an indirect challenge to the general status of the Commission.

With regard to the issue of defence, France like the United Kingdom approaches the IGC from a position of comparative advantage in the military sphere. Few could be unaware of one dimension of this military tradition when President Chirac announced his intention to resume nuclear testing, and carried it through amidst considerable international and even some domestic controversy. Paradoxically, the "Europeanisation" of French (and British) nuclear forces is probably the defence issue least likely to be raised in the 1996 IGC. When the possibility was advanced by the president prior to the first test on 5 September 1995, it was widely seen as an exercise in political damage limitation rather than a realistic option. The extent of overt opposition to the tests among EU member states suggests the nuclear issue is not a promising building-block for the construction of Europe (see chapter 9).

France's non-nuclear military capabilities seem more to the point in the IGC context. In February 1996 President Chirac announced plans for a major restructuring of the armed forces, including significant cuts in troop numbers and the politically radical proposal to end peacetime conscription. In effect, this represents a wholesale modernisation in order to ensure that France remains a major military actor in European security. Its contribution to the IFOR operation, with about 8,000 troops, is only exceeded by the American and British contingents.

Participation in an operation which is unequivocally under NATO command is also a significant indicator of continuing changes in French defence policy, which as recently as the 1991 IGC could be characterised as the European pole in the divisive debates between "Atlanticists" and "Europeanists". Now that American objections to the organisation of a European defence identity have lost their edge, and the commitment of the United States to Europe appears less than eternal, the anti-American (or at least un-American) rationale for French policy has waned very considerably (Grant, 1996).

In December 1995 the French government decided to play a fuller role in routine NATO military consultations, though not as yet returning to the integrated command. This move was presented in the context of the continuing reform of NATO, to include a strengthened "European pillar", a positive relationship with Russia and, as President Chirac put it to the US congress, "the adoption, at the appropriate time, of a Transatlantic Charter" (Chirac, 1996). Following the completion of the controversial nuclear tests, France's position seemed less marked by traditional Gaullist exceptionalism; by the NATO foreign ministers' meeting in Berlin in June 1996 France seemed to accept the view that a European Security and Defence Identity, and the further development of the WEU, were in the first place matters to be tackled in a reformed NATO.

Against the background of these manoeuvres on the high ground of "great power" diplomacy, the French position on the second pillar was in several respects quite different from that promoted in the 1991 Intergovernmental Conference. However, just how different remains to be seen, for it is but one element in the "coalition diplomacy" which generally takes place between France and Germany in devising an overall strategy on major turning points in European integration.

THE EU TRIUMVIRATE AND SECURITY POLICY

The effectiveness of the political leadership offered by the major actors depends on the extent to which their policies converge. Historically, this has not required all three of the EU triumvirate states to combine to pursue a common strategy; the Franco-German partnership has often been sufficient. This partnership has also been a necessary condition of significant integration, and the question whether this will apply in the case of the 1996 IGC is therefore pertinent.

The main part of the answer arguably lies in the prospects for the achievement of monetary union, and is thus outside the scope of this book. But so far as the evolution of the CFSP and defence are concerned, the two governments were slow to reach a joint approach, and it does not suggest a strong convergence of positions which might lead to maximalist reforms.

A Franco-German summit meeting at Baden-Baden on 6 December 1995 did admittedly put the need for a "more visible and more resolute common foreign and security policy" as the first of four priorities for the IGC (France and Germany, 1995). However, this document is couched in generalities: it talks of "clarifying" foreign and defence policy objectives as well as the EU–WEU relationship, and giving the CFSP "greater visibility".

A more substantial paper was agreed three months later (France and Germany, 1996). This contains concrete proposals which can be found in more detail in Appendix VIII. They include the following:

* decision-making procedures to allow for flexibility (constructive abstention, qualified majority voting at the implementation stage), and a strengthening of the power of the European Council to set guidelines, especially concerning WEU actions

* a "forecasting and analysis unit" attached to the Council secretariat and other procedures to ensure greater consistency between the pillars

* greater visibility, through a "new post" (but without defining its political profile)

* a political solidarity clause

* putting Petersberg task-type objectives in the treaty

* the eventual inclusion of the WEU in the EU

* developing a European armaments policy.

This shopping list does not go as far in the maximalist direction as Germany might wish, but it does contain several items which the British have already dismissed out of hand. Yet an alternative combination of major actors exists in the purely military field. A Franco-British summit meeting on 30–31 October 1995 reinforced existing cooperation on defence issues, including joint consultations on nuclear policy. As the two main European contributing countries to the UNPROFOR and IFOR operations in Bosnia, France and the United Kingdom have acquired considerable experience in collaboration at the operational level. But although these developments will no doubt influence future military cooperation, the United Kingdom's insistence on remaining aloof from institutional reform in the IGC means that Franco-British partnership is no substitute for Franco-German leadership on the broader issues.

All of this suggests that the interests of the three largest EU states in the security and defence aspects of the IGC will converge at the practical, operational level rather than in terms of major institutional reforms. For them the outcome of the IGC may be not so much an end in itself as another stage in a broader and more protracted competition for political advantage.

ITALY AND SPAIN

The designation of Italy and Spain as major actors in the EU is not quite as convincing as it is in the cases of Germany, France and the United Kingdom. Italy's population and overall economic performance are on a par with the latter two countries, but its political credibility has been seriously compromised by corruption scandals since the last IGC in 1991. Indeed, the country has been undergoing a difficult period of domestic upheaval, marked by party realignments and resort to non-party, "technocratic" government, and it may be some time before political and constitutional stability is regained.

Spain, too, has experienced corruption scandals in recent years, but on a much smaller scale and they may have been purged by the change of government following the general election in March 1996. Spain's status as a major actor is qualified more by the fact that it is clearly the "smallest of the large", in terms of both population and economic development, and by its relatively recent accession to EC/EU membership in 1985.

Nevertheless, both countries are capable of playing a strong supporting role in the IGC, perhaps in combination with one or more of the triumvirate states. The Italian approach to the second pillar follows a long tradition of adherence to federalist goals, though it must be said that in 1995 the technocratic government under Lamberto Dini aroused criticisms from the centre-left opposition for certain lapses in this respect. It advocated majority voting in the second pillar (with exceptions only for vital national interests) and suggested a foreign policy agenda, to be approved by both the European Council and the European Parliament. On the other hand, its support for a high-profile CFSP secretary-general was seen by Italian federalists as weakening the Commission, to which they would attribute the power of fixing foreign policy objectives. Following elections in April 1996 the new centre-left government under Romano Prodi seems likely to sustain continuity in the country's European policy.

Spanish positions on these issues have been broadly similar. In both the Reflection Group and the WEU consultations on the IGC (both of which were chaired by Spain in the second half of 1995) Spain was in the maximalist camp. However, there is less evidence there of a debate between varieties of Eurofederalism. Public opinion has been generally disillusioned with membership of the Union, and the conservative minority government led by Jose Maria Aznar may add Gaullist nuances to an otherwise expected continuity in European policy.

Both Italy and Spain have sizeable military capabilities, with significant contributions to the IFOR operation, of 2,266 and 1,785 troops respectively. Although Spain was a latecomer to NATO, and remains outside its integrated command structure, this was no bar to the appointment of the Spanish foreign minister, Javier Solana, as NATO secretary-general in December 1995. With regard to the defence issue in the IGC, they both support the gradual merger of the EU and WEU, including the proposal to fix a timetable for its completion at the IGC.

A GREAT POWER OPTION?

Among the more unusual proposals for reform of the second pillar, those of a former British foreign minister, Geoffrey Howe, merit attention when considering the role of the major states in the European Union's foreign and security policy (Howe, 1996). This is not because they are a faithful reflection of government positions — indeed, to many they will appear as more heretical than orthodox. However, they do put the case for the leadership role of the larger countries in a more radical way than is usual, and by doing so underline the tension between the need for an effective collective policy and one which has widespread legitimacy.

Lord Howe sees the tendency of the larger states, particularly France and the United Kingdom, to pursue independent policies as a serious weakness for the EU's international stance. In order to give them a real incentive to use and fully accept the collective discipline of the CFSP, he argues for radical changes in decision-making procedures which would reflect their "actual relative power". This would involve a procedure analogous to that in the UN Security Council. Only the five largest states would retain the right of unilateral veto, but this right would be exercised within a system of qualified majority voting. Hence it would require a wide coalition of smaller states to block a decision agreed by the five large states. As a *quid pro quo* for accepting this "variable veto" for the major countries, smaller states would be exempted from policies to which they objected.

These explicit leadership powers for the large states would also be reflected in the presidency of the Council. So far as the second pillar was concerned, this would be the exclusive preserve of the "big five", rotating on an annual basis. In return the other ten might share the presidency of the third pillar, on justice and home affairs.

The advantage of this scheme, according to its author, is that the major states would be encouraged to act in concert more effectively, thereby giving impetus and direction to the European Union as a whole. The disadvantage, however, is that what may be gained in effectiveness may be lost in legitimacy. Although the smaller states could theoretically combine to block a "great power" consensus, this might be difficult in practice. Moreover, the history of European integration shows an instinctive distrust among the governments of small member states with regard to proposed "directoires" composed of the larger countries. Lord Howe's proposals sit squarely in this tradition, and even if they do represent the optimum from a large state point of view, they would be widely contested were they to be put on the table at the IGC.

CONCLUSIONS

Of the three principal major actors, only Germany has been the source of unequivocally maximalist proposals for reform to the second pillar of the Treaty on European Union. The European policies of both the United Kingdom and France are hotly contested in domestic politics. British policy is unequivocally minimalist with regard to the CFSP, while some French positions in this field appear closer to the British than to the German approach.

Thus concerted leadership at the IGC looks problematic. The second pillar does not seem to be the strongest element in the Franco-German partnership, though both governments can support a series of incremental changes and France's more positive view of NATO will make collaboration easier with regard to defence. Franco-British convergence on the substance of defence cooperation does not lead in an integrative direction, so far as the European Union is concerned.

Of the other two major actors, Italy favours the maximalist end of the IGC spectrum alongside Germany while Spain, under an untried government, may converge with France, which shares its Mediterranean orientation.

Chapter 5
Small States and the IGC: The Alliance Countries

Of the ten small states in the European Union, five are full members of both the military alliances, NATO and the WEU, while the other five have observer status in the WEU. Although one of the latter, Denmark, is also a NATO member, the distinction between the two groupings is an important one for the Intergovernmental Conference, since it marks an initial divergence of views on how far integration should proceed in the field of defence.

This chapter considers the positions on second pillar issues of the first group, the "alliance countries" — Belgium, Greece, Luxembourg, the Netherlands and Portugal. It will explore the questions already raised in chapter 4, on the basis of a further subdivision between:

* the Benelux states (Belgium, the Netherlands and Luxembourg), which have traditionally been the small state champions — and indeed originators — of the maximalist version of European integration

* Greece and Portugal, which have a more recent and in some respects more qualified attachment to European integration.

Before looking at these specific national cases, it is worth making some general points concerning the place of the smaller states in the security policies of the European Union.

Small states in the European Union

Historically, small states, with their relative lack of diplomatic weight and military capabilities, have been prey to the instability and propensity to violence often found in international politics. They thus have a particularly strong common interest in the development of co-operative security regimes, which are rule-bound, and oriented towards "civilian" rather than military forms of power. Membership of an entity like the European Union is in itself a form of preventive security policy, placing the small state in a multifaceted contractual relationship with large and previously aggressive neighbours.

For those small states with harsh experience of invasion, defeat and occupation, membership of a formal military alliance may be seen as a necessary complement to the informal "security community", especially when the latter is only in an embryonic stage. For the smaller member states of both security communities and classical military alliances the stakes may be higher, and the fear of abandonment greater, than for the major actors.

This possibility gives a particular significance to the attitudes adopted by the smaller states in the Intergovernmental Conference. Depending on their specific historical experiences and geopolitical interests, they may have a more active role than would seem to be warranted on the basis of their relatively limited diplomatic and military weight.

BENELUX: THE SMALL STATE MAXIMALISTS

These generalisations would seem to apply to a considerable extent to the Benelux countries — *Belgium, the Netherlands* and *Luxembourg*. Up to 1945 "the cockpit of Europe", the Benelux states subsequently became enthusiastic proponents of both the European Community and a western alliance as responses to the double threat they feared — of Soviet expansion and a further round of Franco-German antagonism. In the post-Cold War era their security policies are framed in both the EU and NATO multilateral settings, which they regard as complementary. All three are contributors to the IFOR operation; the Netherlands provides 2,092 troops, with Belgium and Luxembourg sending 346 and 22 respectively.

CFSP positions
In addition to publishing their individual national views on the IGC, the Benelux governments agreed joint proposals prior to the conference (Benelux, 1996: see Appendix IX). Regarding reform of the CFSP, the Benelux governments highlight possibilities of moving in the direction of majority voting, or at least a relaxation of the need for unanimity, perhaps through a system of "partial consensus". In one of the more detailed national position papers produced by any of the member states, large or small, the Dutch government makes the point that this would still be within an intergovernmental context, without a role for the European Court of Justice or exclusive right of initiative for the Commission (Netherlands, 1995a, p. 19). But even gradual moves away from the consensus principle ought, in this view, to be accompanied by increased democratic control by the European Parliament.

The idea of a reinforced analysis unit also finds general favour, and the option of creating a new, separate body for this purpose is not precluded.

Either way, the Benelux positions stress the importance of the Commission being fully involved in the preparatory stages of CFSP policy-making, suggesting perhaps a clarification of the rather cryptic formulation of Article J 9 of the Treaty on European Union ("the Commission shall be fully associated with the work" in the CFSP).

On the issue of heading such a unit with a secretary-general, there is also a concern lest this post become a pole of institutional rivalry with the external prerogatives of the Commission. The joint paper refers to a senior official, appointed by the Council in consultation with the Commission. However, the fear that a strong secretary-general for the CFSP might also undermine the prerogatives of the rotating presidency of the Council — a fear evident in other small states' positions — is not explicitly advanced as an argument.

Indeed, the Dutch government, in yet another IGC position paper on general institutional reform, characterises the presidency — and especially its external tasks — as "an increasingly onerous burden" (Netherlands, 1995b, p. 25). It declares a provisional support for "team Presidencies", with three states sharing responsibilities for one year. (Of course, as the largest small state in the Union, which if further enlarged will be predominantly composed of small states, the Netherlands might expect to find itself as a team leader in such an arrangement.)

All three Benelux governments support funding of the CFSP by the Community budget as the norm. In their national position papers they emphasise the principle of financial solidarity, that joint actions should be implemented by all member states. Thus, even if there should be some move away from a strict insistence on consensus, all states will have contributed financially. Opting out or "standing aside" from an EU joint action should not be a cost-free option.

Defence policy positions
As full members of both NATO and the WEU, the Benelux states are not preoccupied by any distinction in principle between "article five commitments" to collective defence and the Petersberg tasks. So far as the operational dimension of defence policy is concerned, both Belgium and the Netherlands are in the throes of a significant reduction and restructuring of their armed forces, including the radical step of abandoning peacetime conscription.

The relationship between the European Union and the WEU is the central concern. The Netherlands' traditional preference for an Atlantic rather than a purely European alliance, which was a marked feature of its position in the 1991 IGC, receives less emphasis now that the two positions no longer seem to be mutually exclusive. The Dutch argue that incorporation of the WEU into the EU should be accompanied by an "Atlantic contract" — a direct link between the EU and the north American members of NATO (Netherlands, 1995a, p. 26). With regard to the evolution of the WEU itself, as with the focus of operational military cooperation, the Dutch government is now clearly aligned with its German counterpart.

However, there is no expectation among the Benelux governments that the integration of the EU and WEU can be achieved at the current IGC. The medium- to long-term goal remains the complete merging of the WEU into the EU second pillar. In the meantime, there should be a gradual convergence of the two institutions so that the European Council can "instruct" and not just "request" the WEU to implement military policy. The Benelux countries press for commitment to a timetable for a common defence policy, on the lines of the EMU arrangement agreed at Maastricht; for some, completion of the merger by the end of the 1990s is envisaged.

The preference of these governments is that all member states should at that stage undertake all defence commitments, including a collective defence obligation, though the implementation of the latter remains the responsibility of NATO rather than the WEU. The various options designed by the Reflection Group to accommodate the more reluctant member states are not referred to in the joint Benelux approach, though it does accept that the actual deployment of armed forces is a matter for national governments.

Modest maximalists?

The positions on the second pillar of these three member states show a strong convergence, and it is not surprising that their governments agreed on a coordinated approach to the IGC negotiations. Their overall tradition as promoters of a federal form of European integration can be seen in their openness to majority voting and the role of the Commission, but it is expressed in a decidedly more muted way than on previous occasions. The current IGC is seen as an opportunity for gradual change, in which the Benelux group will align with Germany. So far as defence is concerned, these countries would undoubtedly qualify for any future "hard core" group.

GREECE AND PORTUGAL: LOYAL ALLIES?

The approaches to the Intergovernmental Conference of the other two small alliance states have been influenced by quite different historical experiences. Although long-standing members of NATO (Portugal from 1949, Greece from 1952), they are more recent adherents to the EC/EU,

Greece joining in 1981 and Portugal in 1986. Given dissimilarities in their geopolitical interests, they are treated separately here.

Greece
Greece is clearly the most exposed member state in the European Union; relations with three of its four proximate neighbours are based on perceptions of more or less serious threat. The disintegration of Yugoslavia in 1991 has had very negative consequences. A dispute with the former Yugoslav Republic of Macedonia (FYROM) involved a trade embargo until the autumn of 1995, and relations with Albania have been marked by tension arising from minority questions. However, the underlying source of Greek insecurity remains its fear of Turkey, involving disputed boundaries and the partition of Cyprus.

That experience, reinforced by a populist political culture, has given Greece a reputation as something of a maverick in the European Union's foreign policy, particularly under the highly personalised leadership of Andreas Papandreou. But since Papandreou's replacement by Costas Simitis in January 1996, although both external and internal politics remain fraught, there have been signs of a more measured approach to the CFSP. This is reflected in the new government's contribution to the IGC (Greece, 1996). On the reform of the CFSP itself, Greece supports the "partial communitarisation" of the second pillar, including a more active role for the Commission and a reinforcement of the powers of the European Parliament. There is also support for the extension of qualified majority voting on issues which do not affect "vital national interests".

The most striking element in the Greek position, however, is the inclusion among the EU's objectives of a "solidarity and mutual assistance clause". No other member state gives such concentrated attention to this emphasis on defence in its classical form, the protection of territory and the external borders of the Union. In the Greek case, this is seen as a direct trade-off between reinforced security and economic cohesion, on the grounds that the former would allow Greece to divert significant resources from defence to economic development.

The Greek position on specific defence questions includes the gradual merger of the EU and WEU according to an agreed timetable, the incorporation of the Petersberg tasks into the EU treaty and the formulation of defence policy within the EU, through meetings of defence ministers in the Council. NATO, however, is seen as "the main element in the European security system".

The evident nervousness in Greece's security policy is likely to persist. Within weeks of taking office the Simitis government was faced with a military confrontation with Turkey (itself in the throes of an untidy political succession). The issue — territorial limits in the eastern Aegean — was an old one, and among the recriminations which followed was the complaint that Greece's EU partners had given inadequate support in a crisis which was defused by American rather than EU diplomatic intervention.

The Simitis government, like its predecessors, thus operates in an immediate environment where crisis is the norm, and of course more than any other member state Greece will be sensitive to the course of events in the Balkans. In the latter context, although Greece has not hitherto been noted for its military contribution to international crisis management, it is currently moving in this direction, by sending 236 troops to IFOR.

Portugal

Portugal's much longer history as a sovereign state (and indeed world maritime power in the fifteenth and sixteenth centuries) includes a strong tradition of joining military alliances to compensate for the proximity of its larger neighbour, Spain. Membership of NATO followed this tradition and, like the Netherlands, Portugal has generally seen itself as an "Atlanticist" in previous debates about the development of a European alliance. In practical terms, Portugal, like all the states covered in this chapter, is a contributor to the NATO-led force in Bosnia with 959 troops.

In the past, Portuguese positions on the second pillar have tended to be conservative, and the policy of the Socialist government which took office in October 1995 seems to be in this tradition. The section on the CFSP in its initial statement for the IGC opens with the argument that a move towards "communitarisation" is unrealistic (Portugal, 1996). Rather than propose new decision-making procedures, there is a preference for implementing the neglected possibilities already in the treaty; any relaxation of the unanimity principle must be tightly controlled and limited to exceptional circumstances. Reinforcing the CFSP unit in the Council secretariat would be acceptable, but the creation of a high-profile secretary-general should not undermine the rotating presidency which the Portuguese wish to preserve. Democratic accountability is seen in terms of the national parliaments rather than the European Parliament.

With regard to relations between the EU and the WEU, Portugal's position starts from the retention of NATO as the "fundamental instrument" for collective defence as well as for large-scale missions for international crisis management. The WEU should remain as an autonomous institution, with a role in small-scale crisis management and as the European subset of NATO. Portugal's profile on these issues resembles that of the United Kingdom rather than that of the other small alliance states — a reflection, perhaps, of another alliance in the state's long history.

CONCLUSIONS

As with the major actors, this group of five small alliance states covers a range of positions on the reform of the second pillar. The maximalist arguments of the Benelux countries suggest they will play a relatively activist role in seeking changes during the negotiations. Greece, though susceptible to events in its much less stable environment, is also open to procedural change and an eventual merger of the EU and WEU, in the context of a package deal covering its economic interests. Portugal, on the other hand, has adopted a more conservative approach. But with respect to defence, none of the five has the reservation shared by the third group of member states, examined in the next chapter, the WEU observers.

CHAPTER 6
SMALL STATES AND THE IGC: WEU OBSERVERS

In contrast to the five small alliance states examined in chapter 5, four of the five countries which hold observer status in the WEU share an explicit reservation about membership of military alliances in general. That of the fifth, Denmark, is focused on the WEU itself. These reservations, whatever their origins in each case, are important factors in the defence aspects of the Intergovernmental Conference, and may also indirectly affect negotiations on the broader issues dealing with the second pillar.

This chapter analyses the IGC positions of the WEU observers with the exception of Ireland, which is treated more fully in the third part of the book. In each case it looks at:

* the state's individual foreign policy profile

* its IGC positions on the general questions relating to reform of the CFSP

* the state's military profile, including both self-defence and its contributions to international crisis management

* its IGC positions on the framing of a common defence policy.

Before examining these national positions it is necessary to clarify two terms which recur frequently in this context — "observer status" and "neutrality".

OBSERVER STATUS AND NEUTRALITY

Prior to the 1991 IGC the WEU took the form solely of a military alliance, based primarily on the obligation of mutual assistance in the event of attack on any member state — the Article V commitment. Full membership of the WEU is restricted to countries making that commitment. However, in the WEU's declaration attached to the Treaty on European Union, EU member states not already in the WEU were invited to either join or become observers. In the event, Greece applied for full membership (only finalised in 1995) and Denmark and Ireland became observers when the Maastricht Treaty at last came into force late in 1993. Austria, Finland and Sweden became observers after they acceded to EU membership in 1995.

What does observer status entail? Above all it involves representation in the WEU's regular political consultations, from the six-monthly meetings of the Council of Ministers (including both foreign and defence ministers) to the more frequent routine meetings at ambassadorial and working group levels. Such representation provides an opportunity to monitor the politico-military aspects of European security continuously and in some detail, thus opening a channel of information not found in the EU. Observer delegations are not expected to be mute, and there is thus some opportunity to influence the discussion; however, decision-making is reserved to full members. This is a political arrangement, without legal or contractual obligations.

It is precisely because of the latter characteristic of observer status that the governments which have acceded to it regard it as being compatible with their stance of what is often referred to loosely as "neutrality". In fact, most of these governments have been reluctant to use this terminology in their official statements since the end of the Cold War. Instead, they refer to their "non-participation in military alliances", and even in Ireland where the word "neutrality" survives it is qualified by the adjective "military".

This semantic precision is neither accidental nor trivial. It is based on the definition in international law of neutrality as a status which strictly speaking only has meaning in time of war. In that context, the state which wishes to maintain its right to stay outside the war is obliged to remain outside military alliance with any of the belligerents. It also is obliged to defend its neutrality by force of arms if necessary; neutrality is not, as is sometimes assumed, synonymous with pacifism.

During the Cold War (which in legal terms was not an actual war) the security policies — and often the overall foreign policies — of those European states which wanted to stay outside the rival military alliances attracted the description of "neutrality", and the countries became known as "neutrals". Most of their governments professed to be inhibited from any international commitment which might make it impossible for them to be neutral in a future war between the Cold War blocs. This was one reason for their remaining outside the European Economic Community, which in legal terms did not seem to accommodate that possibility. This can be seen as a form of prudential "neutrality policy", related to the long-term security of those states.

While governments understood neutrality in this way, as a defining characteristic of their foreign policies, the citizens of these states often adopted the term to refer to a cluster of very broad but politically powerful values which transcended the basic *raison d'être* of neutrality — to avoid involvement in a war. Neutrality was assumed to be the basis of the state's autonomy, and even an essential mark of national identity; it was regarded as an indicator of general pacific intent, and even of pacifism; it was seen as an inherent part of the state's acceptability for active roles with regard to international mediation, peacekeeping or development cooperation. In fact, there may be no necessary connection between the claim to neutrality and these values or policies; the record of Canada, Denmark, the Netherlands and Norway (all NATO members) with regard to development cooperation and peacekeeping, for example, has nothing to concede to that of the neutrals.

But public perceptions have a life of their own, and arguably this broader meaning of neutrality still has political significance in Austria, Finland, Ireland and Sweden — which for convenience will be referred to here as the European Union's neutral member states. However, in the context of the formation of a common defence policy in the Intergovernmental Conference, both the broad (public) and the narrow (governmental) meanings of neutrality should be kept in mind.

DENMARK: A VERY SPECIAL CASE

As the only WEU observer which cannot be described as a neutral, Denmark is a special case. Denmark considered joining a possible Scandinavian alliance in 1948, but when that failed to materialise chose to become a founder-member of NATO, rather than stay outside alliance, as Sweden did, in order to be neutral in a future war. As a member of NATO, Denmark accepts the obligation of mutual assistance, subscribes to the alliance's doctrine on nuclear deterrence and plays a full part in the formation of NATO policies.

However, there was little interest in Denmark in developing a west European as opposed to Atlantic alliance, partly because American leadership of the latter was more acceptable than that of France and, especially, Germany. This attitude can be seen throughout the somewhat patchy history of the WEU, and the strict separation of military policy from the European Community's tentative foreign policy consultations (the EPC process) was also a feature of Danish membership of the EC following accession in 1973.

The reactivation of the WEU in the mid-1980s met with a lukewarm reception from the Danish government and overt criticism from the large Social Democratic Party, then in opposition. The WEU's "Hague platform" of 1987, it was argued, represented an undesirable emphasis on nuclear deterrence and the lack of any territorial limitations in the treaty was characterised as an opening for post-colonial military adventures. Many of these political positions were carried over into the post-Cold War period through Denmark's fragmented domestic politics (Petersen, 1994, p. 19 n. 7).

The Danish referendum which rejected the Treaty on European Union in June 1992 led to a "National Compromise" negotiated between the political parties in order to agree a basis for a second referendum, which reversed the decision a year later (Petersen, 1993). This agreement, endorsed by the European Council at Edinburgh in December 1992, included an opt-out on defence which meant, first, that Denmark would not join the WEU without a further referendum and, second, that while it would not participate in planning or executing decisions with "defence implications" it would not block others from doing so.

This politicisation of the protective dimension of Danish security policy has led to a contradiction in policy — the alliance commitment that is rejected in the (largely hypothetical) context of the WEU is still accepted in the context of NATO membership. But this confusion has not been replicated so far as preventive or crisis management policies have been concerned. Denmark is an active supporter of EU enlargement, especially with regard to the Baltic states, a leading development aid donor in world terms and at the forefront of peacekeeping.

CFSP positions
Denmark has always insisted on the intergovernmental nature of foreign policy cooperation, and the government's official position for the IGC maintains that principle (Denmark, 1995, p. 6). However, the same document makes it clear that the government is "prepared to agree to joint actions being adopted even if one or two countries do not wish to participate". In other words, this is a consensus-minus-two procedure in decision-making, in which the Danish government "will argue in favour of a separate decision being taken on the conditions for those countries which do not participate in a joint action".

Denmark also supports the idea of establishing an analysis unit "under the aegis" of the Council and appears to be open to the idea of shared presidencies, but there is no reference to the proposals to "personify" the

CFSP in some way, or indeed to any other aspect of the second pillar's institutional capacity. It may thus be inferred that the status quo is seen as sufficient on these matters.

Positions on defence

One consequence of the defence opt-out which eventually emerged from the ratification crisis in 1992–93 is that the Danish government is in a difficult position on the evolution of issues such as the future relationship between the EU and WEU. It can make its preferences known, but is in effect negotiating with its own public as much as with its partner governments. The Edinburgh agreement is not on the IGC agenda, as the government's position paper makes clear, and can only be changed by a national referendum which would be unlikely to take place until after the IGC.

Nevertheless, the government's short section on CFSP proposals includes a reference to the fact that other EU states wish to develop an' EU role regarding the Petersberg tasks, and this comment may serve to remind Danish citizens that Denmark, too, has an active policy in this dimension of security.

Politically, Denmark has taken forward positions on the crisis over the independence of the Baltic states in 1990–91 and the Chechnya crisis in 1994–95. There is also active participation in the military aspects of crisis management. In 1993, for example, more than 1,300 personnel were deployed in all UNPROFOR areas of operation in former Yugoslavia. A principal feature of the armed forces' restructuring has been the establishment of an "international brigade" with the twin tasks of assignment to NATO's rapid reaction forces and UN- or OSCE-mandated peacekeeping. Denmark is NATO's "lead country" in the peacekeeping aspects of the Partnership for Peace programme and contributes 801 troops to the IFOR operation.

The separate issue of whether Denmark should become a full member of the WEU, though not an issue for the IGC, is bound up with the general security debate in that country. After a period in which it was in effect a taboo subject there have been signs of its reactivation. In May 1995 a report of the independent Danish Commission on Security and Disarmament (SNU) argued that since the ratification crisis justifiable uncertainties had been clarified. American approval of a European Security and Defence Identity, the incorporation of future EU applicants as associate partners in the WEU and the emphasis on the Petersberg tasks all served to legitimise the WEU (SNU, 1995, p. 39). Thus full membership of the WEU was in Denmark's interests: it would provide opportunities to influence transatlantic relations, the integration of new applicants in the EU, the development of the CFSP itself, the evolution of NATO and the debate on peacekeeping (SNU, 1995, p. 36).

Of course, even were Denmark a full member of the WEU it seems unlikely that it would favour a merger of the WEU with the European Union. Its overall lack of enthusiasm for deeper integration suggests a preference for the status quo. Meanwhile the Danish experience offers a foretaste of what a defence opt-out looks like — that, perhaps more than anything else, is what makes it a very special case.

FINLAND: THE LONG VIEW OF SECURITY POLICY

During the Cold War Finnish neutrality policy evolved in the context of a difficult relationship with the Soviet Union, a neighbour which had recently invaded and annexed Finnish territory. Finnish policy was characterised by a relatively non-committal line in east–west relations, a disciplined domestic consensus, an emphasis on national military defence and a very cautious attitude towards west European integration.

The evident constraints in this unbalanced bilateral relationship were removed by the retreat and disintegration of the Soviet Union between 1989 and 1991. Despite short-term costs of adaptation (especially the loss of an advantageous trading relationship with the Soviets), Finland was faced with an opportunity, unprecedented in its history as a sovereign state. Now it could establish a diplomatic profile as an unequivocally "western" country rather than remaining in the penumbra of Russian influence. The decision to apply for EC membership was thus a major turning point in the state's evolution, confirmed by the endorsement of the terms of accession by a referendum vote of just under 57 per cent.

CFSP positions
In contrast to the situation in the other new member states, Austria and Sweden, where public opinion subsequently became disillusioned, there is still majority support for EU membership in Finland. Following general elections in the spring of 1995 a broad coalition government, including Social Democrats, Conservatives, former Communists and Greens, led by Paavo Lipponen (Social Democrat), undertook detailed consultations between government and parliament before publishing its IGC positions in February 1996 (Finland, 1996).

Regarding decision-making procedures the report, which describes the European Union as an "association of independent states", starts on a cautionary note: "political will is of more essential importance than the structure of organisations or the modalities of decision-making". This tone of orthodox intergovernmentalism is softened to some extent by support for the use of qualified majority voting on "questions concerning implementation", and possibly on other matters where the Union's objectives are not in contention. The pillar structure should remain, but measures to improve consistency between the pillars are recommended.

The Finnish report supports the reinforcement of common analysis in the Council secretariat, but has little time for the high-profile "personification" of the CFSP which is seen as a source of potential confusion. There are no CFSP-related grounds for changing the rotating presidency, which retains the primary role for policy implementation. The role of the European Parliament and the question of funding require clarification, but not necessarily in the form of treaty amendment.

Positions on defence
In an official report on guidelines for Finland's security policy, it is now accepted that "the policy of neutrality that Finland followed in the Cold War is no longer a viable line of action" (Finland, 1995, p. 58). However, the report goes on, Finland "continues to observe restraint regarding military alignment", a position justified mainly on the grounds that this is best for stability in northern Europe "in the present circumstances". In other words, in a co-operative security regime Finland's policy of military non-alignment — the term now generally used rather than neutrality — is an important element in the reassurance of an unstable Russia.

Thus the protective dimension of Finnish security policy remains primarily national (though it is also argued that EU membership would at least help deter military threats and political pressures). In official statements there remains a strong emphasis on a "credible national defence", which is still based on the extensive mobilisation of forces trained through peacetime conscription.

The government's IGC report also emphasises the military aspects of crisis management, seen as requiring "a new kind of preparedness". This is seen as the main purpose of the WEU, which would implement EU policy, and would be open to the participation of all categories of states within the WEU network. Finland already contributes to the WEU civilian police force in Mostar. The question of merging the EU and WEU is not viewed as a realistic prospect in the context of the 1996 IGC, though the Finnish government is quite prepared to consider the further development of the EU–WEU relationship, the preferred option being one in which the WEU is subordinated to the European Union as an instrument of military crisis management.

The military aspects of Finland's security policy are also being developed in the context of NATO's Partnership for Peace programme, which Finland joined in May 1994. This arrangement in Finland's case is concerned with the development of its peacekeeping capability, and does not cut across its non-alignment policy. Finnish ministers are not apologetic about their contacts with NATO, which is seen as an essential element in European security, both to sustain American engagement and to provide operational resources beyond the reach of the UN or the OSCE (Norrback, 1995). A contingent of 373 Finnish troops has been deployed in the IFOR operation in Bosnia.

Although the present formulation of Finnish security policy maintains a good deal of its former restraint, the way in which it has adapted to radical changes in the country's immediate environment reflects a view of security policy which is both focused on concrete realities and pragmatic in style. There is not much place for the elaboration of universal values or sentimental rhetoric; security policy is firmly focused on the state's external security, and a long view is taken. Should circumstances change, for better or worse, Finland is likely to be ready to adapt.

SWEDEN: ACTIVISM AND ORTHODOXY

Sweden has by far the longest tradition of neutrality of the WEU observer countries, and not surprisingly this is quite strongly reflected in the country's political culture. However, as state policy, Swedish neutrality has sometimes been more pragmatic than doctrinaire. In 1948 the government engaged in negotiations to create a regional defence pact with Denmark and Norway, and it was after these fell through that modern Swedish security policy was based on national defence and a non-entangling foreign policy in order to maintain a credible neutrality in any future war.

This approach depended on a significant military capability (plus a domestic arms industry) and an economic capacity permitting Sweden to remain outside the European Community. The revelation in 1994 of secret military contingency plans to cooperate with NATO during the Cold War suggests that neither neutrality policy nor political transparency were always quite what they seemed at the time, and there was also tentative consideration of EEC membership in the early 1960s and the early 1970s. Nevertheless, it was not until after the end of the Cold War that economic difficulties triggered the application in 1991 to join the EC.

Sweden has confirmed its long tradition of an activist foreign policy profile in recent years. There has been a strong presence in multilateral institutions, the continuation of significant development cooperation and arms control policies and increasing support for cooperation in the Baltic Sea region. Joining the EU in 1995 and operating through the CFSP is part of this pattern. However, public support for EU membership has fallen significantly from the 52 per cent approval in the referendum in November 1994; although foreign policy as such hardly accounts for this disillusion, future attitudes towards the CFSP may be affected by it.

CFSP positions

The section on the second pillar in the Swedish government's report on its "fundamental standpoints" is introduced by an emphasis on the need for an EU capacity to intervene at an early stage in crisis management (Sweden, 1995, p. 26). However, for Sweden that does not imply radical change to the CFSP decision-making procedure: "there is no question of abolishing the right of veto for foreign and security policy decisions". On the other hand, there is an openness to considering (unspecified) modifications to the unanimity rule "in questions of more limited scope", which may be necessary especially in the context of further enlargement.

Better preparation of decisions through a reinforced planning and analysis capacity is favoured, with a preference for the Council secretariat as its location, and allowing "some scope" to the Commission. But the Swedish view of the personification of the CFSP is lukewarm; if there is to be such a post, it should be "of a limited nature" and not cut across the external roles of the presidencies of either Council or Commission. All in all, the report reflects a cautious but not doggedly minimalist view regarding institutional reform in this field.

Positions on defence

Sweden's current military policy combines a strong interest in developing its preventive and crisis management aspects and the retention of a purely national position regarding the protective (i.e. self-defence) aspect. Thus participation in NATO's Partnership for Peace programme (which Sweden joined together with Finland in May 1994) is justified on the grounds that it is "exactly the kind of practical co-operation which in itself is confidence-building, and in addition adds to our capacity to carry out peacekeeping operations" (Hjelm-Wallen, 1995).

Contributions to actual peacekeeping operations have been considerable, particularly in the Yugoslav crisis. In early 1995 Sweden deployed some 1,300 troops in the three UNPROFOR operations in Croatia, Bosnia and

FYROM. This involved two innovations; the first was participation in a joint Nordic force (Nordbat 2) which included two NATO states (Denmark and Norway), and the second was the deployment of combat equipment. Sweden's contribution to UNPROFOR's successor, the NATO-led IFOR, consists of 830 troops, while the civilian side of this operation is headed by a former Swedish prime minister, Carl Bildt. There is also a contribution to the WEU civilian police force in Mostar.

This interest in "peace promoting activities" is strongly reflected in the Swedish government's IGC report where it is seen as the most appropriate focus for the development of the WEU. The government declares its readiness to "take part in the implementation of certain measures of this kind, but such participation must be based on a decision taken at the national level in each specific case". It also makes plain the necessity for a UN or OSCE mandate, and improvements in the operational capacity of the WEU.

The report is non-committal on the future relationship between the European Union and the WEU, but insists on the need to maintain the distinction between "cooperation in the peace-promotion area" (i.e. the Petersberg tasks) and mutual defence guarantees. On the latter point Swedish policy retains more than a flavour of former orthodoxy, though the word "neutrality" is used only in the strictest technical sense. Participation in common defence is ruled out: "Sweden's policy of non-participation in military alliances, aiming at the possibility of being neutral in the event of war in our vicinity, has not changed" (Sweden, 1995, p. 30).

This position was elaborated in an earlier report by the Swedish Parliamentary Defence Commission (1995). It reflects the assumption that "in the current situation an armed attack against Sweden is highly unlikely", but nonetheless recommends a concept of "total defence" based on popular support and the maintenance of conscription and state of the art armed forces.

Two questions may be posed about the long-term viability of this approach. First, as the introduction to the parliamentary report concedes, the Green Party and the Left Party do not participate fully in the current consensus on security policy (and the Social Democrats have divided views on the EU more generally). More importantly, there appear to be doubts among the military leadership as to whether proposed expenditures on defence will be sufficient to sustain a credible national defence in the long term (*The Economist*, 9 September 1995).

So far as the IGC is concerned, however, the continuation of a policy of non-alignment would seem to be the bottom line of Sweden's position. If for no other reason, the general public apprehension about the new member state's EU policy is likely to constrain the government from considering full membership of the WEU.

AUSTRIA: FEDERALISM, EVENTUALLY?

An explicit emphasis on neutrality was a distinctive feature of Austria's foreign policy following the restoration of full independence in 1955. This derived partly from the circumstances surrounding the State Treaty of that year and the adoption of the Swiss model of "permanent neutrality", with its constraining legal definition. The model was immediately interpreted more freely by Austria than by Switzerland (for example, by joining the UN), but the interpretation was still expressed in terms of a legalistic tradition which was more marked than in Finland or Sweden during the Cold War period.

Neutrality came to be associated with an activist foreign policy, especially under Chancellor Bruno Kreisky, and in domestic politics with the much more general successes of the rehabilitated Austrian state, economy and society. However, following a series of economic reversals in the mid-1980s Austria became the first of the Cold War neutrals to seek EC membership, a policy change which required a good deal of debate, both internally and in Brussels, about the compatability of neutrality and accession to the EC/EU.

In the accession negotiations this question was resolved by a joint declaration with the other applicants and the existing member states pledging willingness to participate fully in the CFSP as defined in the Treaty on European Union. The provision in Article J 4.4, "that the policy of the Union . . . shall not prejudice the specific character of the security and defence policy of certain Member States", which covers the maintenance of Ireland's military neutrality, was considered sufficient to accommodate Austria. This position was endorsed by 66.6 per cent of the vote in the accession referendum in June 1994.

CFSP positions

A set of guidelines for the IGC was adopted by the Social Democrat (SPO)–Peoples Party (OVP) government in May 1995 (Austria, 1995). With regard to decision-making procedures, Austria advocates a cautious transition to majority voting in the second pillar, at first through implementing decisions within the framework of joint actions (already allowed for) and the possibility of some sort of consensus-minus-one arrangement.

As with most other member states, the reinforcement of the planning and analysis capacity of the Council secretariat is supported, but the Commission is also encouraged to make more use of its (non-exclusive) right of initiative in the CFSP. The role of the presidency is maintained in preference to either a high-profile individual or team presidency serving for longer terms.

The Austrian document also devotes attention to the need to clarify the major instruments of the CFSP (common positions and joint actions) as well as the financing procedures. There is no enthusiasm for extending the role of the European Parliament in this domain.

The political presentation of these guidelines was remarkable, at least so far as the OVP was concerned, for a federalist gloss not found among the other WEU observer countries. Thus the then vice-chancellor, Wolfgang Schussel, lauding a "European Union committed to the principles of federalism", contemplated a Europe with "functioning security structures" and the goal of Austria being in the "leading group" on all dimensions of integration, including external security (Schussel, 1995). Even allowing for the long-term perspective of this speech, it marks Austria — itself a federal state — as potentially the most maximalist of the states examined in this chapter.

Before turning to Austrian positions on defence in the IGC, the evolution of attitudes towards neutrality during the last five years merits attention. Formerly viewed as the bedrock of Austrian foreign and security policy, the doctrine of permanent neutrality has become "increasingly problematic for more than one reason" (Neuhold, 1995, pp. 6-9). It has lost its principal "conflict of reference" (the Cold War) and the associated bridge-building; its military rationale, based on the possibility of general interstate war, has little relevance to the threats on Austria's borders, which have derived mainly from the spillover, including very large numbers of refugees, from the conflict in former Yugoslavia.

Positions on defence
Austria's exposure, to both the low-level risks of instability in central and eastern Europe and military threats arising out of a possible revival and extension of armed conflict in south-eastern Europe, is not surprisingly reflected in an interest in the potential of the WEU's Petersberg tasks. The government guidelines preceded the formulation of the WEU's own options for future EU–WEU relations, but it is clear that at the very least Austria favours closer links. On a practical level, the government has designated "Prepared Units (Prepun)" as forces which it would be prepared to make available for Petersberg tasks; these forces are also envisaged as playing a

role in Austria's Partnership for Peace with NATO, which was agreed early in 1995. Austria has sent 286 troops to IFOR, and there has also been a contribution to the WEU civilian police force in Mostar.

On the other hand, the question of a commitment to collective self-defence in the IGC context is uncertain, principally because of continuing popular support for the broad idea of neutrality (Neuhold, 1995, p. 17). The political parties are currently divided on the issue. The Social Democrats, led by Chancellor Franz Vranitsky, have traditionally shown a preference for maintaining neutrality, though the issue is the subject of some internal debate. The OVP is not so committed, and includes active advocates for a change, while the third party, Jorg Haider's Freedom Party, which opposed entry to the EU, nonetheless advocates joining NATO.

The increasing signs of strain within the Austrian party system, with an indecisive election in December 1995 failing to resolve tensions between the two main parties, make it difficult to provide any clear prognosis of where they stand individually on the evolution of security policy. In March 1996 the coalition agreement of the renewed SPO/OVP government (still under Chancellor Vranitsky) contained a commitment to consider all options by the spring of 1998 at the latest. This includes the possibility of full membership of the WEU, an option which does not appear on the agenda of the other observer countries, but only time will tell whether that decision might be taken within the context of the Intergovernmental Conference.

A JOINT APPROACH: FINNISH–SWEDISH PROPOSALS ON CRISIS MANAGEMENT

Within the WEU observer category there exists a group of like-minded Nordic member states (involved in their own long-established consultative network with the non-EU Nordic states, Iceland and Norway). Has this the potential to bring joint positions to bear on the IGC, along the lines hitherto practised by the Benelux countries? Given the singularity and domestic political sensitivity of Denmark's position, a wholly inclusive and explicitly coordinated approach may be unlikely, but shortly after the Intergovernmental Conference started the Finnish and Swedish governments made a joint proposal on crisis management (Finland and Sweden, 1996).

The proposal focuses on the need for an enhanced EU role in military crisis management. The full text of the proposal is in Appendix X, but it is worth summarising its main features to illustrate the point that the observer countries are not confined to a passive role, even with regard to military policy. The Finnish–Swedish memorandum envisages the incorporation of the Petersberg tasks into the EU treaty as a task of the CFSP, a reinforced link between the EU and WEU so that the former may empower the latter, and participation in planning and operational decision-making by all contributing states on an equal footing.

However, this is far from being a wholesale merger between the European Union and the WEU. The WEU may still act independently of EU policy where the CFSP has not reached agreement; the EU will not attempt to duplicate its role in military planning. The proposal assumes that collective defence commitments are separable from cooperation in military crisis management, and that any enhanced EU role in the latter will require a UN or OSCE mandate. The commitment of forces in any specific case depends on voluntary decisions by national governments.

CONCLUSIONS

Two general conclusions can be drawn about the national attitudes towards the reform of the second pillar of the four WEU observer countries examined above.

First, their positions on changes to CFSP procedures and structures show common features. There is a conservative approach to the inter-governmental nature of the second pillar, but also an openness to some modification of decision-making; there is support for reinforcement of the Council secretariat's capacity to prepare policy decisions, but not for the personification of the CFSP or radical changes to the prerogatives of the presidency. If Austria sometimes hints at a more ambitious approach, it is not certain that the necessary domestic consensus will be available.

Second, notwithstanding the persistent reservation concerning mutual security guarantees in the WEU (their defining attribute as a group), there is a clear willingness by these countries to develop the WEU as a framework for their participation, on a case-by-case basis, in international crisis management. This is wholly consistent with their actual contributions and previous record in this field. Hence the Finnish–Swedish proposal may well prove to be more than just another straw in the wind.

CHAPTER 7

SECURITY POLICY IN THE IGC: A PRELIMINARY PROGNOSIS

The negotiations in the Intergovernmental Conference may be completed by the summer of 1997 or, at the latest, by the end of that year. Ratification of any new treaty or treaty amendments will take at least a further twelve months. Against a background of continuing uncertainty in many of the major elements in world affairs, and remembering the confusion which attended the ratification of the Maastricht Treaty, it is clearly impossible to predict the final outcome.

It is possible nonetheless to sketch a preliminary prognosis. In order to do so this chapter:

* examines the IGC itself as a political process

* summarises the range of national attitudes to the CFSP and defence policy

* introduces the "sixteenth voice" in the IGC — the Commission's preferences with regard to security policy

* and considers whether the most likely broad outcome of the IGC may be some form of differentiated integration.

THE SETTING: THE IGC AS POLITICAL PROCESS

The formal arrangements for the conduct of the first phase of the IGC were straightforward. The subject-matter of the conference was divided into three broad categories. The first — "bringing the Union closer to its citizens" — covers citizenship, justice and home affairs (the "third pillar"), the environment and employment policy; the third deals with changes to the Union's institutions. The second "chapter" concerns the EU's external action, with the main focus on the CFSP and the security and defence dimension.

Negotiations took place at monthly meetings at foreign minister level, on the basis of weekly meetings between the foreign ministers' specially designated representatives. The Italian presidency of the Council, which opened the conference in Turin on 29 March 1996, scheduled three ministerial meetings and ten representative meetings prior to the European Council at Florence on 21–22 June, at which an interim report was presented. A measure of democratic accountability was provided by special briefing procedures for the European Parliament, and by the governments' reporting to their own parliaments, mainly through the relevant committees.

Following this opening round, which completed a "first reading" or tabling of all the major themes, the negotiations resumed under the Irish presidency. It is possible that the broad shape of the final bargains will have emerged by the European Council in Dublin in December 1996, but the "end-game" may well be postponed to the Dutch presidency in the first half of 1997, or even to the succeeding term of Luxembourg.

Indeed, the overall timetable depends on political context rather than administrative routine. Tactics and timing are of the essence, and the principal factor is probably the electoral politics of the major member states. Both France (with parliamentary elections in the spring of 1998) and Germany (with federal elections in the autumn of that year) have strong incentives to seek as short an IGC as possible. However, the key event is the next British general election. Given the present government's role as champion of die-hard minimalism, its partners in the IGC may prefer to postpone the end-game in the hope of dealing with a more amenable British position after the election. This could be delayed to the late spring of 1997 (and any new government would need time to play itself in), but the government's precarious parliamentary majority might disappear before that.

A further element of uncertainty lies in the ratification process, involving the confirmation of the treaty within a period (generally twelve months) by all member states and by the European Parliament. The method of ratification depends primarily on the individual member state's constitutional arrangements, and in the past for most states that meant endorsement by a parliamentary majority. However, the greater than anticipated politicisation of the Maastricht Treaty, following its initial rejection in the first Danish referendum, delayed ratification and arguably damaged the credibility of the treaty.

In the longer term this may have the effect in more countries of increasing pressures to resort to the much more demanding method of endorsement by popular vote. Even where this is not the case, the conjunction of IGC ratification with other contentious decisions relating to EU integration — the move to a single currency and the need to agree a new five-year budget are the most obvious — is likely to influence the ratification debates. In the final analysis, European integration is domestic politics, in fifteen different countries.

THE RANGE OF NATIONAL ATTITUDES TO THE CFSP AND DEFENCE

Summarising the state of play in the blueprinting process in the opening phase of the IGC, it is clear that there is a wide range of national attitudes towards reform of the second pillar of the Treaty on European Union.

With regard to the general characteristics of the CFSP — whether it remains a strictly intergovernmental form of cooperation or whether it acquires some effective measure of qualified majority voting — the position appears as follows. There is a maximalist group, which calls for the latter approach, led by Germany with the concerted support of Belgium, the Netherlands and Luxembourg. Assuming policy continuity in spite of domestic political change, Italy and Spain will also adopt this "pre-federalist" stance. At the other extreme of the spectrum, the United Kingdom champions a thorough minimalism.

Most of the remaining member states do not seem wholly convinced of the merit or feasibility of departing from intergovernmental procedures in the second pillar, but may not wish to share British dogmatism on that point. In their openness to discussing and perhaps even adopting some change to procedures and structures, they may be seen as "incremental adjusters".

The position of France is particularly important. France is closer to the United Kingdom than to Germany both as a military power and in its insistence on intergovernmentalism in the CFSP, but in its general negotiating strategy can play the pro-European card in a way which gives the initiative to joint Franco-German positions. On this occasion, the Franco-German compromise on the CFSP may seem to blunt the maximalist emphasis on majority voting, but it does leave an opening for incremental adjustments and perhaps for the reintroduction of more ambitious proposals.

So far as the "unfinished business of Maastricht" — the common defence policy — is concerned, there is also a wide range of views. The differences between advocates of a European or Atlantic defence which prevented agreement in 1991 have become blurred since then. The United States has accepted and promoted a European Security and Defence Identity and France has moved much closer to NATO. Neither change, however, has been developed to the point where the shape of a new defence regime is clear. Indeed, pending the development of the west's overall relationship with Russia and the process of NATO reform and enlargement any such clarification may lie well beyond the scope of the IGC. It bears repeating that NATO is "the other place" in which European security policy is taking shape.

What can be said at this stage is that NATO is still the primary focus of multilateral military policies, with regard to both collective defence and the new challenges of crisis management. This is as true for non-NATO countries as it is for NATO members — even states without aspirations to NATO membership, such as Austria, Finland and Sweden, participate in the Partnership for Peace and in the NATO-led operation in Bosnia. Given the adaptation of NATO, there is no question of EU countries agreeing to a standalone supranational common defence. In short, the IGC will not complete the "unfinished business" of Maastricht.

In the IGC context, the principal issue is the relationship between the EU and the WEU. It should be remembered that there must be some form of relationship, given the inclusion of the WEU in the Treaty on European Union as "an integral part of the development of the Union" (TEU, Article J 4.2); the question now is what this is to mean. Maximalists envisage agreement on an eventual merger of the two, perhaps within a stated schedule. This camp is composed of CFSP maximalists, but on this question also includes France and Greece. The minimalist champion — with particular conviction, given its emphasis on military capabilities — is again the United Kingdom, now more ready to work operationally through the WEU (as a subset of NATO) but only so long as it is not subordinated to the European Union.

The position of the WEU observer countries might at first sight seem to be eased by a minimalist outcome. Their reservations about accepting WEU collective defence commitments may be more easily accommodated if the EU remains primarily a "civilian power"; their willingness to contribute military support to crisis management could probably be realised within any of the options for a WEU–EU relationship. However, the Finnish–Swedish wish to make the WEU subordinate to the European Union for the purposes of crisis management is not on the British agenda. The WEU observers will also face questions about their commitment to the overall solidarity of the Union.

On the whole, then, the possibility of consensus on a radical new departure among member states on the second pillar seems remote. The Conclusions of the European Council in Florence in June 1996 bear this out. Among the aims for the negotiating phase of the IGC, they include the following: "the possibility of whether the unanimity rule can be relaxed"; "the possibility of including in the Treaty objectives corresponding to the Petersberg tasks"; "closer links between the European Union and the WEU, also with a view to defining the question of their future relations following the results of the June NATO meeting in Berlin"; and "a possible political solidarity clause" (European Council, 1996b, pp. 9–10).

This is hardly a manifesto for a federal security policy. The determined minimalism of the United Kingdom is only the most obvious obstacle to reform; even the most clearly committed maximalists seem if anything less sure of their case than they were in the 1991 IGC. This more modest approach is reflected in the positions adopted by the Commission, which also participates in the negotiations as, in effect, the "sixteenth voice" at the table.

THE "SIXTEENTH VOICE": THE COMMISSION

Although the Commission does not have a determining role in what is after all an intergovernmental negotiation, its participation at all levels of the discussions may be influential. It was also required to submit an "opinion" at the outset of the IGC, thus giving it the opportunity to present a vision of the EU's common interests which is not beholden to national concerns.

One of the three major headings of this document is "A clear identity on the world scene" (the others, matching the main categories in the IGC, are "A people's Europe" and "Institutions for the enlarged Europe"). The Commission includes proposals for reform to trade policy and emphasises the need to reinforce consistency in foreign policy between the treaty's pillars and the various institutions, but its main focus is on the CFSP and the issue of security and defence (Commission, 1996b, paras. 23–35).

So far as the CFSP is concerned, the Commission supports the one point of consensus reached in the preliminary rounds of "blueprinting", the joint analysis unit, without being dogmatic about its location so long as it includes personnel from the Commission. It also sees preparation as being facilitated by the introduction of a permanent "Political Committee" of senior officials, on the lines of the well-established arrangements in the first pillar. Although it calls for greater "visibility" for the CFSP, it does not favour an overall supremo at the highest level, but stresses the dual role of a reinforced presidency and the Commission.

On the key issue of decision-making procedures, after recommending clarification of the distinction between the main policy instruments, "common positions" and "joint actions", the Commission shows its maximalist colours by stating the view that qualified majority voting should be the norm in the CFSP. But it also concedes (as do maximalist member states) that military decisions require specific rules, and it seems to support the Franco-German proposal for flexibility in order to avoid specific action by some states in the Union's "general interest" being blocked by a minority (Commission, 1996b, para. 31).

With regard to common defence, while acknowledging that "NATO remains at the centre of Europe's defence arrangements", the Commission calls for several changes (Commission, 1996b, paras. 34–5). These include incorporation of the WEU into the Union "according to a settled timetable", writing commitments "aimed at restoring or keeping peace" into the EU treaty, and ensuring that defence ministers play "an appropriate role" in the EU Council. The provision of a "solid industrial base", involving better integration of the armaments industry into the single market, is also recommended.

The Commission's position, then, is clearly on a par with those of maximalist member states, but the presentation of its proposals is relatively modest compared to its federalist advocacy in the 1991 IGC. The aim of the proposals — "to empower the Union to act rather than react, the better to defend the interests of its people" — is clear, but it is anything but clear whether they will be accepted.

AN AGENDA FOR DIFFERENTIATED INTEGRATION?

It was argued in chapter 3 that the most likely choice of overall strategic direction for the European Union lay between a minimalist option which would maintain the status quo and a form of flexible or differentiated integration. In the latter arrangement a majority of member states (the "avant-garde") would be able to undertake more ambitious joint commitments without being blocked by a reluctant minority; the minority would not be obliged to follow, but the parameters of this differentiation would be circumscribed so as to maintain the long-term, overall solidarity of the Union.

The diversity of national positions on both the CFSP as such and the possible shape of a common defence policy suggests that this broad approach may be the most that can be achieved in this IGC. After all, the existing situation, particularly in the field of defence with the intricate relationships between the EU, WEU and NATO, reflects a high degree of de facto flexibility. It does not follow, however, that the compromises entailed in formalising such differentiation will be readily identified or accepted. On the contrary, they beg several very large questions which will have to be faced one way or another by the Intergovernmental Conference.

First, if a majority is allowed to commit the Union (but not all its members) to a particular action, on what basis is this majority composed? Is it a means of circumventing the incapacity of one member state or will it also include the possibility of varying "coalitions of the willing"? On the other side of this coin the question arises as to what conditions attach to abstention, particularly in the light of all member states' overall commitment, inherent in their treaty obligations, to the solidarity of the Union. Several of the proposals for flexibility refer to the "absentees" being required to maintain political and financial solidarity, a condition which only looks workable in the context of their inability rather than unwillingness to participate in the proposed action.

So far as security policy is concerned, the EU's role in military matters could take a variety of forms under the heading of differentiated integration. The commitment to an eventual "common defence policy" already exists in the Treaty on European Union, but how far should the Union move now beyond the present operational limits of the exercise of its "civilian power", in the fields of prevention and the non-military aspects of crisis management? Does this imply contracting out military functions to the WEU as such, or to ad hoc "coalitions of the willing", at the cost of having at best a form of remote control over their implementation? Or should some or all of these functions be incorporated in the European Union itself?

A more general dilemma surrounds the concept of differentiated integration when applied to the whole range of activities encompassed by the European Union. By allowing for varying commitments in the short to medium term, more flexible arrangements run two opposing risks in the long term. On the one hand, a proliferation of "special cases" may reduce the legitimacy of the Union as a whole, leading to its eventual disintegration. On the other hand, however, it risks dividing the member states into distinct, and eventually exclusive, groups of countries based on quite different levels of commitment. The prospect of the negotiations themselves leading to such an outcome, following a crisis between advocates of maximalist and minimalist positions, cannot be ruled out.

Thus, although the preparation of the 1996 IGC has involved more extensive "blueprinting" than was the case prior to the previous IGC in 1991, the negotiations themselves may prove to be testing for all those involved. For Ireland, a country which has hitherto preferred to keep a low profile on its security policy options and which has been wary of differentiation on economic grounds, the Intergovernmental Conference promises to bring some difficult and unfamiliar questions into the public domain.

PART III

IRELAND AND EUROPEAN SECURITY: ISSUES AND OPTIONS

CHAPTER 8
THE DEBATE IN IRELAND

The final part of the book focuses on Ireland. Irish security policy demonstrates several characteristics similar to those in the three other EU member states which remain outside military alliances, but can only be fully understood in the context of the country's own historical experience, geopolitical location and domestic political debate. These themes are summarised in this chapter; chapters 9–11 explore in more detail the major questions arising for the Irish government and people in the course of continuing adaptation to the new and less stable security environment. Chapter 12 then summarises the options facing Ireland in the Intergovernmental Conference, and comments on what is at stake.

This chapter examines the case of Ireland under the following headings:

* the origins and significance of the "neutrality reservation", as manifested in different ways in state policy and perceptions of popular values

* the presentation of security policy in the most comprehensive statement of Irish foreign policy, the White Paper published in March 1996

* Ireland's positions on the IGC second pillar issues

* the domestic debate on security policy.

THE NEUTRALITY RESERVATION: STATE POLICY AND POPULAR VALUES

The exposure of Ireland to major European conflicts since statehood was achieved in the early 1920s has been relatively limited. The official designation of the Second World War period as "the Emergency" symbolised the extent to which the country escaped the horrors of total war; similarly, it remained far from the notional military front of the Cold War.

The direct security risks the Irish state faces in the post-Cold War era, apart from the conflict in Northern Ireland, are in the low-level category — drug smuggling, fishery protection and environmental pollution (a special concern being the safety of British nuclear establishments close to the Irish Sea). On issues like these, Ireland subscribes to a broad concept of common security with its neighbours. The means to achieve it may not always be readily agreed, but they will be negotiated both bilaterally and in the context of the European Union.

As the fate of the Irish economy has become inextricably entwined with the economic integration of the European continent, it is the beginning of wisdom to understand that the broad security interests of the larger entity are increasingly the principal context in which Irish security interests will be framed. However, the peculiarity of the country's historical experience should not be forgotten; nor should the fact that for some its geographical location still ensures a significant physical, and even psychological, distance from the major sources of political instability in or near Europe.

Irish governments, like those of most small states, have generally claimed a strong commitment to the preventive dimension of security policy. The promotion of an international rule of law, the legitimacy of the UN and OSCE, and a reduced reliance on military instruments are stressed. On the other hand, commitment to protection is limited, and national defence policy has a low profile. The public image of the small professional Permanent Defence Forces centres on a strong tradition of participation in international crisis management by contributing to United Nations peacekeeping operations, but protection of the territorial integrity of the state often seems to be taken for granted. More importantly, the option of a commitment to collective self-defence, by joining a military alliance, has been rejected.

It may seem paradoxical that the persistent and deliberate abstention from military alliances — in official terminology, the stance of "military neutrality" — tends to be the primary point of reference for public discussion of international security issues in Ireland. If the state's behaviour during the Second World War combined a formal observance of neutrality law with an informal, covert bias towards the allied powers, such bending of the rules was hardly an Irish monopoly. However, Ireland did diverge more noticeably from the practice of other European neutrals during the Cold War period, especially in turning a blind eye to what they saw as the incompatibility of involvement in west European integration and a stance of neutrality. This anomaly demonstrated that, particularly where international pressures are relatively diffuse, "neutrality" may be defined as much by perceptions and values in domestic politics as by the more general behaviour of states (see chapter 6).

The neutrality reservation has been deeply embedded in national political culture throughout this century. For the Irish nationalist movement neutrality was synonymous with an anti-imperialist (and specifically anti-British) world view. In fact, when Ireland actually practised a declared neutrality during the Second World War the government of Eamon de Valera covertly acted according to a "certain consideration" for British interests, thus breaching the rules of strict impartiality. But by 1945 the public perception was one of a successful neutrality which had kept Ireland free from the horrors of total war.

This gap, between an essentially instrumental view of neutrality policy held by the government on the one hand, and a broader quasi-ideology of neutrality in public debate on the other, became a latent tension in Irish political life. However, external pressures were never so great that a radical change in policy or public attitude occurred. The possibility of military alignment in the Cold War was at first precluded in the late 1940s, ostensibly by the dispute with the British government over Northern Ireland. The Irish government claimed it could not join NATO while Northern Ireland remained in the United Kingdom; the British and American governments were at one in not encouraging the inclusion of such a potentially disruptive and militarily unimportant member. The exploration of the possibility of a bilateral alliance with the United States shortly afterwards by the foreign minister, Seán MacBride, suggests that the government had no principled commitment to neutrality as such (Fanning, 1979), but the public perception to the contrary was rarely discouraged.

The decision by the Fianna Fáil government of Seán Lemass to apply to join the EEC in 1961 in effect made neutrality conditional on the extent of European integration. Lemass himself indicated that "we are prepared to go into this integrated Europe without any reservation as to how far this will take us in the field of foreign policy and defence" (Salmon, 1989, p. 217). The 1970 White Paper on EEC membership recognised "that as the Community evolves towards its political objectives, those participating in the new Europe must be prepared to assist, if necessary, in its defence" (Ireland, 1970, p. 8). Subsequent governments, irrespective of party configuration, have left this door open, but in practice there was little concrete incentive to change policy during the Cold War era.

In opposition, political parties showed little inclination to pursue the implications of broad hypothetical commitments which had no immediate relevance. However some, especially in Fianna Fáil and the Labour Party, on occasion tended to present the maintenance of military neutrality as a matter of fundamental principle rather than one of means and contingencies, and they consequently criticised the government of the day for allegedly allowing its erosion. This attitude, though at odds with the political commitment to eventual participation in common defence, could constrain official policy in quite significant ways. An important example was Ireland's ratification of the Single European Act in 1987, which was accompanied by a national declaration asserting the status of military neutrality in explicit terms that had hitherto been avoided. This development was mainly a result of domestic politics, including the tensions within the Fine Gael/Labour Party coalition which had negotiated the Single European Act and Fianna Fáil's sceptical view of its implications for neutrality when in opposition. Following the unexpected constitutional crisis leading to the referendum of May 1987, Fianna Fáil — now in Government — supported the Act, as qualified in its view by the neutrality declaration.

Although domestic debate on neutrality has been infrequent and has not generally been a major determinant of electoral politics, recent governments have promised to submit any change in policy to a referendum. The Fianna Fáil/Labour Party coalition (January 1993–November 1994) and the Fine Gael/Labour Party/Democratic Left government which came into office in December 1994 both included this commitment in their agreed programmes. One effect of this might seem to be to give military neutrality a quasi-constitutional status, in that policy change requires the same method of popular endorsement as a constitutional amendment. However, in considering whether the constitution should bind the state to a policy of neutrality, the Constitutional Review Group (1996, p. 93) concluded that "neutrality in Ireland has always been a policy as distinct from a fundamental law or principle".

Nevertheless, because neutrality touches on broad political values, some of which have little direct relevance to security policy, it can serve as a symbol of general political orientations. What are these values which tend to legitimate the neutrality reservation? A first set of ideas relates to a broadly political, rather than legal, concept of *sovereignty*. Neutrality is seen as a symbol of national identity, much as British attachment to parliamentary sovereignty or the monarchy and German anxieties about the national currency mark the limits of international collaboration in those countries. In Ireland's case the symbol has a particularly emotive connotation, in representing the struggle of a small nation against a dominating neighbour.

This view may be extended from a specific rejection of British influence to that of any alliance involving large states. In such a collaboration it is assumed that the national interests (if not the inherently imperialist instincts) of the great powers will outweigh the collective good of security. These assumptions about alliance are often associated with a second set of ideas centred on *anti-militarism*. General fears of an expansionist European military superpower are supplemented by the proposition that defence integration implies conscription to a European army, and support for nuclear deterrence (Maguire and Noonan, 1992). In Ireland the issue of conscription refers back to the experience of imperial subjugation rather than any subsequent national defence — it crystallised opposition to British rule in 1917. Although national conscription is an institution now in decline in many European countries — and supranational conscription is a myth — the historical association is powerful, if inappropriate. The opposition to nuclear deterrence is of course more recent, evolving in parallel with the anti-nuclear movement in many industrialised countries, especially during the later stages of the Cold War. The strictly anti-militarist motivation in this case is reinforced by a widespread distrust of nuclear technology — and in practice that is primarily focused on the nearest, that is the British, nuclear establishment.

A third strand in the popular justification for Irish neutrality is the concept often referred to as *positive neutrality*. Here it is assumed that neutrality enhances, or is even a necessary prerequisite of, Ireland's commitment to preventive policies. The pursuit of policies of Third World aid, support for human rights, and contributions to UN activities, including peacekeeping, are often legitimised in this way. The fact that several world leaders on these dimensions of a "positive" foreign policy are members of NATO (countries such as Canada, Denmark, the Netherlands and Norway) has done little to disturb the illusion that there is some necessary connection between "positive "and "neutral".

When weighed in the balance against the claims of solidarity with fellow EU member states, these values give the word neutrality a much greater resonance than might be expected when viewed primarily as a function of the overall European security environment. This residual affection for neutrality is present to some degree in all of the EU "neutrals" (and perhaps in a subliminal way in the political life of other member states). In Ireland, it is the starting point for any reassessment of security policy.

THE FOREIGN POLICY WHITE PAPER

Until very recently foreign policy issues in Ireland often seemed to come into the public domain more by accident than by design. Parliamentary procedures for policy oversight were casual; the parochial nature of party politics gave few incentives for politicians fully to engage in an aspect of public policy with limited electoral rewards. It was not until 1993 that a joint committee of both houses of the Oireachtas (parliament) was established in order to encourage a more systematic approach to parliamentary accountability in this field.

The decision in February 1994 by the Minister for Foreign Affairs and Tánaiste, Dick Spring, to prepare a White Paper on foreign policy was a further innovation in this belated democratisation of foreign policy. The project, which involved an unusual process of consultation through public seminars, was a long time in coming to fruition, the White Paper being published a few days before the convening of the Intergovernmental Conference at the end of March 1996.

This document is by far the most comprehensive statement yet produced of Irish policy positions and their underlying rationale (Ireland, 1996). Its scope is broader than that of security policy as such, but because of its insistence on "the need for a comprehensive approach to security that goes beyond the purely military dimension" (para. 4.64) a concern with security policy pervades the greater part of its contents. Moreover, the whole thrust of the White Paper rests on the fundamental proposition that "in order to prosper and to ensure its security, Ireland must engage with other nations in a common effort to maintain a stable framework for international relations . . ." (para. 2.38).

The three functional dimensions of security policy — prevention, crisis management and protection — provide a preliminary framework for the analysis of the broad orientations and specific commitments in the White Paper. The positions adopted in each of these categories in turn explain Ireland's approach to the debate on the second pillar in the IGC.

Preventive policies
Not surprisingly, given that Ireland is a small state, the emphasis on multilateral organisations is one of the most obvious features. The UN is seen as "imperfect, but irreplaceable"; its inadequacy in the face of the increased demands placed on it since the end of the Cold War is recognised but reform remains a key objective (paras. 5.5, 5.9). The OSCE is described as "uniquely placed to develop further its existing role as a focal point for European security cooperation" (para. 4.27). But above all, the European Community's role to "overcome age-old European rivalries" (para. 4.54) is a constant theme, along with "the extent to which Ireland, together with its fellow member states, has come to express its foreign policy through the medium of the European Union" (para. 2.29).

In the field of military preventive policies a whole chapter is devoted to disarmament and arms control (chapter 6). The basis of Irish policy is a level of armaments lower than that maintained by most European states, and no national armaments industry as such, though like any modern economy Ireland produces goods which have both civilian and military applications. Priority objectives include the complete abolition of nuclear weapons and other weapons of mass destruction, together with a call for greater attention to the transfer of conventional weapons. The means to these ends involve the greatest possible participation in the mainly UN framework, especially including the opportunities to develop a concerted approach through the EU's Common Foreign and Security Policy.

Non-military preventive policies also loom large, with an increasing focus on human rights policy and maintenance of the well-established emphasis on development cooperation (chapters 8, 9). However, in the specifically European context the most significant section is that dealing with the future enlargement of the European Union (paras. 3.129–54). This is described as one of the five major challenges facing the EU. The government claims its attitude to be "open and positive", and considers that "enlargement will enhance European stability and confidence" (para. 3.146). Nevertheless, much is made of the parameters within which enlargement should proceed. The abolition of existing EU policies for agriculture and redistributive programmes through the policy of economic and social cohesion is emphatically not seen as a necessary corollary of enlargement; nor is the abandonment of the Union's unique supranational system of policy-making.

Contributions to international crisis management
Ireland's existing tradition in this context, participation in UN peacekeeping, is the subject of a separate chapter in the White Paper (chapter 7). Drawing on recent experience of the often difficult circumstances of post-Cold War peacekeeping, the government identifies the general factors on which decisions to participate will be made (para. 7.13). Particular attention is paid to the conditions under which contributions will be made to "enforcement" operations; these include legitimation by the Security Council and, in the case of operations mandated to multinational forces not directly under UN command and control, a strict and supervised conformity to Security Council decisions (paras. 7.31–2).

The development of the OSCE, as a regional complement to the UN in international crisis management, is supported in the White Paper, but the most significant proposals under this heading relate to the ways in which the government sees Ireland being involved with NATO and the WEU. These proposals hinge on the attitudes towards NATO's Partnership for Peace and the WEU's definition of its crisis management role in the "Petersberg tasks" respectively (see below, chapter 10).

The objectives of the Partnership for Peace, described as a "co-operative security initiative", are seen as consistent with Ireland's approach. It is argued that participation would have several advantages, including the consolidation of what is in itself a confidence-building measure with the potential of enhancing operational capabilities in peacekeeping, air–sea rescue and humanitarian missions, and dealing with drug trafficking (para. 4.49). The government then states its intention to "explore further" the possibility of participating, following further consultations, but there is no decision to join.

The tentative nature of this formulation is underlined by making any commitment conditional on a set of principles which are also applied to the question of participation in crisis management in the WEU context outlined below. This covers contributions which might be made on a case-by-case basis by either the army or civilian police. However, this possibility is confined to the first two of the Petersberg tasks — humanitarian and rescue tasks, and peacekeeping. "Petersberg three" — tasks of combat forces in crisis management, including peacemaking — is explicitly ruled out (para. 4.88).

Policies of protection

The cautious formulation of commitments to the military aspect of international crisis management may well be justified in the light of the difficulties inherent in that type of security policy. However, it may also owe a good deal to Ireland's position on the classical issue of defending the state against attack from an aggressor. Here, the White Paper is at pains to maintain Ireland's distance from a commitment to collective self-defence. The government makes it quite clear that it will not be proposing that Ireland become a member of NATO or the WEU (para. 4.10). It also repeats the commitment, which has been a feature of successive governments since 1993, to "put the outcome of any future negotiations that would involve Ireland's participation in a common defence policy to the people in a referendum. This will ensure that Ireland's policy of military neutrality remains unchanged, unless the people themselves decide otherwise" (para. 4.115).

In presenting its position on the retention of "military neutrality" the White Paper goes further than the blunt minimalism of previous official statements in at least commenting on the context in which the policy is relevant. The position itself is partly based on a classical expression of national interest, in the proposition that "in the event of a major international or European conflict the security of the State could best be preserved by the adoption of an attitude of neutrality" (para. 4.11). However, after referring to the significant reduction of the risk of such a contingency since the end the Cold

War, the document does not explore just what military neutrality might involve in the new circumstances.

Another strand in the justification for military neutrality appears to be its popularity: "the majority of the Irish people have always cherished Ireland's military neutrality, and recognise the positive values that inspire it, in peace-time as well as in time of war". Here the rationale moves beyond national interest in the claim that military neutrality "has provided the basis for Ireland's wider efforts to promote international peace and security" (para. 4.4). This view comes close to the idea that neutrality has been a *necessary* element in the pursuit of the "positive values" that inspire it. On the other hand, in an earlier section of the White Paper, that logic seems to be rejected: "many have come to regard neutrality as a touchstone of our entire approach to international relations, even though in reality, much of our policy is not dependent on our non-membership of a military alliance" (para. 2.26).

Unusually for Irish policy statements to do with neutrality, the White Paper refers quite extensively to the phenomenon of the contemporary military alliance, particularly in its section describing NATO. Previously at best a "non-institution" in the Irish debate, NATO is now acknowledged to be "the principal defensive alliance in Europe" with "an important bearing on Ireland's security environment" (para. 4.32). There is also reference to the changes which NATO has undergone in relation to a greater role in prevention and crisis management, particularly in the IFOR operation in Bosnia (paras. 4.36–40).

IRELAND'S IGC POSITIONS

Ireland approaches the Intergovernmental Conference as a country which "has benefited enormously from membership of the European Union" (para. 3.8). One of the four main benefits of integration — and one which is too easily taken for granted — is "the success of the Union in preserving peace and contributing to stability, not only within its own borders but beyond" (para. 3.179). The general tone of the White Paper is positive, an added element being provided by Ireland's responsibility as president of the Council for chairing the IGC during the second semester in 1996.

With regard to the issues arising in the context of the first pillar of the Treaty on European Union, Ireland could be considered as being close to maximalist positions, particularly in its defence of the central role of the Commission and its readiness to consider the extension of qualifed majority voting in the first pillar (IEA, 1995; Scott, 1996). What, then, are its positions with regard to the second pillar?

CFSP positions

The White Paper takes a cautious line on the key issue of decision-making. After making the point that sensitive foreign policy issues require the broad backing of member states if a concerted Union position is to be credible, it argues that more use could be made of the existing provision for using qualified majority voting to implement policies already agreed by consensus (para. 3.199). The key to more effective decision-making is in fact seen in the development of a central analysis unit, a proposal which assumes by far the greatest prominence in Ireland's shopping list (paras. 3.200–3).

Notable by their absence are any significant references to other aspects of the CFSP agenda, such as the personification of the second pillar, the question of shared presidencies, the funding of the CFSP or the role of the European Parliament. At first sight this gives the impression that on the spectrum of national positions on the second pillar Ireland is midway between the British and the German–Benelux poles. However, the broader context of Ireland's interests in IGC reform, in which the consolidation of the supranational policy making system is strongly supported, suggests that there will be at least an open mind on most aspects of CFSP reform. In this respect, Ireland will not be significantly different from the other non-alliance member states.

Positions on defence

Given the retention of military neutrality, the White Paper approaches the issues to do with a common defence policy with considerable circumspection. It argues that involvement in the first two Petersberg tasks of the WEU would be both "a concrete contribution to European security" and "a sign of solidarity with our European partners and neighbours" (para. 4.86). The reluctance to undertake "Petersberg three" commitments indicates a strong reservation about the use of force in international crisis management.

The government then spells out three options for the development of Ireland's relationship with the WEU. The first option, to seek full membership, would be incompatible with the existing policy of military neutrality and might require a parallel accession to NATO (paras. 4.105–7). The second option is to maintain the status quo as an observer, with the rather restricted influence that this entails (paras. 4.108–9). The third option is to deepen military cooperation in the context of international crisis management, as outlined above (paras. 4.110–1).

Given the rejection of the first option elsewhere in the White Paper, together with the attention to the identification of the conditions under which the first two Petersberg tasks might be approached, it is clear that the third option is the government's preferred approach to involvement in a common defence policy. The six principles underlying it are:

* constructive participation in the IGC

* compatibility of any common defence policy with UN and OSCE principles

* compatibility with the broader role of the UN in international security

* a comprehensive co-operative security framework for Europe, avoiding new divisions

* the situation of military policies within a broad approach to security

* compatibility with Irish disarmament and arms control objectives (para. 4.114).

It is not surprising, in the light of these heavily qualified indications of how Ireland's relationship with the WEU might develop, that there is no explicit preference stated as to what shape the broader relationship between the European Union and the WEU should take. It is reasonable to infer, however, that a merger of the two bodies as currently constituted (with a mutual security guarantee at the heart of the WEU) could only complicate matters from an Irish point of view.

THE DOMESTIC SECURITY DEBATE

The initial political response to the White Paper showed that the military aspects of security policy were liable to be conflated into arguments about the fate of Irish neutrality rather than that of European security. Indeed, following the first suggestion (at a White Paper public seminar in February 1995) that policy adaptation might involve a working association with the military alliances, even if only in respect of peacekeeping, a retrenchment of attitudes was evident. In May 1995 the parliamentary Joint Committee on Foreign Affairs failed to agree a common position for its own contribution to the White Paper, anticipating a fraught debate following its publication.

The traditionalist critique
In its foreign policy programme, published in November 1995, the main opposition party, *Fianna Fáil*, set its face against those "who want to edge Ireland closer to full participation in an existing military alliance" (Fianna

119

Fáil, 1995, p. 5). While the party would be prepared to put Irish forces "at the disposal of the European Union under the auspices of the Common Foreign and Security Policy for the purposes of helping in situations of crisis management", there was no reference in this document to the role of the WEU (as expressly allowed for in the Treaty on European Union) to implement such a policy. This apparent oversight was corrected in subsequent statements; thus, for example, the party leader, Bertie Ahern, saw no objection to "becoming engaged in a voluntary ad hoc way in particular tasks run by the WEU that we have traditionally involved ourselves in under UN auspices" (Ahern, 1996).

Fianna Fáil's foreign policy programme saw Ireland's involvement in NATO's Partnership for Peace as neither necessary nor appropriate. Indeed, this issue aroused most heat following the launch of the White Paper, serving as a lightning conductor for a wholesale rejection of military alliances. The Fianna Fáil foreign affairs spokesperson, Ray Burke, represented PFP as "second-class membership of NATO" and seemed to suggest that even a limited association with NATO would tar Ireland with the nuclear brush (*The Irish Times*, 28 March 1996). The party leader, Bertie Ahern, called for a referendum before a decision to join PFP, which he claimed would be seen "by other countries as a gratuitous signal that Ireland is moving away from its neutrality and towards a gradual incorporation into NATO and Western European Union in due course" (*Dáil Debates*, 28 March 1996).

In addition to arguing that PFP was the thin end of the wedge of full NATO membership, Fianna Fáil maintained that Ireland had different geopolitical considerations to other non-alliance countries which were close to sources of instability. This qualification of the principle (endorsed by a Fianna Fáil Taoiseach at the CSCE summit in 1992) that European security was "indivisible" was matched by an insistence that economic benefits already gained from EU membership were not a favour "which we will have to repay by other means" (Bertie Ahern, *Dáil Debates*, 28 March 1996).

The focus on PFP was reinforced when the smallest government party, *Democratic Left*, also opposed Ireland's participation (and thereby made explicable the tentative formulation of the issue in the White Paper). In the Dáil Kathleen Lynch claimed it would be incompatible with "a positive neutrality" and "would lock Ireland into a militaristic view of the world". Partnership for Peace, she argued, merely served as a vehicle for NATO to "establish its control of security arrangements in post-Cold War Europe" and NATO for its part was "an American-led militarist alliance" (*Dáil Debates*, 28 March 1996). The smallest opposition party, the *Green Party*, followed a similar anti-militarist approach.

The radical critique

Opposition criticism of the White Paper for not going far enough in adapting to the new security environment was confined to the *Progressive Democrats*. The party spokesperson, Des O' Malley, recalling the axiom attributed to Seán Lemass that "a Europe worth joining is a Europe worth defending", argued that the White Paper focused only on the "feel good" aspects of security policy. He doubted whether military neutrality would be credible in the event of an attack on another EU member state.

Further parliamentary reactions to the security policy issues raised by the publication of the White Paper did not develop beyond these very general initial positions by the time Ireland assumed the presidency of the Council in July 1996. The fact that one of the government parties and the major opposition party had opposed participation in the PFP heightened sensitivities about neutrality, in a context coloured by domestic party calculation. The result was, for the time being at least, an uneasy lull in the security debate.

Public opinion

In the past, public opinion polls have shown the significance of neutrality as a political symbol. On the eve of the referendum on the Maastricht Treaty in 1992 a review of the intermittent data up to that point concluded that neutrality remained a significant political symbol, but with a loosely defined content and no very clear social or political profile (Marsh, 1992). Using Eurobarometer data published in the spring of 1993, another analysis found that the highest levels of opposition to a common defence policy came from both the least and best informed among those polled (Sinnott, 1995, p. 8).

A poll conducted during the European Parliament election campaign in 1994 raised the possibility of Ireland becoming involved in a common defence, thereby forgoing neutrality. A minority of 30 per cent was in favour, 63 per cent were opposed, and the uncommitted category was as low as 7% (*The Irish Times*, 3 June 1994). Yet only five months later another poll, commissioned by the RTE television programme *Tuesday File* (24 October 1994), found that 51 per cent were prepared to see Ireland take part in a common European defence, and 56 per cent agreed with support for another EU member state if it was attacked. But when the question referred explicitly to neutrality only 37 per cent were in favour of changing Ireland's policy, as against 46 per cent for its retention and 17 per cent undecided. Clearly the answer will vary according to the way the question is posed, and one of the most pertinent points about Irish opinion polls on international security policy is their rarity.

Conclusions

With regard to the Intergovernmental Conference, there are obvious broad similarities between Ireland's approach and that of the other three neutral WEU observer countries. On the question of reform of the CFSP, they all share a cautious attitude to decision-making procedures, based on incremental qualification of its intergovernmental nature. The most ambitious reform contemplated is an enhanced analysis capacity in Brussels.

So far as the definition of a future common defence policy is concerned, Ireland, like the others, shows an interest in selective participation in international crisis management. The question of seeking full membership in the WEU (or in NATO) is clearly not on the agenda.

Where Ireland does differ from the other neutral countries is in the pace of its adaptation to the military aspects of post-Cold War security. Finland and Sweden joined the Partnership for Peace almost two years before the Irish political system started to get to grips with the underlying issues. Austria, Finland and Sweden, in addition to their PFP commitments, have contributed to the innovative arrangements for military support to the Bosnian peace process. Ireland's involvement is less direct, being confined to monitoring and civilian policing aspects which come under the aegis of the UN and the EU.

This suggests that the necessary conditions for policy innovation in the military field may be relatively weak in Ireland. Neutrality has become more politicised at the parliamentary level in recent years, and party positions are such that it cuts across the overall government–opposition alignment. The consequent tendency to procrastinate is reinforced by the country's relatively low level of direct exposure to the most dramatic security risks.

The domestic debate so far has been characterised by an evident residual distrust of military alliance and, particularly in the context of the PFP question, a reluctance to accept that alliances themselves may be adapting to changed circumstances. The concentration on neutrality as such tends to foreclose an examination of many of the specific issues pertaining to the development of a co-operative security regime, involving both military and non-military means.

The following chapters explore these issues in more detail, as "matters arising" (or which should, eventually, arise) in the Irish security debate. Their resolution — by the government, political parties and, ultimately, the general public — will shape Ireland's security policy at the Intergovernmental Conference and beyond. The analysis, using the broad headings of protection, crisis management and prevention, identifies the major trends in general policy adaptation, and explores the implications these may have for Ireland. The starting point is a closer look at what is for the Irish debate ostensibly the most sensitive dimension of security policy, that of protection. What are the changing roles of military alliances? What is the place of nuclear force? Does political solidarity in the European Union require a commitment to collective defence?

CHAPTER 9
MATTERS ARISING: PROTECTIVE POLICIES

The most obvious point of contention in Ireland's security debate is the significance to be ascribed to the stance of "neutrality", and to its converse, military alignment. As aspects of international political behaviour, both these phenomena derive from the protective dimension of security policy. They both assume the existence of military threat and the possibility of war, and see conflict in terms of military instruments; the first seeks to avoid entanglement in conflict, while the second entails a strategy of collective deterrence to avoid war, and if that fails, a collective defence. From that vantage point, it may seem paradoxical that even with the disappearance of the Cold War the relative merits of neutrality and alliance are still contested with such apparent emotion.

It is therefore appropriate to begin this examination of current security issues by asking how significant the protective dimension now is, and whether the attention it receives in the Irish debate is actually justified. To that end, this chapter explores the following themes:

* the persistence of military alliances, and their adaptation to purposes other than their traditional role of collective defence

* the reduced, but ambiguous, significance of nuclear force in a co-operative security regime

* the proposition that political solidarity in the European Union requires a commitment to collective defence, and hence the end of military neutrality.

THE PERSISTENCE OF MILITARY ALLIANCES IN EUROPE

One thing is quite clear in the position of "military neutrality" — it means not being a member of a military alliance. In those countries, like Ireland, which have become accustomed to this policy it is often inferred that military alliances are undesirable in themselves. In this view, for example, they may be seen as expressions of militarism, the institutional forms of a mind-set unduly focused on the resort to force. Thus it is an illusion to regard alliances as "defensive"; rather than being a solution to the problem of insecurity between states they become a part of it, creating and sustaining spirals of mutual distrust.

In the context of a co-operative security regime, it is argued, military alliances are particularly inappropriate. There is no adversary to ally against, and the exclusive membership of alliances runs against the grain of the overall requirement of inclusiveness. Even in an adversarial environment, alliances are inherently unstable. Members have to cope with two opposing fears: that they will be abandoned in the event of a threat against them which does not impinge directly on their allies' interests or, alternatively, that they will be entrapped in alliance commitments against their own interests. European history provides many examples of the high costs of alliance membership, even in those cases where the overall purpose of a military coalition was ultimately achieved.

However, these general arguments against alliance have to be considered in the context of the specific circumstances prevailing in Europe today. It is an observable fact that most European governments see alliance as an important and viable instrument of collective policy. By examining the recent evolution of NATO and the WEU in more detail, it is possible to understand why this should be so, and to explore the question of whether the institution of military alliance itself is changing.

Why does NATO still exist?
Following the disintegration of the Soviet Union and its European alliance, the Warsaw Pact, it was sometimes assumed that there was no longer any reason for the existence of NATO — the "enemy" had simply disappeared. Was the organisation's survival beyond the achievement of its original purpose anything more than a combination of bureaucratic inertia and vested organisational interests?

Such motivation cannot be discounted (institutions do tend to outlive their original purpose), but such an explanation does not do justice to the persistence of NATO. Unlike the Warsaw Pact, seen by the majority of its members as an instrument of Soviet control and occasional coercion, NATO has survived for several reasons:

* Its members value it as a hedge against an uncertain future. There may be no rival blocs now, but the emergence of future blocs cannot be ruled out. In the meantime some degree of threat may be seen in the policies of several "rogue states" — militarised states which explicitly reject international norms (for example, Iraq, Libya, North Korea).

* NATO states may also still see membership broadly as a "confidence-sustaining measure" in their own intra-alliance relations. The sensitive question of German rearmament was easier to handle in an alliance context during the Cold War; the potentially greater military profile of Germany in the years to come may likewise prove more acceptable in this setting. The alternative — a "renationalisation" of defence policies — might rekindle apprehension about great power ambitions.

* NATO remains the main formal institutional channel for, and expression of, the continuing engagement of the United States in European security. In the increased uncertainty as to the extent and durability of American engagement, the alliance's political role in this respect may now be more rather than less important.

* Most of the governments of the post-communist states in central and eastern Europe are anxious to become members of NATO for all of the above reasons. They do not fear Russian aggression, but do not wish to be pulled back into a Russian sphere of influence or remain in an ambiguous "buffer zone"; they wish to deal with their largest central European neighbour, Germany, in a multilateral context which includes the other large European states and the United States.

* NATO still represents the most advanced form of peacetime multinational military cooperation, offering a high level of standardisation with regard to joint commands, equipment and interoperability of forces. There is an increasing economic incentive to cooperate, in the context of declining national defence budgets. Indeed, it may not be an exaggeration to say that defence policies are now shaped more by finance ministries than by their colleagues in foreign or defence ministries. During the Cold War not even the larger European members of NATO possessed a sufficient military capability to ensure the defence of their national territories; now, the military requirements of the new challenges of international crisis management may likewise be beyond the capacities of individual countries. Thus, in addition to its original core function of collective self-defence, NATO is now acquiring a new role as the most important single framework for the collective adaptation of military force in Europe. This significant — and as yet incomplete — aspect of the adaptation of NATO is examined in more detail in chapter 10.

The WEU: the alliance within the alliance

In the fluid circumstances of European security the roles of other European alliance groupings remain to be defined. The Commonwealth of Independent States is very loosely organised and its military commitments (in the Treaty of Tashkent, 1992) are as yet unrealised; its significance lies mainly in its potential as a focus of future Russian influence with most but not necessarily all of the other former Soviet republics. The WEU also has the characteristics of a "paper alliance", with a legal base and political structure but little in the way of its own military capability. If in the overall historical context it served as the catalyst for the creation of NATO, it nevertheless remained in the shadow of the larger alliance throughout the Cold War.

Arguably the WEU still is "the alliance within the alliance". This is the formal position, reflected in the WEU declaration attached to the Treaty on European Union where it is described as "a means to strengthen the European pillar of the Atlantic Alliance". Its dual role in the evolution of both NATO and the European Union is still far from clear — hence the rather vague concept in that declaration of a "European Security and Defence Identity" which will somehow, sometime pull all these institutional entities together.

In January 1994 the NATO summit meeting developed the relationship further, through the concept of Combined Joint Task Forces. This refers to a multinational, combined services (air, land, sea) force created for a specific mission (Barry, 1996). From a WEU point of view, this device allows WEU crisis management operations to use NATO (i.e. partly American) assets such as command structures, airlift capabilities and perhaps intelligence in operations where the United States itself might not wish to become involved.

Translating this idea into workable procedures has not been easy; indeed, the CJTF mechanism was not finally agreed until June 1996, being largely dependent on France's move back towards the NATO fold. In the meantime, the actual involvement of the WEU in the Balkans has been on a very small scale and rather experimental in character. A share in coordinating the naval embargo in the Adriatic and sanctions implementation on the Danube, together with the provision of civilian police for the EU administration of Mostar, fell a long way short of the image of an embryonic European army. The de facto CJTF in Bosnia — for this is what the Implementation Force amounts to — is led by NATO, not the WEU, and even in the event of an American withdrawal it is not clear whether the WEU as such would be the next framework for an international force in the region.

The idea that full membership of the WEU for the central and east European countries might be a feasible alternative to their wish to join NATO does not hold much water either. So long as the WEU members' collective defence commitments are in effect underwritten by the United States, it is hard to see how a state could be a full member of the WEU without being a full member of NATO (though the converse is possible — witness the cases of Iceland, Norway and Turkey).

Thus the development of the WEU from being "an alliance-in-waiting" to being an entity comparable in scope to NATO is unlikely so long as the latter is a going concern. Short of a dramatic reassessment by the United States of its interests in European security leading to a withdrawal from NATO, the WEU seems likely to develop mainly as the operational military framework for the European Union's policies of crisis management.

Are the UN and the OSCE alternatives to military alliances?
Some Irish critics of NATO and the WEU argue that the appropriate international organisations to deal with security are the United Nations and any relevant inclusive regional bodies, such as the OSCE in the case of Europe. Their composition and, so far as the UN is concerned almost universally agreed, legal basis give these institutions superior legitimacy to more narrowly based alliances.

In principle, the point seems appealing. At first sight the UN offers a system of true *collective* security, binding on all parties, which is superior to the conditional commitments of co-operative security. However, a closer examination shows that in such a system any member state may in principle be obliged to use force at the behest of the UN against any other member which breaks the rules. This is hardly different in effect from the mutual assistance obligations of an alliance commitment; the obligation of collective security, in which in the last resort the UN takes sides, overrides the option of strict neutrality.

In fact, the UN has never come close to realising its potential in this regard, and the OSCE has hardly even aspired to it. In practice neither organisation provides collective security; nor do they necessarily have a strong capacity to act particularly where the military instrument is concerned. Where the OSCE and especially the UN play an essential role is in assisting member states to define legitimate mandates for international action. Their relevance lies in providing political authority for international crisis management rather than military protection for their members.

During the last five years, when the demand increased significantly for such mandates (and consequent actions, including those of a coercive nature), the institutional capacity of the UN has clearly been inadequate. That is not to detract from its several successes (for example, in Cambodia), but to recognise its inherent limitations. Of course these reflect the diversity of national interests, the level of distrust and the jealously guarded prerogatives of the member states. By the same token, the amelioration of these negative factors is an important task for the long term. There is nothing to preclude

— and indeed much to recommend — the reform and further development of the UN and the OSCE as frameworks in which, over time, the felt need for military alliances becomes less acute.

In the short to medium term, however, it is unrealistic to expect countries which value alliances to regard the UN and the OSCE as viable replacements. These are the necessary legitimators of international crisis management, but they are only part of a broader range of multilateral networks which channel political influence and organise military force. For European governments, it is not a question of choosing between institutions with comparable scope and effectiveness, but rather of trying to mesh the complementary roles of disparate institutions more successfully.

This untidy and often uneasy coexistence of security organisations with quite different characteristics and origins is a "given" of the current security regime. There may be regrets for missed opportunities to reform the multilateral system more radically at the end of the Cold War, but the need for further adaptation in the future is more to the point. And that goes for military alliances as well as the other organisations.

The adaptation of military alliances
In the Irish security debate it is not always appreciated that the military alliances in contemporary Europe are in a fuzzily defined transitional stage, with elements of their original purpose combined with new functions. They play some sort of role in each of the main dimensions of security policy. They retain their traditional role in the long-term protection of their member states; by providing for deterrence of, and ultimately defence against, future enemies they behave in a familiar way. But their other roles may not be so clearly understood. The elaboration of forms of association with former enemies (NACC, PFP, WEU associate partnership) is an element of reassurance and long-term conflict prevention. The involvement of NATO, and on a smaller scale the WEU, in Bosnia illustrates their utility in crisis management.

The commitments involved in these roles vary considerably. So far as the preventive and crisis management aspects are concerned, both member states and interested non-members undertake a wide range of tasks, many of which do not involve the deployment of armed forces. Where participation does involve such risks it is on a case-by-case basis by individual governments. These commitments are examined in more detail in chapter 10.

On the other hand, the traditional commitment to collective self-defence is more demanding. A mutual assistance guarantee is a legally binding promise to provide military help to a fellow member state which has been attacked (see Appendix VI). In practice, the policy of the alliance is geared towards ensuring that this contingency does not arise in the first place. The operational emphasis is on the provision of a collective military posture strong enough to deter potential adversaries from attacking a member of the alliance. Successful deterrence by definition avoids the actual use of force in collective defence.

To date NATO's security guarantees have never been put to the ultimate test. Its supporters have often given credit for this happy outcome to a particular form of deterrence — the threat of retaliation by nuclear weapons. During the Cold War that threat was mutual, and was a central feature of the relationship between the opposing military blocs. That the security guarantee was nuclear came to be taken for granted by alliance governments, but it is pertinent to ask what relevance this nuclear orthodoxy has in the different circumstances prevailing today.

THE NUCLEAR ISSUE

For those countries, like Ireland, which have eschewed the nuclear option for any purpose, whether civilian or military, the nuclear dimension of defence policy often appears to be at best a dangerous anachronism. For many people in these societies one of the main objections to joining an alliance is that it implies a commitment to nuclear deterrence. In alliance member states, which during the Cold War became accustomed to thinking of nuclear deterrence as a lesser evil than actual defence, this issue appears less pressing (though in some cases substantial minorities oppose nuclear weapons). There remains a considerable gap between the two positions, the more so given the increasing ambiguity about the role of nuclear force.

The persistence of nuclear weapons
Since the end of the Cold War the apparatus of mutual nuclear threat between the major nuclear powers, the United States and Russia (as successor-state to the former Soviet Union), has been significantly reduced. NATO's land-based nuclear stockpile has been reduced by over 80 per cent. A treaty-based programme of verified disarmament is under way, and existing weapons are no longer officially aimed at specific targets. In a co-operative security regime nuclear force is no longer the hard currency of European security.

However, reduction has not meant elimination. The implementation of agreed cuts is both expensive and slow, and the ratification of further agreements is uncertain. Although France and the United Kingdom are also reducing their strategic programmes, the case for retention of at least some nuclear capability is the orthodoxy among the governments of nuclear states.

The argument is usually put in the form of a hedge against the possibility of the breakdown of co-operative security. It is an argument which can be applied to all forms of weapons of mass destruction (including chemical and biological weapons) as well as the missile technology relating to their delivery (Neville Brown, 1995). However, in the context of nuclear weapons the debate has a particularly sharp public profile, largely because of controversies about the safety of nuclear technology in civilian as well as military guise.

For some proponents of nuclear orthodoxy, there is now a tendency towards "existential deterrence", whereby possession of these weapons is enough to deter potential adversaries. Moreover, the ultimate goal of complete nuclear disarmament is seen as unrealistic, both because the technology cannot be disinvented and because it would not be possible to prevent a state "breaking out" of a future non-nuclear regime. In this view, there will always be a case for the indefinite retention by existing nuclear possessors of a minimum nuclear deterrent (Quinlan, 1993).

The counter-argument, that a break-out would be controllable in a mature non-nuclear regime (MccGwire, 1994), offers a more benign view of the long-term prospects of co-operative security. Either way, the arguments about the "ultimate" fate of nuclear disarmament are couched in a time-scale of twenty to thirty years while a non-nuclear regime is negotiated and implemented. Where does that leave the policies of the nuclear states in the interim?

At first sight official positions seem to reflect a policy of "less of the same" — a considerably reduced emphasis on the nuclear factor, but little change in the rationale for possession of nuclear forces (Witney, 1994–95; Yost, 1994–95). A minimum deterrent will be kept in being, just in case of a future threat to the survival of the state. But there has also been an interest in the possibility of what is known as "sub-strategic" deterrence, in which "nuclear weapons are seen as usable instruments of war" which may be deployed in regional conflicts where the nuclear possessor's territorial defence may not be directly at stake (Rogers, 1996, p. 27).

Sub-strategic deterrence does not appear in the official declaratory policy of the nuclear powers. Given the ruling of the International Court of Justice (ICJ) in the Hague in July 1996, that the threat or use of nuclear weapons is contrary to international law except in the extreme case of self-defence, it does not seem to have much of a future in nuclear doctrine. This ruling may only be an advisory opinion, but as the first-ever legal restriction on nuclear weapons its impact on international norms is likely to be significant.

Nuclear orthodoxy is also being questioned more widely, even amongst political–military establishments. A former director of the London-based International Institute for Strategic Studies, Sir Robert O'Neill, has taken the governments of existing nuclear possessors to task for their reluctance to revise nuclear policy (O'Neill, 1995). He argues that even in the short to medium term possession has increasing disadvantages. It has no utility in countering actual or potential non-nuclear threats, and the possibility of nuclear proliferation by smaller powers would be more effectively dealt with by conventional force under UN authority.

In addition, public opinions will be even less willing to support nuclear weapons programmes as the evidence of technical and human error becomes more rather than less compelling. Since the disintegration of the Soviet Union, which led willy-nilly to the proliferation of nuclear arsenals in the hands of new and weak states, the strict controls of the Cold War era have become more difficult to maintain. At the same time, the potential threat posed by smaller near-nuclear states, such as North Korea and Iraq, has only been contained (so far) by sustained diplomatic pressure and, in the latter case, in part by conventional war and continuing embargoes of relevant equipment.

In the long term, therefore, the nuclear question may be more appropriately seen as a matter for the preventive approach rather than as the bedrock of military protection. Indeed, the focus has shifted to some extent from the elaboration of nuclear doctrines by the possessor states and their allies to arms control frameworks, such as the Nuclear Non-Proliferation Treaty (see chapter 11). Nevertheless, in the medium term the utility of nuclear force will remain on the agenda of collective defence, especially in Europe, which remains the major concentration of nuclear force.

Nuclear issues in the EU defence debate

The nuclear policies of EU countries cover a wide range of positions. At one end of the spectrum is the solidarity they showed on the issue of indefinite extension of the NPT at the 1995 review conference. Indeed, this was based on one of the joint actions adopted under the new CFSP procedures, and demonstrates the potential of the EU as an effective diplomatic actor (Muller and van Dassen, 1995).

However, agreement on the approach to non-proliferation is not replicated when it comes to positions on nuclear doctrine. At first sight little appears to have changed in this respect. In 1987, for example, the WEU's "Hague Platform" justified nuclear weapons on the grounds that they were necessary to "confront a potential aggressor with an unacceptable risk"; in 1995 the same organisation's "common concept" on European security (framed by all of the then twenty-seven participants in the extended WEU network) repeated the formula, adding that "the independent nuclear forces of the United Kingdom and France, which have a deterrent role of their own, contribute to the overall deterrence and security of the Allies" (WEU, 1995b, p. 31, para. 158).

A footnote to this paragraph reminds the reader, however, that Austria, Finland, Ireland and Sweden were not party to these decisions. In his national statement following the presentation of the document at Madrid, the Tánaiste, Dick Spring, made it clear that "we do not subscribe to the language on the role of nuclear deterrence" (Spring, 1995). It may be inferred that the remaining twenty-three WEU countries do still in principle accept a role for nuclear forces, including those of France and the United Kingdom, though the twenty-one non-nuclear states among them have no say on the nuclear policies of the other two. What is not so clear, though, is how, or even whether, they wish French and British nuclear weapons to be incorporated in a future European defence policy.

From an alliance point of view, the residual nuclear guarantee is still American, for the relevant military capability is still American. The British and French governments have always insisted their much smaller nuclear forces remain under independent political control, and in spite of bilateral consultations between the two governments since November 1992 it is not clear what this will amount to in terms of national doctrines or co-operative policies in the long term. When President Chirac gave his blessing to the proposition that France's nuclear deterrent was a necessary element in a future European defence (see chapter 1), the context of his argument — the row following the unilateral resumption of French nuclear testing — made it appear mainly as a self-serving exercise in political damage limitation. Ten of France's EU partners opposed the tests at the UN General Assembly, including six NATO allies (Belgium, Denmark, Italy, Luxembourg, the Netherlands and Portugal), whose governments had no difficulty in acccepting the American nuclear guarantee. Germany, Greece and Spain abstained, leaving France supported only by the other European nuclear power, the United Kingdom. Subsequent French signals of an eventual reintegration into a reformed NATO gave credence to the view that for France nuclear policy was an instrument to gain greater influence in that context.

The position of Germany on the possible Europeanisation of British and French nuclear forces is of particular interest, in the light of the long-standing tension in German policy between the renunciation of national nuclear forces (a necessary reassurance to former victims) and an insistence on nuclear guarantees as a prerequisite of American engagement in European security. The German government was not among President Chirac's many vocal EU critics in the summer of 1995, and there were even reports of consideration being given to his proposals by the majority government party, the CDU/CSU.

These straws in the wind probably had more to do with the overall requirements of establishing a satisfactory Franco-German entente following the election of the unpredictable Jacques Chirac than with German security policy. The latter is still based on the importance of the American nuclear guarantee as the essential "coupling" mechanism between the United States and its European allies. There is no serious public pressure to revisit what were very divisive nuclear debates during the Cold War period; nor is this seen as an issue which will further the cause of deeper European integration (Kamp, 1995).

The nuclear card, then, is only to be expected at some stage in the game that major states play — seeking advantage in alliance politics. It does not follow that it will be the decisive element in the formation of a common defence policy, for hesitations about creating a European nuclear force are hardly going to be transient ones. Even its supporters can provide no compelling arguments that it is either necessary or desirable in present circumstances. The utility of nuclear force is ambiguous, and the concept of "extended deterrence", whereby a nuclear state guarantees the security of non-nuclear allies, is inherently difficult: the nuclear power has to concede some measure of national control of its forces; the non-nuclear recipient has to accept a new form of dependence on, and leverage by, the former.

All of that proved difficult enough in the context of American nuclear dominance during the Cold War, when all concerned shared a common perception of threat from the Soviet Union. Since then there has been little to suggest that the British or French governments are really prepared to concede their independent nuclear status, one of the few areas of comparative advantage (as they would see it) over Germany. There is nothing to suggest other countries see this issue as a major priority in the development of a co-operative security regime. In short, the Europeanisation of nuclear forces is not on the agenda, formally or otherwise, of the Intergovernmental Conference.

MILITARY NEUTRALITY AND EUROPEAN SOLIDARITY

The persistence of both NATO and the orthodoxy of nuclear deterrence may be partly explained by the fact that the end of the Cold War did not involve an immediate or total transition to a secure and stable environment for European states. Hence the traditional motivation for military protection did not wholly disappear, and neither did the policy instruments devised for that purpose. But there is also a quite different argument for a collective defence commitment of the traditional kind — the proposition that the requirements of political solidarity in a fully integrated European Union include a formal commitment to defend that Union. This view is much more likely to be raised at the Intergovernmental Conference than questions of nuclear doctrine, and is therefore a more relevant consideration for the security debate in Ireland.

The debate on "core Europe"

The inclusion of security and defence in the maximalist vision of European integration, however aspirational it may have been in practice, is not new. Indeed, before either the Council of Europe or the European Coal and Steel Community (ECSC) — the "Community of the Six" — was established, a "Treaty of Economic, Social and Cultural Collaboration and Collective Self-Defence" — the foundation treaty of what later became the WEU — was signed at Brussels on 17 March 1948. Likewise the European Defence Community, rejected by the French National Assembly in 1954, was envisaged as a complement to the existing ECSC and a projected European Political Community.

Of course, the fate of these precedents testifies to the sensitivities involved in integrating the field of security, and especially its military dimension, defence. Nevertheless, it has been a constant, particularly in Germany's European policy, and the CDU/CSU paper which launched the IGC debate in September 1994 reflects this continuity. It regards the creation of a common European defence as "a matter of much greater urgency than envisaged in the Maastricht Treaty . . . it should be done now, rather than 'in time' as stated in the Treaty" (CDU/CSU, 1994, p. 11).

In so far as a strong European Union is seen as an essential element in creating stability throughout Europe, the authors of the CDU/CSU paper were motivated by considerations of security policy as such. But they were also concerned with the need to counteract the tendency to fragmentation in a larger and more diverse Union; in the most controversial part of their paper they resurrected the idea that a "core group" of countries, which would "participate as a matter of course in all policy fields", was necessary to sustain the integrative process.

The debate on "core Europe" is unlikely to be resolved in the short term, as many member state governments see it as unnecessarily divisive. However, it could well be an important element in the dynamics of the Intergovernmental Conference itself, and has a more lasting importance in that it raises the question of political solidarity in a particularly acute way.

Any form of cooperation implies some degree of solidarity or, to put it at its most basic level, a willingness to assist partners in difficulty. This principle is already expressed in the opening article of the Treaty on European Union, where the Union's "task shall be to organise, in a manner demonstrating consistency and solidarity, relations between the Member States and between their peoples" (TEU, Article A). It has been implemented in the form of EU policies of economic and social cohesion, of which Ireland has been a major beneficiary during more than twenty-three years of membership. If security and defence are included in the Union's basic remit — and the Treaty on European Union does so, however ambiguously — it is difficult to resist the argument that reciprocal commitments should apply across the board. From the point of view, say, of a German citizen the question is a simple one: should not Ireland, financially assisted by German subsidies, pledge its assistance to Germany in the event of an attack against Germany?

Viewed in this light, the question of how far a country is willing to go in making commitments to security policy may be a significant factor in the much broader "issue-linkage" which takes place in negotiations among EU member states. A successful negotiation leading to an overall package deal requires a complex process of give and take which can involve policies which are not functionally related. In the current Intergovernmental Conference there are core policy areas as well as potential core countries — as well as defence, participation in European Monetary Union (EMU) and the dismantling of border controls under the Schengen Agreement are generally regarded in this way. Any government will need to ensure that the best possible balance is maintained in the IGC between its security policy interests and those in other fields.

Nevertheless, there are arguments against pushing the logic of the core approach to its limits. The development of the European Union, particularly at this stage of its existence when an identifiable hard core consists of perhaps only one-third of its member states, might be hindered rather than enhanced by emphasising such a potentially divisive approach. With regard to security policy in particular, the existing division of labour, whereby NATO looks after "hard security" (and especially collective defence) and the EU concentrates on its comparative advantage as a "civilian power", may be the most realistic option for some time to come. The basis of a transatlantic bargain on security is clear — in terms of military capabilities "Europe" falls far short of the United States, and the latter is not about to become a member of the European Union. The insistence on a full EU defence now pays too much attention to the dogma of a union which is deemed "incomplete" until it has acquired all the classical but perhaps in some respects outmoded attributes of statehood.

In fact, the potential proponents of a core approach — the member states with a maximalist orientation in the IGC — have lowered their sights. Some have proposed a political solidarity clause in the treaty, though it is hard to see precisely what could be added to the actual and implied commitments it already contains. More generally, they seem to be working towards a compromise where there is sufficient "flexibility" in the policy-making system to permit an "avant-garde" or "coalitions of the willing" to act for the Union without being blocked by the incapable or unwilling (see chapter 7). This differentiated integration would allow a member state like Ireland to remain outside a collective defence commitment, thus preserving the position of military neutrality.

Nevertheless, a government advancing such a case may be pressed to explain the reasons for its reservations about expressing political solidarity in the form of a mutual security guarantee. Where it is unwilling to make a commitment in one area it may also be pressed to compensate by a greater commitment elsewhere, in order to sustain the overall political solidarity of the Union.

CONCLUSIONS

The protective dimension of security policy, with its concentration on the organisation of military power to deter adversaries, is no longer the dominant theme of European security. But it has not disappeared altogether, and three aspects have some relevance for the Irish security debate.

First, the persistence of NATO at least in part reflects its members' reluctance to abandon a collective instrument which might have to be reinvented in the face of any future threat. However, NATO has also survived because it serves other purposes, relating as much to its members' political relationships as to their military policies. In the military domain, its future may depend more on its ability to adapt to the needs of international crisis management than on territorial protection. Given the extent to which NATO already has adapted, the WEU appears more likely to develop as a European branch of NATO than as a standalone military alliance acting for the European Union.

Second, nuclear issues — not so long ago the currency of European security politics — have also receded into the background. However, nuclear countries are in no hurry to abandon that status altogether, though the rationale for the possession of nuclear force may become less clear in a co-operative security regime. There is little sign of a serious debate on the question of creating a "European" nuclear force.

Third, the issue of a mutual security guarantee — the key commitment in a military alliance — may be raised in the context of the IGC, but not so much because there is an urgent need for military protection as because it is seen by most member states as a normal corollary of political solidarity.

To what extent are these themes being absorbed in the Irish security debate? The concentration on a traditional distaste for NATO and the WEU tends to obscure the point that, irrespective of whether Ireland is a member of these alliances or not, they are an inherent part of the institutional arrangements in the evolving security regime. In addition, the capacity of the alliances to adapt their role, especially towards international crisis management, opens the possibility of non-alliance countries like Ireland being associated with some of their activities. This question is explored further in the following chapter.

The persistence of the nuclear issue, though in a minor key, provides a challenge but also an opportunity to non-nuclear states to assist in multilateral attempts to influence the debate on controlling and reducing the risks of nuclear confrontation. This question is arguably part of the long-term preventive dimension of security policy. To insist on regarding nuclear doctrine as the determining feature of European military alliances, thereby consigning them to a limbo of political incorrectness, is unlikely to be a productive strategy. It will hardly engage the attention of the alliance members on what is left of the nuclear question, and bars the development of collaboration with the alliances on other, and arguably more relevant, aspects of security policy.

Paradoxically, it may be when an alliance commitment is proposed as a requirement of political solidarity in the broader context of European integration that the retention of military neutrality is most difficult to justify, assuming that the overall goal of integration is accepted. However, in the context of the Intergovernmental Conference the extent of consensus on a future common defence policy is so low that there appears to be little significant pressure for non-alliance states to engage in full alliance commitments at this stage.

CHAPTER 10
MATTERS ARISING: INTERNATIONAL CRISIS MANAGEMENT

The most obvious dimension of European security policy since the end of the Cold War has been that of crisis management. Unfortunately it has made an impression not so much for its successes — such as the peaceful dismantling of the Soviet empire — which tend to be taken for granted, as for its failures, such as the protracted wars in former Yugoslavia. The use of force, often without scruple, has exposed the weaknesses of the orthodox conventions of international intervention. Their legal and institutional bases have been ambiguous, and the commitment of the members of "the international community" has been inadequate.

Although the development of a co-operative security regime in the long term relies mainly on a strategy of political confidence-building and non-military policy instruments, in those situations where the use of force is a reality the military dimension of security policy can rarely be avoided. This chapter thus concentrates on the difficulties governments face in trying to devise an effective response to the risk, and in some places the actuality, of political violence which persists in and around post-Cold War Europe.

The emphasis here on the military aspects of crisis management (as distinct from non-military means such as arbitration, mediation and economic inducement) is not accidental. This type of intervention is uncertain in its effects; far from being a panacea, it often involves choosing the lesser evil. But when force is being used, and threatens to spread, this choice may be unavoidable. The inclusion of crisis management on the agenda of the Intergovernmental Conference reflects the increasing salience of crises in Europe since the constraints of the Cold War were removed, as well as a general uncertainty as to how crisis management should now be conducted. For Ireland, with a long tradition of participation in military crisis management in the context of UN peacekeeping, a reassessment of recent changes in this field is a particularly relevant part of the overall security debate.

The main themes covered in this reassessment include:

* the question of political authority for international intervention

* the changing nature of military crisis management

* the increasing significance of NATO and, potentially, the WEU in this field

* the unavoidable dilemmas facing countries which wish to contribute to what is an inherently risky but arguably necessary element of security policy.

POLITICAL AUTHORITY FOR INTERNATIONAL INTERVENTION

Perhaps the most fundamental problem with international crisis management lies in the uncertain source of political authority to intervene in the first place. International norms point in different directions. The principle of non-intervention, reflecting the traditional claim to absolute national sovereignty, is deeply embedded in the UN Charter (Article 2.7) and at first sight rules out a direct role for the international community. However, during the last twenty years this has increasingly been qualified by the proposition that some consequent threat to the (international) peace, or other claims, especially relating to human rights, may justifiably override this strict insulation of the domestic jurisdiction (van Eekelen, 1995, pp. 10–20).

This unresolved tension at the legal level has been accentuated by the fact that most crises of the post-Cold War era have been primarily "internal", that is they arise within domestic jurisdictions rather than as conflicts between states. The waters are further muddied by the strong possibility that, alongside even the most self-evident conditions justifying an intervention, there exist ulterior motives to do with the national interests of at least some of the intervening states. Finally, where there is a strong threat, or actual use, of force in a crisis, the establishment of political authority is not sufficient in itself without the deployment of effective military capability.

It is tempting to see all this as the exclusive responsibility of the global security institution, the United Nations. Certainly the UN is the primary locus of the search for political authority because it is the most inclusive of all multilateral institutions — a UN Security Council mandate has generally been seen as a *sine qua non* of legitimate intervention. However, the real providers of legitimacy for any intervention are the member states of the UN, in their adherence to the obligations of the Charter. The member states are also the providers of military capability. Whether there is any international intervention in response to a crisis, and whether it succeeds or fails, will thus depend on the sum of the actions of the member states.

In practice, there is also an increasing role for a third, intermediate, level of political authority. In fact, Chapter VIII of the UN Charter has always envisaged "regional arrangements" playing an active part in maintaining security; indeed, Article 53 allows the Security Council to use regional agencies for enforcement action under its authority. More recently, a mandate from the OSCE has also been regarded by its member states as a sufficient legal base for action, though it is not yet clear precisely how this will work in practice.

Given both the political diversity and the microscopic resource base of the UN system, regional institutions such as the OSCE and the European Union tend to provide the catalyst for particular groups of states to come to common views on specific cases of crisis management. For the same reason, NATO and, on a smaller scale, the WEU have become organisers of military capabilities in this field.

THE CHANGING NATURE OF MILITARY CRISIS MANAGEMENT

Peacekeeping plus?
Ireland's primary involvement in the military aspects of international security has been as a contributor to UN peacekeeping. Between 1958 and 1995 Irish military personnel completed over 42,000 tours of duty in twenty-nine UN missions (Macdonald, 1995). There is thus a familiarity with this type of activity which sometimes leads to the conclusion that it is the only appropriate commitment for a small state professing military neutrality, and that there is some necessary connection between neutrality and peacekeeping.

This assumption is one of several which merit closer investigation in the light of the changes which have taken place with regard to international crisis management since 1989. During the Cold War, UN-authorised interventions in response to crises generally took the form of what is now often referred to as "traditional" or "classical" UN peacekeeping (the war in Korea being the obvious exception to this rule). Peacekeeping, which was not actually envisaged when the Charter was being drawn up, came to consist of lightly armed multinational missions, depending on the consent of all parties to the dispute and operating as an impartial stabilising factor. Typically, these missions were on the margins of the primary Cold War antagonism, and the contributing countries tended to be small to medium powers. However, military neutrality was never a general precondition of participation, as witnessed by the leading role played by some of the smaller NATO members.

Much has changed during the last six years. The unblocking of the UN Security Council led to a phase of increased activism which saw more experimentation than during the previous forty-five years. This has taken place within the existing Charter provisions, since Charter amendment is so cumbersome, and the concepts and technical terms are still evolving (Boutros-Ghali, 1992, 1995). Recent trends include the following developments (Malone, 1995):

* the preponderance of internal conflicts, which cut across the Charter's legal exclusion of an unsolicited UN role within national jurisdictions

* more complex mandates combining a wide range of civilian and military activities

* more large-scale operations, involving a significant increase in personnel (in 1987 the total was not quite 10,000 — by 1993 it was over 75,000)

* greater public pressures to prioritise humanitarian operations

* involvement in "democratisation", through support for elections

* promoting human rights

* developing new legal mechanisms, such as the war crimes tribunal on the former Yugoslavia

* the regionalisation of international crisis management.

There have been considerable problems in trying to meet the increased demand for UN crisis management. The attitude of the major actors has often been ambivalent; in particular, the experience of the United States in Somalia in 1993, when elite troops were killed in a futile attempt to disarm a local war-lord, led to an abrupt and damaging decline in American public and financial support for the UN. The organisation's humiliation in Bosnia has already been described (see chapter 1); more successful operations cannot disguise the basic weaknesses which have been exposed in the UN's capacity with regard to international crisis management.

Several of these have to do with its military capacity. The UN's "financial" crisis — at root a question of political confidence rather than the non-existence of financial resources — means that potential contributors have been reluctant to bear the costs of delayed reimbursement. The operation in Bosnia was not provided with the military means to implement its mandate until the summer of 1995, by which time its credibility was in doubt. The lack of a rapid reaction capability, based on preassigned standby forces, has been widely noted. So too has the difficulty of achieving effective military interoperability among up to forty different national contingents, with very different military cultures, levels of training and discipline.

In fact, all of these weaknesses were present to some degree throughout the development of traditional peacekeeping, though mitigated by the smaller scale of the operations and the more limited range of contributing countries. Traditional peacekeeping only appears theoretically coherent in retrospect, and by contrast with the even more confused situation of recent years. But if the military dimension of international crisis management is always likely to bear the stamp of improvisation and pragmatic evolution, the need to establish at least some basic ground rules for present and future operations is a priority for all concerned.

The central dilemma in this debate concerns the appropriate level of force. Existing international norms, as we have seen, leave much open to interpretation. Traditional peacekeeping, evolving outside the UN Charter, is based on the consent of the host state's government and the use of force by the peacekeeper only in strict self-defence. Chapter VII of the Charter allows for "enforcement" — that is a UN war — against an aggressor state. However, the response to many crises may not fit easily into either of these categories, especially where the conflict is internal and there may be neither external aggression nor a viable host government. In these circumstances the concept of enforcement is particularly problematic, and there is still no clear definition of what it should entail.

How does the international community deal with this "middle ground"? One option has been to extend the traditional practice, to allow for more "robust" self-defence by the peacekeeper or even a disproportionate response to deter future obstruction, but at the same time trying to remain within the constraints of consent. Others argue that making consent the key determinant of the level of force simply renders the peacekeeper hostage to the most obstructive party to the dispute, and that a new concept of military crisis management is necessary (Gow and Dandeker, 1995).

In practice, of course, this debate is shaped by events. The military operation which started in Bosnia in December 1995, though authorised by the UN, is conducted under the command of NATO, but with the participation of many non-NATO countries. There is a "peace" to keep — the Dayton Agreement — but the force is both mandated and equipped to respond to violence in a more robust way (i.e. with stronger capabilities and less restrictive rules of engagement) than has been associated with traditional peacekeeping. This, it has been argued, might be more appropriately described as "stability support" than as peacekeeping or enforcement (Freedman, 1995). Finally, the military operation is complemented by a civilian programme of political and economic reconstruction of even greater complexity.

A NEW ROLE FOR MILITARY ALLIANCES IN MULTILATERAL CRISIS MANAGEMENT?

Changing NATO? Crisis management and the Partnership for Peace
In chapter 9 it was argued that one of the most important signs of the adaptation of the remaining European military alliances was the greater role being played by NATO in crisis management. The fate of the IFOR operation is likely to be a major test of this approach; both as a political condition of American involvement and as military organiser of a large-scale and complicated form of "peace support", NATO's role is pivotal. The alliance has to establish and sustain a working military relationship not only among its own sixteen members but with even more non-NATO states (including, most significantly, Russia). Equally, NATO's function as the framework of military activity must be coordinated with a very complex effort of civilian "peace-building", under the aegis of other multilateral organisations and involving the holding of elections, economic reconstruction, the repatriation or resettlement of refugees and the monitoring of human rights.

What does NATO bring to this that is not readily available in other institutional frameworks, and especially the UN? NATO officials point to the following capabilities (Lightburn, 1996):

* a highly developed common command and control structure, based on common procedures and a high level of interoperability

* specific military assets, such as an airborne early warning force, intelligence-sharing arrangements, and rapidly deployable naval and air forces

* the provision of forces on a scale and degree of readiness not available elsewhere

* extensive planning capacity

* a framework for political consultation.

Time — and future experience in Bosnia — will tell whether these advantages can successfuly be brought to bear in the field of crisis management. A further consideration is the significant level of involvement by non-NATO countries. Inclusiveness — a basic condition for co-operative security — has already been a feature of the alliance's recent history, from the establishment of the North Atlantic Cooperation Council at the end of 1991 to the launching of the Partnership for Peace programme in 1994. These schemes attempt to meet the security fears both of the former Soviet Union's victims and of its much reduced and unstable successor-state, the Russian Federation.

For these countries, participation in the NACC and the PFP is justified on the broad political ground that it reinforces inclusiveness and reassurance; in effect, it is a confidence-building measure and as such an element in the long-term preventive approach to security policy, rather than the short-term contingencies of crisis management. However, much of the substantive military cooperation that takes place within these arrangements has to do with developing the conceptual basis and operational enhancement of peacekeeping. The PFP, in particular, has evolved into a framework for "cultivating a multinational peacekeeping capability, in which the constituent elements are interoperable and trained to the necessary minimum standards" (Williams, 1996, p. 104).

In the Irish debate on security policy, fears have been expressed that there is a serious risk of entrapment in such participation: "Ireland could find itself sucked into foreign interventions under the guise of 'making' peace" (Fox, 1995, p. 3). This proposition is based on the fact that the reference to peacekeeping in the objectives of the PFP "Framework Document" also includes other missions "as may subsequently be agreed", and is followed by the objective of greater interoperability between NATO and non-NATO forces.

The governments of other non-alliance states have not discerned any mechanism of entrapment in this, especially given the wholly voluntaristic way in which individual PFP commitments are defined. The quasi-automatic engagement in alliance warfare which is implied by a mutual assistance guarantee — the "article five" commitment — simply does not arise. Each partner marks the limits of its involvement; in Finland's "presentation document", for example, the emphasis is on preparation for peacekeeping under the authority of the UN and/or the OSCE, search, rescue and humanitarian operations and environmental protection. But any interest in collective defence is explicitly ruled out: "Through participation in Partnership activities Finland is not seeking a new defence solution. Finland pursues a policy of military non-alliance and independent defence" (Finland, 1994).

Military interoperability — depending on common operational concepts and procedures, and common command, control and communications systems — is an unexceptionable objective in any multinational military operation. In spite of attempts to achieve it in the UN context, success has been limited by the general reluctance to provide the UN with the necessary resources. Finally, the PFP as such is in any case not the operational setting for actual crisis management operations, and participation in the latter, such as IFOR, depends on the decision of each national government.

The institutional division of labour: a role for the EU/WEU?
If the implementation of military "peace support" operations, however defined and labelled, is not the exclusive province of the UN, the question arises whether the EU as such, or the WEU on its behalf, has a distinct role in this regard. The basis for the WEU's involvement in crisis management is the declaration agreed at Petersberg, near Bonn, on 19 June 1992. The Petersberg Declaration indicates that "we [the full WEU member states] are prepared to support, on a case-by-case basis and in accordance with our own procedures, the effective implementation of conflict-prevention and crisis-management measures, including peacekeeping activities of the CSCE or the United Nations Security Council" (WEU, 1992, I.2).

In the section on "Strengthening WEU's operational role" the document then describes what subsequently became known as the "Petersberg tasks":

* humanitarian and rescue tasks

* peacekeeping tasks

* tasks of combat forces in crisis management, including peacemaking.

The first category is generally taken to refer to the provision of relief to beleaguered civilians, though if a broad interpretation of "humanitarian" is accepted (such as the need to respond to a gross violation of human rights), the task may be far from straightforward (van Eekelen, 1995, p. 13). The second category seems clear enough, assuming "peacekeeping" is understood as traditional peacekeeping. The meaning to be ascribed to the third Petersberg task, however, is not so clear.

The term "peacemaking" is also found in the contemporaneous attempt by the UN to redefine the rules of the game; there it refers to the whole range of policy instruments which might be brought to bear on disputes involving armed conflict (Boutros-Ghali, 1992, pp. 24–7). In the WEU context, with its reference to combat forces, "enforcement" would be a more appropriate term (van Eekelen, 1995, p. 43).

Since these documents appeared both the experience of crisis management and the debate as to how it should be conducted have resulted in new lessons and even new language. After Somalia and Bosnia few governments and international organisations could be so sanguine about the possibilities and costs of the military dimension of crisis management. There is surely a case for reviewing and clarifying the terminology of the Petersberg tasks at the Intergovernmental Conference, whether they remain in an autonomous WEU or are incorporated in some way into the Treaty on European Union.

In the interim, the actual role of the WEU in crisis management has not in fact expanded very much. The military dimension of the Bosnian peace process is the business of NATO. The latter organisation's readiness to implement the concept of Combined Joint Task Forces, which allows for NATO assets to be used under a WEU command, represents a potential increase in the WEU's capacity, yet there appears to be no significant enthusiasm for realising that possibility in Bosnia. The contrast could hardly be greater with the attitude at the beginning of the Yugoslav drama in the summer of 1991, when the President of the European Council declared the "hour of Europe" was at hand. European governments now accept that a crisis on that scale requires an American presence, and the future role of the WEU may be restricted to operations on a smaller scale. It may be that the WEU will in effect acquire the role of a collective "gendarmerie", or armed police, leaving enforcement to NATO.

DILEMMAS FOR CONTRIBUTORS

In the continuing debate on military crisis management at the Intergovernmental Conference (and elsewhere, for this debate is likely to be a perennial fixture on the diplomatic calendar), contributing countries face at least four difficult issues.

First, there is the question of *the separation of the legitimacy and control of operations*. Ireland has traditionally based its policy on the proposition that its defence forces would only serve in a UN-authorised *and* UN-commanded mission. This has not been explicitly expressed in the enabling legislation, but has been part of the orthodoxy when it came to justifying specific contributions. The change in the Defence Act in 1993 to permit participation in the revitalised mission in Somalia (UNOSOM II) allowed for participation under an enforcement mandate, but the government preserved the insistence on only joining a UN rather than coalition force.

Does this inhibition merit further consideration in the light of subsequent experience? In fact, the foreign policy White Paper appears to go in this direction. It does not rule out participation in a UN-mandated multinational mission, but refers to the need to establish strict control of the mission (Ireland, 1996, para. 7.32). Also, recognising the need for the development of peacekeeping capacity by regional organisations, the Irish government is considering the necessary legislative changes to allow for participation in this context by both military forces and civilian police (paras. 7.34–5). Arguably, such a change would be no more than an adjustment to accepted international practice. It is noticeable that the other EU military neutrals (Austria, Finland and Sweden) do not see their military non-alignment as precluding participation in the NATO-led IFOR in Bosnia.

A second question relates to *the military capacity of the contributing country's defence forces*. The more complex and often more dangerous circumstances of contemporary crisis management require the best in terms of equipment, training and interoperability with other national contingents. Here, the increasing emphasis on multinational cooperation by EU partners which are members of NATO and the WEU, both at the preparatory stage and potentially in specific operations, offers new possibilities of enhancing the national capabilities of the non-alliance countries.

Reservations about being seen to associate with alliances must be set against the potential costs of depriving national contingents of the best available preparation. Until recently, the organisation of the Irish army, while allowing for the constant commitment of between 800 and 1,000 troops overseas, did not permit the provision of readily available standby forces (O'Carroll, 1995, pp. 57–60). The failure to exploit opportunities to train through multinational exercises, in the context of PFP, is all the more surprising given the difficulty in providing serious field training at home.

The third difficulty is *the risk of what is sometimes called "mission creep"* — a tendency to broaden mandates and authorise threats of force without providing the appropriate means. This can lead to a form of entrapment, as illustrated only too often in the case of the so-called "safe areas" in Bosnia. Indeed, the whole experience of UNPROFOR showed how difficult it is to avoid being pulled into the quagmire of internal conflict while at the same time trying to limit national commitments.

There are no easy answers to this problem, particularly for contributing countries without direct access to the mandating authority. Paradoxically, maintaining maximum influence in this respect might be easier in the context of an EU/WEU-controlled operation than in a conventional UN-led mission; political access to the highest levels of authority by a small EU member state like Ireland could prove to be more direct and effective in that framework than with regard to the UN Security Council in New York. However, if a UN mandate is to be a necessary condition of a legitimate intervention, there remains a strong incentive to reform the Security Council, both to make its own membership more representative of the changing distribution of power and to make its procedures generally more transparent.

Finally, there is the question of *the country's reputation as a viable contributor* to military crisis management. It has been argued that recent developments, and particularly the increasing role played by the major powers and military alliances, compromise the legitimacy of international interventions. In these circumstances, the argument goes on, the possibility of participation in NATO's Partnership for Peace programme will greatly damage "Ireland's reputation as an independent and neutral peacekeeper" (Fox, 1995, p. 4). What evidence is there to support this assertion?

It is true that the significantly greater involvement of the major states in recent operations marks a change from the Cold War practice, when they were regarded as too self-interested (as ideological opponents or neo-imperialist predators) to be accepted as impartial peacekeepers. They will no doubt continue to carry this historical baggage for some time to come. Yet the felt need for the major actors' direct participation is very considerable. It is required by the sheer scale and complexity of many operations; the complaint in recent years has been that the "great powers" do too little rather than too much. Arguably, the involvement of NATO in Bosnia will ultimately be judged by its ability to sustain the Dayton Agreement rather than as a manifestation of western imperialism.

Likewise, the future reputation of individual contributing countries is likely to hinge on their professional performance rather than on general Cold War stereotypes or association with the overlapping networks of multilateral diplomacy. Even during the Cold War Ireland's reputation was probably based as much on the fact that it was a small state as a neutral one. Several of the paragons of traditional UN peacekeeping have been NATO members, such as Canada — often regarded as the "market leader" in this approach — Denmark and Norway. Over time the professionalism and impartiality demonstrated in their commitment came to count for more than their Cold War alignment; there is little reason to suppose that this will not be the real basis for a contributor's reputation in future multinational operations mandated but not conducted by the UN.

Involvement in the military dimension of international crisis management will no doubt continue to raise such questions, for even at the best of times it has always borne the mark of improvisation and experimentation. Multinational intervention is inherently a high-risk business, both in military operations in the field and in political commitment. But then the only low-risk alternative is to look on and be no more than a spectator.

Conclusions

It is often remarked that, instead of facing the threat of mutual annihilation by contending military blocs, Europe must now cope with the actuality of armed conflict. Thus the military aspect of security policy has not disappeared, but is rather being channelled in new directions.

This has led to a change of emphasis in international norms, in ways which underline the inherent tension between principles protecting the state and those protecting the individual. The consequent and continuing adaptation of international organisations has been marked by attempts to establish a new division of labour between the universal framework, the UN, and regional organisations. This is an aspect of security policy where practice necessarily drives theory, and where the need for engagement is urgent.

After six years of experimentation with mixed results, the role of NATO has come to the fore, as a framework for multinational intervention in the most acute European conflict, in Bosnia. This reflects both a continuing European dependence on the presence of the United States and the unique assets of NATO as an organiser of military cooperation, including the contributions of non-NATO states in both the PFP and IFOR. The potential role of the WEU, as the military arm of the European Union, is also on the agenda, but is likely to be restricted to smaller scale operations.

These developments pose several urgent questions for Ireland. Should peacekeeping contributions be made outside the traditional context of operations conducted entirely within the UN framework? What reforms are required within the UN? Does Ireland have the necessary military capability to make a contribution, and what adjustments might be necessary to the state's defence policy? What relevance, if any, does military neutrality have with regard to Ireland's reputation as a credible peacekeeping country?

These questions are not, of course, exclusively addressed to Ireland, and many small states, including other non-alliance countries, have already adapted their policies in quite significant ways. The Irish debate, on the other hand, has remained at a primitive stage. The confused response to the foreign policy White Paper, summarised in chapter 8, failed to get to grips with many of the relevant issues. Paradoxically, it is precisely in that aspect of security policy where the country's contribution has hitherto been most clearly defined, and where new thinking is most urgent, that adaptation has taken second place to a preoccupation with the perils assumed to be posed by "nuclear alliances".

In a co-operative security regime, the central emphasis is on the long-term prevention of conflict through a strategy which is inclusive and non-threatening. One of the difficulties inherent in this approach is that it is so comprehensive in terms of the range of public policies it covers that it is all too easy to lose focus on its essential elements. This is a problem for the analyst as much as for the governments involved, and rather than surveying the whole range of policies this chapter will select two major themes to illustrate the issues which arise.

The first theme encompasses attempts to reduce the traditional emphasis on military instruments, looking at the ways in which the EU member states try to arrive at common approaches to nuclear non-proliferation and arms export controls. The second theme is broader, and in its own way even more challenging, because of its far-reaching effects on the interests of all EU member states, including Ireland. This is the attempt to consolidate the stability of Europe through the further enlargement of the European Union.

The significance of the European Union for the security of the whole continent is more evident on this dimension of security policy than it is with regard to protection or crisis management, in which military alliances retain an important role. Thus before exploring the specific issues in detail, it may be helpful to recapitulate the EU's existing capabilities in conflict prevention, and comment on ways in which the policy-making framework might be enhanced at the Intergovernmental Conference.

THE EUROPEAN UNION AND CONFLICT PREVENTION

With the end of the Cold War, the European Community (and later the European Union) became the principal source of "civilian power" in the attempts to stabilise the former Soviet empire. It has been the major channel of multilateral economic and political support for post-communist transition, and its member states have made the greatest material contribution. Acting together, in the framework of the Common Foreign and Security Policy, they have been able to agree on measures, such as the Stability Pact, which are clearly based on a strategic vision of long-term prevention. The promise of future membership is a powerful inducement to work for common standards of democratic behaviour across the continent.

That said, the Union's activities in this field have often lacked coherence, and have proved difficult to sustain. A non-governmental organisation with a brief for conflict prevention, Saferworld and International Alert, has suggested that the Intergovernmental Conference should consider specific reforms of the CFSP in order to improve the EU's conflict prevention capacity (Rummel, 1996). These include several of the proposals already submitted by other sources, but three have a particular bearing on conflict prevention. First, the CFSP objectives should be revised to make explicit the Union's primary role and comparative advantage with regard to preventive policies. Second, the proposed common analysis unit should include a "conflict prevention department", with access to information which would enable it to give early warning of increasing tension. Finally, the possibility of a "centre for active crisis prevention" in the European Parliament (already proposed by a former French prime minister, Michel Rocard MEP) should be incorporated in this changed institutional context.

Institutional reforms on these lines are hardly radical, and they reflect the fact that the European Union already is a vehicle for co-operative conflict prevention. As such, it is also a catalyst for the reinforcement of other multilateral security institutions, such as the OSCE. Thus the implementation of the EU's Stability Pact, agreed in 1995, became the responsibility of the more broadly based OSCE. But much more could be done; for example, agreement to fund the OSCE's high commissioner on national minorities on a more substantial basis would be a serious investment in long-term prevention. Other specific aspects of the preventive strategy also demonstrate that there is a long way to go to exploit the European Union's potential more effectively.

THE MILITARY DIMENSION: NUCLEAR DISARMAMENT

The non-proliferation approach

The Cold War coincided with the development of nuclear technology, and was characterised by the stockpiling of nuclear weapons and the deployment of delivery systems. The consequent arms races both threatened the stability of the mutual deterrence between the nuclear powers and were increasingly seen as dangerous in themselves. The Nuclear Non-Proliferation Treaty of 1968 put the issue on the international agenda, checked the number of formal nuclear powers and established procedures to monitor and control proliferation. However, it was followed by the emergence of several "threshold countries" (undeclared or near-nuclear states), increased nuclear arsenals among nuclear powers and a sterile debate between possessors and Third World countries which saw the regime as yet another form of discrimination against them.

The end of the Cold War was associated with negotiations between the two main nuclear possessors, the United States and the Soviet Union, leading to agreements on considerable cuts in, but not the elimination of, these arsenals. The utility of nuclear force as an instrument of military protection has not been conceded (see chapter 9). Hence the NPT process retains its relevance. The main result of the most recent review conference, which concluded in May 1995, was the indefinite extension of the treaty itself, in spite of demands to adopt limited extensions (which many non-nuclear countries saw as the best way to keep the pressure on the nuclear states to disarm). There will still be regular reviews of the non-proliferation regime, however, and there are signs that the old cleavage between rich industrialised nuclear countries and a non-nuclear Third World — an oversimplification of the actual state of affairs at the best of times — may be succeeded by a more complex alignment in the debate (Simpson, 1995).

There may also be more compelling pressures on nuclear possessors (and within their own public opinions) which could lead to incremental tightening of the non-proliferation regime. The first test is agreement on a Comprehensive Test Ban Treaty by the end of 1996; a minimum deterrence regime might be a medium-term goal (in about ten years), while further steps towards a mature non-nuclear regime over maybe a further twenty years would represent the long-term programme for this process.

Expectations of success in this field should be framed in the light of two considerations. First, nuclear capability is only one element in the category of weapons of mass destruction; biological and chemical technology must also be controlled, as must the means of delivery. Second, the pace of arms control and disarmament depends on the degree of trust engendered in the overall co-operative security regime, and the process is not irreversible.

What, then, can a small state like Ireland contribute to that process? Mainly its role is to support the development of the various elements of the international regime wherever possible. In the NPT process, for example, a common approach to the overall shape of the regime at the 1995 review conference was agreed by the EU states (including two nuclear possessors,

France and the United Kingdom). This showed that, up to a point, the common interest of EU member states in non-proliferation could be effectively harnessed in the form of a CFSP joint action, and to that extent the European Union's collective diplomatic weight could be brought to bear on a major preventive measure.

But the EU's presence, together with its utility as a framework for nuclear disarmament, is limited. Where its member states' interests diverge, particularly between nuclear and non-nuclear countries, other coalitions must be formed, outside the CFSP context. This is not precluded by EU obligations. Already there is evidence of enhanced pressure for nuclear disarmament from a group of medium and small industrialised states, the so-called "G 10" (actually eleven countries in 1995, including Australia, Austria, Canada, Denmark, Finland, Hungary, Ireland, the Netherlands, New Zealand, Norway and Sweden). The presence in this group of four NATO member states and six EU member states is a reminder that the ambiguities of nuclear doctrine cut across formal political and military alignments.

THE MILITARY DIMENSION: ARMS EXPORTS AND THE DEFENCE INDUSTRY

One concern frequently expressed in Ireland is the impact of arms sales on regional and internal conflicts outside Europe. The issue is raised not so much in the context of European security policy (as defined in terms of traditional European conflicts and interests) as in that of development policy in the Third World. The role of several EU member states as major arms exporters, and the possibility that the EU as such may encourage this trade, is seen in very negative terms. For some critics it is an unacceptable consequence of a residual neo-imperialism; for others, it also represents the vested interests of a dangerous "military–industrial complex".

The question of arms exports is inextricably bound up with that of arms production; they are in effect two sides of the same coin. They both focus on the activities of defence industries with large R&D budgets and significant implications for employment, and a very particular relationship with the process of European integration.

Are defence industries being "Europeanised"?
Although arms export controls are dealt with in the CFSP, in the context of the 1996 IGC the issue of the defence industry arises in the first pillar, in relation to the EU's single market. Under Article 223 of the EEC Treaty of

1957 national military defence procurement remains the business of the individual member states, thus keeping national defence industries out of the single market.

Since the end of the Second World War this jealous protection of defence industries has been the norm in the major states and to a lesser extent in a few smaller states which could just about sustain their own defence producers, including neutral Sweden and Austria. An insistence on self-sufficiency in armaments for security reasons, generally leading to the production of surpluses, was matched by commercial considerations in disposing of those surpluses. For a long time neither the pressures of external competition, especially from the United States, nor the military requirement of NATO standardisation, nor even the potential economies of scale to be gained by cooperation succeeded in altering this situation to any significant degree.

The cooperation that has taken place has generally taken the form of ad hoc multinational ventures between defence manufacturers working within very different national contexts. The two biggest national industries, the British and French, have opposed traditions (free market and *dirigiste,* respectively) regarding the relationships between government, defence companies and their internal and external markets (De Vestel, 1995, p. 37). There have also been attempts to coordinate national defence procurement policies in a more formal and consistent way. Thus NATO's Independent European Programme Group (IEPG) was revitalised in 1984 to promote more effective R&D investment, standardisation and interoperability, and the development of a "two-way street" arms trade with the United States.

In 1992 the IEPG — still the only European body dealing with armaments issues — was transferred to the WEU and renamed the Western European Armaments group. It is composed of the ten full members of the WEU and the three associate members (Iceland, Norway and Turkey), and in November 1994 it proposed it should become the basis of a full-scale European armaments agency (De Vestel, 1995, pp. 95–102). The joint Franco-German position paper for the IGC repeated and reinforced the proposal for a European armaments agency (France and Germany, 1996).

Simultaneous attempts by the Commission to include national defence industries in the single market have been resisted by member state governments. The Commission's proposal to abolish Article 223 failed at the 1991 IGC, in spite of the fact that, in addition to the then increased incentive to move towards political union and achieve economies of scale, European defence industries were facing substantial contraction with the end of the

Cold War. For the 1996 IGC, the Commission has returned to this theme. Pointing out that between 1988 and 1992 defence-related employment in the twelve EC states fell from 1.6 million to 1 million, it argues that the primarily national approach risks the collapse of important branches of the defence industry in Europe; rationalisation, on the other hand, could lead to significant savings (Commission, 1996a).

It is by no means certain that this will lead to a truly Europeanised defence industry, based on integrated policies and including the abolition of Article 223. At most, the open procurement of "dual-use" products (goods with both civilian and military applications) might be brought into the single market in the short term. A more far-reaching reform is likely to take much longer, for several reasons. Some experts think the post-Cold War incentive for rationalisation is not in fact as serious as the Commission imagines: the convergence of national defence structures is bound to take time; armaments programmes have lead-times of up to thirty years; and the political framework for the development of a common European defence policy is only at an embryonic stage (De Vestel, 1995, pp. 104–5).

Implications for Ireland
Ireland has no significant national defence industry as such, though like any other modern economy it produces some dual-use goods (AfrI, 1996). At first sight it has only a limited interest in the issue of a European defence industry, as a small-scale consumer. Irish interests in limiting and controlling arms exports have generally received greater attention. For some time they have been pursued in the context of United Nations measures, such as the Register on Conventional Arms and efforts to develop more effective codes of conduct in the international arms trade.

Membership of the European Union provides added value to this aspect of preventive security policy. Participation in the CFSP is an increasingly important element in the development of arms export regimes, by bringing the debate directly to the major arms producers within that process and even in building consensus on a concerted approach in the UN. In 1992 the European Council agreed general criteria governing arms exports, though these have yet to be clarified in a code of conduct. In December 1994 a regulation on the control of dual-use goods (not covered by Article 223) was agreed, to be implemented by July 1998. The possibility of further linkages between arms production and export controls within the EU framework thus merits attention.

It is not very clear, though, what long-term strategy will best lead to the required result — the control of the arms trade. The tension between the two objectives — the rationalisation of defence industries and the regulation of their exports — may lead to paradoxical effects from any given approach. For example, if the maintenance of Article 223 does indeed cause national defence industries in the EU to self-destruct sooner rather than later, the overall consequence will be to make EU countries even more dependent on external suppliers which are even further removed, so far as arms control is concerned, from the influence of EU member states. The removal of Article 223, on the other hand, might strengthen the defence industries in the EU, but by bringing them out of their national sanctuaries and into a common regulative regime it could also facilitate efforts to press for more effective regulation of exports.

However, there are few expectations of significant change to Article 223 in the Intergovernmental Conference, and the notion that issues of arms production and export controls are susceptible to a quick fix in the shape of institutional reform is illusory. When major producers are incapable of keeping their own national rules as was the case, for example, with regard to British exports to Iraq prior to the crisis of 1990, regulation of the arms trade is clearly a matter for the long haul.

As in the case of nuclear proliferation, the issue will have to be pursued in several multilateral settings, in collaboration with like-minded governments wherever they may be found. The European Union is not the only focus for this approach, but it may prove to be one of the most significant points of engagement in the long term. The very fact that it includes states which are at the same time both major arms producers and contributors towards Third World development policy makes it a relevant arena for attempts to control arms exports.

ENLARGEMENT OF THE EUROPEAN UNION: THE CENTRAL ISSUE?

Enlargement as security policy
Historically, negotiations for membership of the EC/EU have been conducted primarily in terms of the economic costs and benefits for both the EC/EU and the applicant countries. That is not surprising, given the scope of the collectivity's policies; after all, motivation for joining what has generally been seen as "a rich man's club" has usually been strongly economic.

But membership has not been exclusively about economic goals. The motive of achieving security *among* the member states (as well as against external threats) was prominent from the outset. In 1950 the rationale for the proposed European Coal and Steel Community was to incorporate Germany in a mesh of economic interdependencies, leading to a level of political solidarity which would make future war between Germany and France inconceivable. For western Europe, this was to create a "security community . . . in which there is real assurance that the members of that community will not fight each other physically, but will settle their disputes in some other way" (Deutsch, 1957, p. 5).

The first enlargement of the EC, adding Denmark, Ireland and the United Kingdom in 1973, stressed economic issues (though the inclusion of the last named as a counterweight to Franco-German domination was an important subtext for several member states). The addition of Greece (in 1981) and Portugal and Spain (in 1986) was very much about security; it was a significant part of the consolidation and stabilisation of the new democratic regimes in those countries. Even the three well-established democracies which joined in 1995 (Austria, Finland and Sweden) were motivated by security concerns, especially in the cases of Austria and Finland which border the unstable post-communist world.

Indeed, it is above all the goal of bringing stability to that part of Europe which now makes the further enlargement of the European Union perhaps the key element in preventive security policy. Already ten post-communist countries, plus Cyprus and Malta, have intimated their wish to become EU members, raising the prospect of a Union with perhaps double the number of states it now caters for.

This would add more than 100 million to the existing EU population of 370 million, greater economic, social and cultural diversity, and new strains on political structures and policies. But if enlargement were to succeed in the stabilisation of the continent, that achievement would be quite extraordinary. It would be, literally, unprecedented in terms of bringing peace by peaceful methods — a voluntary rather than an imposed peace. By the same token, however, the cost of failure could be very high, and likewise on a continental scale.

Exposure of the applicants
The extent to which the applicant and would-be applicant countries are exposed to a variety of security risks has been analysed in some detail in the IEA's interim report on security (Keatinge, 1995, chapter 3). A brief geographical survey will serve to recall the main characteristics of their predicament.

The three small Baltic states, Estonia, Latvia and Lithuania, are the only republics of the former Soviet Union widely regarded as "western", though not always in Russia. Disengagement from Russia's sphere of influence is hindered by the existence of Russian-speaking minorities and residual Russian military interests, in addition to the strains of economic transformation and the development of the institutions of a democratic state.

Bulgaria, the Czech Republic, Hungary, Poland, Romania and Slovakia are perhaps less vulnerable to negative effects of Russia's difficult transformation, but have considerable problems of economic and political adjustment of their own. These include the rehabilitation of former communists, the establishment of the rule of law, the privatisation of economic interests, and in several cases serious difficulties with regard to ethnic minorities. Slovenia has been the only republic of the former Yugoslavia able to join this category of potential EU members; depending on the outcome of the peace process in Bosnia, the others, together with Albania, might expect to join the enlargement queue at a later date.

The Mediterranean applicants, while not suffering the strains of post-communist transformation, are exposed to the more diffuse risks in their region. In addition, the partition of Cyprus in the context of the underlying animosity between Greece and Turkey is an acute security problem in itself.

More generally, it may be said that the basic conditions for establishing a security community among these countries in the long term consist of three levels of stability — domestic, regional and geopolitical (Gambles, 1995, p. 3). Domestic stability requires a reasonably open civil society and the continuity of legitimate authority from one government to the next. Regional stability implies formal and informal institutions of peaceful conflict resolution. Geopolitical stability means the creation of an effective co-operative security regime to include and reassure states outside the security community that its security is not at the expense of theirs.

The European Union — through the obligations of membership, and even potential membership — has the capacity to influence all of these levels of stability. For example, the EU is the major source of economic and technical assistance for the rest of Europe and, together with the Council of Europe and the OSCE, defines the standards of a modern democratic market economy. The EU Stability Pact provides a framework for moderating minority issues in the region. With regard to the third level, geopolitical stability, it has been argued that EU enlargement represents a less threatening alternative to the incorporation of these countries in NATO (which many of them also seek), in view of Russian opposition to NATO enlargement. That said, however, it is unlikely that EU enlargement will happen easily, and the pace at which it occurs will be a matter of contention.

EU enlargement policy

The European Union has negotiated "Europe Agreements" with ten central and eastern European countries — Bulgaria, the Czech Republic, Estonia, Hungary, Latvia, Lithuania, Poland, Romania, Slovakia and Slovenia. The European Council in Copenhagen in June 1993 in effect agreed their membership in principle, but in practice imposed strict conditions, especially the ability to take on the obligations of membership. Cyprus and Malta must meet the same conditions.

The Union has also drawn up a "comprehensive pre-accession strategy", based on the development of the bilateral Europe agreements, financial assistance (the PHARE programme), a "structured dialogue" with EU institutions (i.e. regular meetings at all levels), and preparation for integration into the single market (Commission, 1995b, pp. 3–4). These policies are subject to regular reassessment by all concerned.

But what does it all add up to? Optimistic expectations raised in the euphoric climate of the early 1990s have long subsided. The route to domestic stability in central and eastern Europe has been uneven, regional stability has been overshadowed by the awful example of Yugoslavia, and geopolitical stability has been unnerved by the nationalist rhetoric of Russian politics. The EU, for its part, has hardly fulfilled the anterior promise of "1992" — the completion of the single market.

There is bound to be a danger of disillusion among the applicants, and the risk of the dilution of original commitments by EU member states, in a strategy which calls for sustained effort over several decades. According to one study, this strategy will require at the very least the serious implementation of the Europe Agreements; possibly some form of "partial membership", whereby full participation in the second and/or third pillars of the Maastricht Treaty would precede that in the first pillar; and very long transitional periods built into full membership (Wessels, 1995, pp. 396–403). Anything less, such as a loose association confined to a free trade regime without collective political and economic disciplines, would be a recipe for continued instability. In any event, in "setting the limits of the geopolitical space" the EU has to avoid the gratuitous alienation or exclusion of Russia (Gambles, 1995, p. 109).

The implications for Ireland: costs and benefits

The requirements of EU enlargement are contested between the existing member states. There is a definite difference in emphasis, for example, between the British argument that it does not imply either radical institutional reform to the EU or a significant increase in the overall ceiling to the EU budget, and the German insistence that considerable adjustments to the existing EU will be necessary.

Each member state will have to assess its priorities in this regard. For Ireland, the pressure to concede much greater market access, especially in agricultural products, is an obvious area where the cost of further enlargement materialises — the more so in the context of arguments that such access will be the final straw for the Common Agricultural Policy. Likewise, the future of economic cohesion policies is at stake, foreign direct investment may be diverted and some Irish companies are already vulnerable to low-cost competition from the applicant countries (IBEC, 1995, pp. 11–13).

Less tangible costs include the added complexity of EU decision-making and perhaps even the relative loss of political influence for a small member state in a significantly expanded Union. On the other hand, actual benefits are already accruing in the realisation of new commercial opportunities in countries where Ireland had negligible interests ten years ago. Over time a successful enlargement process could increase such opportunities exponentially.

However, the principal prize of further enlargement is simply the political stability of the European continent. In the long term this is no less relevant to Ireland than it is to states in much closer physical proximity to existing sources of instability. Consider the most likely alternative to a successful enlargement: the marginalisation of the weaker states, deprived of multilateral assistance and increasingly dependent on strong neighbours; the consequent creation of an exclusively German hegemony in central Europe; a regression to relatively unconstrained power politics among the major actors, often at the expense of small states; and a continent riddled by adversarial relations between states, and criminality and environmental destruction between and within societies.

The stakes involved in EU enlargement are high, and the demands it imposes are correspondingly severe. It does require a measure of altruism among existing member states, but it can equally be justified in terms of enlightened self-interest.

CONCLUSIONS

The end of the Cold War has provided an extraordinary opportunity to make the preventive approach to security policy the central strategy in a co-operative security regime. In principle, this approach provides the best available environment for a small state like Ireland, and shows to advantage the role of a collectivity like the European Union which can mobilise significant economic and diplomatic resources.

In practice, however, the implementation of this essentially "civilian power" cannot be taken for granted. The EU's policy-making framework often lacks coherence and focus. In the field of disarmament and arms control, national interests still diverge in significant ways, and residual fears and vested interests can be seen among the member states of the European Union. Nevertheless, with regard to both nuclear non-proliferation and the export of conventional arms, the CFSP has provided a framework to raise these issues and, in some cases, to act on an emerging common interest.

The issue of the future membership of the European Union is in itself probably the single most important element in long-term prevention. Here, the range and diversity of interests are even greater than in the case of demilitarisation. Political will has to be sustained over the long term, in the face of frequent democratic competition. The costs of enlargement will inevitably disturb existing policy gains, but would be more than compensated in the long term by the extension of the existing EU "security community" throughout Europe. For Ireland, which is less directly tied into the predicament of those countries most in need of preventive security, the main political obstacle to sustaining a commitment to the preventive approach may be that of complacency.

CHAPTER 12
OPTIONS FOR IRELAND

Change, and adaptation to change, have been persistent themes in this analysis of European security. The European continent has moved from a starkly defined Cold War confrontation to a more confusing and multidimensional array of risks and challenges. Governments have on the whole adapted their individual and collective approaches to security policy in a positive way, to the point where it can be said that a co-operative security regime exists. But continuing instability, together with a propensity for, and in some places the actuality of, political violence, means that the future of this regime cannot be taken for granted.

In these circumstances the need to adapt remains paramount. The 1996 IGC is part of this process of adaptation, and arguably a particularly important part given the unusual concentration of political and economic resources in the Union. Behind the often arcane issues to do with institutional structures and procedures in the second pillar of the Treaty on European Union lie several basic questions concerning the EU's place in the emerging security regime. That there may be more than one answer was demonstrated in the survey of the member states' national approaches in Part II of this study.

Like all other European states, whether or not they are members of the EU, Ireland has been faced with the question of how to adapt to the new security environment. In several important respects the Irish debate is at a less advanced stage than in most comparable states, particularly where the military aspects of security are concerned. Many of the matters which might be expected to be on the agenda, as outlined in chapters 9–11, have been presented in the government's foreign policy White Paper, but such public debate as has occurred has more often than not been conducted in terms of stereotypes dating from the Cold War and before.

Against that background, it is perhaps easy to forget that adaptation implies both the possibility of, and responsibility for, making policy choices. In the field of security policy these choices are not confined to the European Union, but as the primary international setting within which Irish foreign policy is framed and conducted, the Union's own policy-making framework, including the IGC, is where Ireland's choices will be critical.

This chapter, therefore, returns to the IGC, in order to identify the options for Ireland, and to suggest what consequences might follow from each. It concludes with comments on what is arguably the basic choice — between the general orientations of passivity or engagement. But first, it is necessary to recall the context within which the IGC is taking place and the broad parameters which will determine the limits of choice.

THE RANGE OF CHOICE FOR THE EUROPEAN UNION: THEORY AND REALITY

The governments represented at the IGC can, in theory, choose from a wide spectrum of broad options for the future of the European Union. The range of possibilities includes: a strategy of renationalisation of policies hitherto dealt with jointly; a minimalist adjustment to the status quo; more ambitious commitments by some of the member states in some key policy areas in a form of differentiated integration; and progress towards the completion of a comprehensive federal agenda, in which the Union would acquire the main attributes of statehood (see chapter 3).

The analysis of the extensive "blueprinting process" to date suggests, however, that in practice the parameters of the negotiations are more limited. The positions at either end of the range of choice do not seem to be realistic. All the member states have at least some important vested interests in integration, however sceptical they may be about taking on more ambitious commitments. Thus a strategy of overt renationalisation, quite apart from reneging on treaty commitments, would entail very high risks even for one of the larger member states. At the other end of the spectrum, in spite of the stated preference of several governments for a move in the federal direction, there is clearly no overall consensus on this option.

Hence the conclusion was reached in chapter 7 that the most ambitious outcome of the IGC would be one in which forms of differentiated integration receive even greater attention than at present. In this scenario negotiations focus on the conditions under which member states can opt in or out of joint activities which are decided and implemented in a more integrated way. The problem is to find a balance between the maintenance of overall solidarity and a flexibility of commitment which will not unravel existing mutual obligations to the point where *disintegration* occurs.

The survey of national positions on the reform of the CFSP and the further definition of a common defence policy shows that second pillar issues are a significant point of contention in the IGC (see chapters 4–7). Given the continuing flux on the ground, especially in crisis flashpoints such as Bosnia, together with the parallel adaptation of other multilateral security institutions such as NATO, the political context of the Intergovernmental Conference is one of considerable complexity.

IRELAND'S OPTIONS AND THEIR LIKELY CONSEQUENCES

Ireland's overall interests in EU membership, and their bearing on the government's strategy at the IGC, have been analysed in more detail elsewhere (IEA, 1995; Scott, 1996). For nearly a quarter of a century membership has offered a clear balance of advantage in material terms, especially through the redistributive effects of the Common Agricultural Policy and the increasing emphasis on the strategy of economic and social cohesion. More generally, policy-makers have appreciated the enhanced opportunity the EU gives to small states to manage the strains of economic and political interdependence in a multilateral system which offers disproportionate access to political influence. All of this has made Ireland a supporter of integration so far as the first pillar of the Maastricht Treaty is concerned.

Options
As we have seen, however, this does not apply in quite the same way to the second pillar, especially where it touches on military matters. The long experience of neutrality, for all the ambiguity between state policy and public perception, has made this an area of critical choice. An analysis of Ireland's options on this aspect of the IGC is therefore most relevant where the possibility of significant policy change seems to arise. This is most readily seen in the context of the possible positions which can be taken towards the WEU. Indeed, this is one place in the government's foreign policy White Paper where a range of choice is explicitly presented (Ireland, 1996, paras. 4.105–11).

In addition to the three options outlined in the White Paper, the further possibility of "withdrawal" from the existing relationship with the WEU will be considered below, in order to complete the full range of theoretical possibilities. In ascending order of commitment, these may be summarised as follows:

* *Withdrawal:* the existing arrangements for observer status in the WEU would be ended. Ireland would also opt out of the EU decision-making process in the CFSP wherever the possibility of WEU involvement was raised.

* *Status quo:* Ireland would continue to be represented as an observer at WEU meetings, at both ministerial and official levels. However, there would be no participation in military operational matters, such as planning, exercises or actual missions.

* *Crisis management:* in addition to participation in political consultations as an observer, this option includes the possibility of participating in selected crisis management operations under the aegis of the WEU, at the instigation of the European Union, on a voluntary basis.

* *Full commitment:* Ireland would join the WEU as a full member, accepting a commitment to collective defence in addition to voluntary participation in crisis management operations.

Each of these options has different implications for Ireland's place in the European Union, with regard to both security policy as such and the country's overall interests. While any assessment of these implications is necessarily speculative, it is possible to suggest in broad outline where the choice of a particular option will lead.

Consequences

The first option is consistent with a renationalisation of the European Union. Although a withdrawal from WEU observer status might not in itself imply reneging on treaty commitments, the inference that Ireland would have nothing to do with any aspect of a common defence policy, however defined, would probably be seen as a repudiation of the commitment already made in Article J 4.1 of the Treaty on European Union to include "the eventual framing of a common defence policy".

It is not clear what, if any, legal consequences would flow from this, since the second pillar does not lie within the remit of the European Court of Justice. The political consequences, however, would probably be severe. Assuming that no other member state makes a similar choice — and there is no indication that any will — Ireland would be in an isolated position. A total lack of influence on any joint policy involving military measures, including those to do with international crisis management, is self-evident. Abstention would be the weakest possible base from which to oppose what might be seen as future "militaristic" developments within the EU–WEU nexus. It is possible that the marginalisation of a member state taking this option would also reduce its influence on the formulation of joint policies to do with non-military aspects of preventive security. A small state which would, in effect, be only a semi-detached participant in the CFSP process as a whole would be unlikely to be taken seriously by either its partners or third parties.

It is also probable that the adoption of this approach would have negative effects on Ireland's overall interests in the European Union. The outcome of this Intergovernmental Conference, like its predecessors and indeed like much of the general policy-making process within the European Union, will reflect a package deal. This involves tactical linkages between issues which might not otherwise be connected but which are balanced in such a way as to produce something for everyone. It is likely that the withdrawal option would be taken by other member states as an overt rejection of the overall solidarity already achieved; hence any special pleading Ireland might make with regard to redistributive policies, such as economic and social cohesion, would meet indifference at best, and possibly outright opposition. At the very least, it is certain that this choice would make Ireland a clear candidate for the slow lane in a differentiated Union.

Largely for these reasons, the option of withdrawal from any involvement with the WEU does not appear in the government's foreign policy White Paper; nor is there evidence to suggest it would command serious support in the Dáil. It serves nonetheless as an indicator of what might follow if distaste for "defence" is pushed to the point where it becomes the main determinant of the limits of Ireland's membership of the European Union.

The second option, maintenance of the status quo, would obviously be compatible with a minimalist vision of the future of integration in the EU. Less obviously, it just might get by in a very cautious approach to differentiated integration. There is no question of formally reneging on existing commitments. Ireland could still contribute to those peacekeeping operations which remained wholly under an exclusive UN command.

However, this option would probably still lead to a loss of influence as compared with the present situation, as the WEU itself is likely to expand its activities to some degree, if only to be given responsibility for small-scale crisis management operations. The other WEU observers, too, are unlikely to remain fixed on the status quo. Even the complexities of the Danish opt-out on defence are not irreversible, and in any case as a full member of NATO Denmark is already significantly more committed to military cooperation than is Ireland. The more directly comparable non-alliance WEU observer countries, Austria, Finland and Sweden, are all clearly in favour of moving in the direction of EU–WEU involvement in crisis management. Hence sticking with the status quo would leave Ireland in an isolated position.

One effect of this would be to marginalise Irish contributions to common security policies. Even with regard to UN peacekeeping, for example, the state's traditional role might be significantly circumscribed over time. Further regionalisation of the UN's efforts, that is peacekeeping by proxy under a UN mandate, will tend to give organisations such as the WEU more scope for defining the rules of the game, raising the standards of multinational military cooperation through joint procedures and exercises and conducting actual operations. In those circumstances Irish peacekeepers might find themselves at a disadvantage, with less opportunity to influence policy or avail of better training. This could even expose them to a greater degree of risk in the UN operations they did undertake than would otherwise be the case.

So far as Ireland's broader interests in the EU are concerned, the status quo option would clearly signal an unwillingness to make any serious move on a core issue, and thus would be seen as a correspondingly clear signal that Ireland had no real case to be considered as a candidate for a possible overall "avant-garde" group of member states. That would not necessarily be a determining factor with respect to Irish ambitions to participate in other important avant-garde projects, such as EMU, but it would hardly be helpful.

On the other hand, this option promises the least line of resistance when it comes to the ratification of an amended treaty. There is no question of any commitment to collective defence, nor of any form of operational military cooperation. This option would not in itself require a referendum, and if a referendum was necessitated by some other aspect of the IGC it would be difficult to make a case that military neutrality was any more at risk than it had been.

The essence of the third option is that it envisages the possibility of crisis management operations being undertaken by the WEU, and being open to the equal participation of all EU member states, including WEU observers, on a voluntary basis. This model of security cooperation sits squarely within the overall approach of differentiated integration, offering some move towards the maximalist aspiration for a substantive common defence policy but maintaining the minimalist reservation against a commitment to collective defence. It is no accident that it was the subject of an IGC proposal by two WEU observer countries, Finland and Sweden (see Appendix X).

By adopting the option of involvement in EU–WEU crisis management, and engaging in the most urgent element of security policy, Ireland would be in the mainstream of policy adaptation. The country's existing military assets — the defence forces' considerable experience and professional expertise in peacekeeping — would be brought more fully into a framework of European military cooperation, operating with, but not within, a military alliance. This would be broadly similar to what the other EU neutrals are already doing in the context of NATO's Partnership for Peace programme and the IFOR operation in Bosnia. A willingness to adapt in this way might even enhance the state's influence on non-military aspects of security policy.

By exploiting the possibility of differentiated integration in an adaptive rather than reserved way, Ireland would demonstrate a willingness to stay within the parameters of a broadly defined solidarity. That would not meet the charge that the refusal to commit to collective defence represented a fundamental gap in the Union's overall credibility, but it might deflect accusations of a failure to reciprocate in some way.

Of course, it is precisely by avoiding a collective defence commitment that this option preserves the existing position of military neutrality. On that score, it would also seem to avoid the exercise of the government's commitment to hold a referendum following a change in neutrality policy. However, given the probability that a post-IGC referendum will be held anyway (as a consequence of another issue or as an act of general political prudence), the crisis management option may give rise to domestic controversy. Although Fianna Fáil seems to accept it in broad outline, some of the arguments it uses against participation in the Partnership for Peace could also apply to the WEU, an institution which is after all as closely connected to NATO as it is to the EU. Those who view neutrality as a broad value in itself (rather than as a position which only has meaning in a particular contingency), together with those who oppose European integration in any case, are likely to argue this option is the thin end of a militarist or federal wedge. Those who do not take that view will point to the fact that there is little real pressure at the thick end of the wedge.

With regard to the fourth option, full commitment to WEU membership, there would be no doubt on that score. There would certainly be a referendum, because this option certainly means the end of the policy of military neutrality. Two less obvious points are also worth noting. First, as the foreign policy White Paper itself remarks, for some NATO states "membership of the WEU implies membership of NATO also" (Ireland, 1996, para. 4.107). Second, although a full commitment to defence might be considered a necessary element of a federal European Union, it would not of itself lead to this end. After all, the most determined opponent of a federal Europe, the United Kingdom, has long accepted the disciplines of a military alliance.

That said, choosing the fourth option would put Ireland convincingly in the category of potential core or avant-garde countries. The state's presence in all the existing multilateral security organisations would arguably also enhance its influence on the military aspects of security policy (including those of a preventive nature) to a greater extent than under any other option.

However, on the basis of existing political party positions and the intermittent and often ambiguous findings of public opinion polls there appears to be insufficient support for this option. The government's foreign policy White Paper raises it only to conclude elsewhere in the same document that it will not be proposed. The range of realistic choice in the IGC, on this key question of Ireland's relationship with the WEU, therefore seems to lie between the second option — maintaining the status quo — and the third — participating, on a voluntary basis, in EU–WEU crisis management.

PASSIVITY OR ENGAGEMENT?

The options examined above focus on a specific, though important, aspect of security policy, defined largely by the context of the European Union's process of adaptation, the Intergovernmental Conference. The choice there is about the further development of a particular agency, the European Union, and a particular policy instrument, the military. But although it does not refer directly to the whole range of questions which determine international security (of which the issues discussed in chapters 9–11 were only a sample), it is clearly an important part of the overall question of adaptation.

From the point of view of the government of an EU member state negotiating in the IGC on behalf of its people, consideration of the broader context of the adaptation of security policy is essential. Here, the central question is this: in what ways, and to what extent, should we be engaged in the current attempts to develop a co-operative security regime in Europe?

In the case of Ireland, the people themselves may ultimately face this question in a ratification referendum. The answer is not predetermined; there is a real choice to be made between two basic orientations — passivity or engagement. The image of Ireland as an actively internationalist small state has some credibility, especially in the field of development cooperation in the Third World, but it is not always convincing when it comes to security policy. The durability of neutrality, however loosely defined or practised, has set limits to the state's engagement in this field. Several elements in the current debate on security policy tend to reinforce these limits, and could have the effect, whether intended or not, of assigning Ireland to a rather passive role.

One such element is a measure of indifference, deriving perhaps from the fact that Ireland is at present less exposed to security risks than those European states in close proximity to sources of instability. This can take the form of what is almost an iron law of geopolitical exceptionalism, where it is inferred that Ireland's security interests do not require involvement in all the available inclusive multilateral networks. That suggests a narrow and myopic view of Ireland's interests. If, for example, Russia's transition is not successful, Ireland, like Finland, will have to pay the price in terms of greater multinational crime, lost commercial opportunities and a possible regression to a Europe characterised by military confrontation and arms races. It will happen more quickly with regard to Finland, but not much more quickly. The realities of interdependence, for good or ill, are likely to have the edge on the privilege of insularity.

A second factor inhibiting full engagement in security cooperation is suspicion — but suspicion not so much with regard to the risks of instability or conflict as concerning the institutions designed to meet those risks. This fear of entrapment is most evident in attitudes towards military alliances, assumed to be inherently malign in effect, irrespective of their stated intent or membership. The instinctive distrust of NATO, which is such an obvious feature in the Irish security debate, is a curious counterpoint to the unusually close commonality of values, interests and exchanges of all sorts which Ireland enjoys with NATO member states. A similar fear is evident in the vision of the European Union becoming a future "European superpower", which would deploy the conscripted troops of a European army on imperial adventures around the world.

Of course, it would be imprudent, at the very least, to consider joining a military alliance or agreeing to an increase in the powers of the European Union without first looking carefully at the small print of the relevant obligations. Indeed, the IGC provides an opportunity to do just that with respect to the EU. But the rules of international institutions cannot be evaluated in the abstract. A close look at the actual performance of these institutions is also necessary, rather than depending on the projection of selected historical stereotypes. If one thing is clear about the confusion which has followed the end of the Cold War it has been the reluctance rather than the eagerness of the surviving superpower and its allies to resort to the threat or use of force in the face of open challenges to the international rule of law. As for the European superpower, whatever slight credibility this vision might have had in 1991, it is clear from the positions being discussed in the current Intergovernmental Conference that it is a decidedly mythical creature now.

Reluctance to become involved more closely in the military aspects of security cooperation may also be reinforced by a perfectionist, if not utopian, attitude towards international institutions. This often takes the form of the argument that the more inclusive the institution, the more it should be the primary focus of the international community's joint efforts. Thus, rather than working through the European Union or the military alliances, Ireland should concentrate its efforts on the United Nations or, if regionalism must be acknowledged, the OSCE.

The problem is, however, that while the inclusiveness of these institutions provides legitimacy for international action, the other side of the coin — the diversity of interests they represent — often makes it difficult to develop a framework for action. In practice, effective multilateralism relies on smaller groups of like-minded states both to mobilise political will in the UN and, increasingly, to implement its mandates. Confining the pursuit of Irish security interests to a United Nations which itself is in obvious need of reform would simply be a recipe for ineffectiveness or, ultimately, irrelevance if the UN itself progressively contracts out its crisis management tasks to regional organisations.

Finally, there is the view that further engagement by Ireland in the military aspects of European security would detract from the aims and implementation of policies of development cooperation. For example, the Irish Association of Non-Governmental Development Organisations, Dochas, opposes participation in the Partnership for Peace and WEU crisis management on these grounds (Dochas, 1996, pp. 20–7). This line of argument is often based on the assumption that neutrality is in some way a necessary basis for a successful Third World policy. At a more general level, it assumes a direct trade-off between resources applied to defence and those applied to development. But that begs the question of how an insecure Europe is to conduct a serious development policy — indeed, it might even be argued that a secure Europe is a prior condition for such a policy. So far as the military aspect of crisis management is concerned, a more effective multilateral effort on the part of European states could well be in the interests of developing countries, either by reducing the burden on the UN itself or by supporting their own regional organisations.

Indifference, a fear of entrapment, an unrealistic view of international organisations and an incomplete analysis of the relationship between security policy and development cooperation — all of these factors work in the direction of a cautious and limited involvement in co-operative security; in short, a relatively passive approach. What, then, are the arguments for becoming more engaged?

The general proposition that human agencies are responsible for their environment can be applied here. States, too, have a responsibility for ensuring that their security environment is so far as possible compatible with their values and interests. Whether the motivation is seen in terms of a "cosmopolitan" morality in which altruistic goals to some extent transcend state interests, or whether it is a projection of an enlightened self-interest, responsibility implies engagement.

For small states this solidarity with the outside world is particularly important, since it is manifestly in their interest to sustain an environment in which power rivalries are contained and an international rule of law is developed. The question remains just how this is to be achieved, for the political organisation of the international environment cannot be taken for granted. That has been especially true since the Cold War ended at the beginning of this decade, and the need for the adaptation of international procedures and policies has been acute.

Arguably, the Irish state has never been so well placed as it is now to contribute towards the development of a more stable, and ultimately more equitable, environment, through the shaping of the evolving co-operative security regime. It is already an experienced member of the European Union, which is one of the central poles of attraction of the regime; a doubt remains about how, or even whether, to engage further with the other main pole, the Atlantic alliance. A total engagement through a commitment to collective self-defence may be for many people an adaptation too far, though perhaps the option merits a more serious consideration than it has yet received. The Partnership for Peace programme and selected participation in future WEU crisis management also offer forms of engagement which are arguably at the same time less constricting and more immediately relevant to the construction of a co-operative security regime.

The choice between passivity and engagement, and indeed much of the current Irish debate, has tended to focus on the military aspect of security policy. That is not accidental; nor is it just the result of a parochial obsession with neutrality. Since the end of the Cold War there has been an increase in the use of force in and around Europe, "defence" is on the IGC agenda, and the meaning of neutrality can no longer be taken as self-evident. Yet it must also be remembered that beyond the Intergovernmental Conference, and beyond whatever arrangements are made on the military side, the question of engagement will be posed in the broader context of the future role of the European Union, and particularly its enlargement. This may prove to be even more challenging for future Irish governments. It will affect the whole range of public policies now determined in part by the interdependence of European states. And, so far as the security of these states is concerned, unlike the special case of dealing with emergencies through crisis management, the need to sustain measures of long-term prevention will always be with us.

◌ Bibliography

AfrI (Action from Ireland) (1996). *Links: Ireland's Links with the Arms Trade and Military Industry*, Dublin.

Ahern, Bertie (1996). Speech of the leader of Fianna Fáil at Oxford, 10 May.

Allin, Dana H. (1995). "Can Containment Work Again?", *Survival*, Vol. 37, No. 1, (Spring).

Asmus, Ronald D., Richard L. Kugler and F. Stephen Larrabee (1995). "NATO Expansion: The Next Steps", *Survival*, Vol. 37, No. 1, (Spring).

Asmus, Ronald D. and Robert C. Nurick (1996). "NATO Enlargement and the Baltic States", *Survival*, Vol. 38, No. 2, (Summer).

Astrom, Sverker and Leif Leifland (1994)). *A Historic Choice: The Consequences for Swedish Foreign and Security Policy of Membership or Non-membership of the European Union*, Official Report of the EC/EU Commissions: Foreign and Security Policy, Stockholm.

Austria (1995) Leitlinien zu den voraussichtlichen Themen der Regierungskonferenz 1996, Austrian government, 30 May.

Barnier, Michel (1995). "The European Union: Looking Ahead to the Next Ten Years". Speech by the Minister Delegate with responsibility for European Affairs, Bonn, 26 October.

Barnier, Michel and Werner Hoyer (1995). Article on the CFSP (no title), *Le Monde*, 8 December.

Barry, Charles (1996). "NATO's Combined Joint Task Forces in Theory and Practice", *Survival*, Vol. 38, No. 1, (Spring).

Belgium (1995). IGC Note of the Government of Belgium, 13 October.

Benelux (1996). Memorandum of Belgium, Luxembourg and the Netherlands for the IGC, March.

Boutros-Ghali, Boutros (1992). *An Agenda for Peace*, United Nations, New York.

Boutros-Ghali, Boutros (1995). Supplement to An Agenda for Peace: Position Paper of the Secretary-General on the Occasion of the Fiftieth Anniversary of the United Nations, 25 January.

British Labour Party (1995). *The Future of the European Union: Report on Labour's position in preparation for the Intergovernmental Conference 1996*, October.

Brown, Michael E. (1995). "The Flawed Logic of NATO Expansion", *Survival*, Vol. 37, No. 1, (Spring).

Brown, Neville (1995). *Ballistic Missile Defence: a British perspective*, London Defence Studies, 27, London.

Bulmer, Simon and William E. Paterson (1996). "Germany in the European Union: Gentle Giant or Emergent Leader?", *International Affairs*, Vol. 72, No. 1, (January).

CDU/CSU — Fraktion des Deutschen Bundestages (1994). "Reflections on European Policy", 1 September.

CDU/CSU — Fraktion des Deutschen Bundestages (1995). "A European Union Capable of More Effective Action in the Field of Foreign and Security Policy", 13 June.

Challenge 96: IGC Intelligence Service, Belmont European Policy Centre, Brussels, periodical 1995–96.

Chirac, Jacques (1996). Address before the Congress of the United States, 1 February.

Commission (1995a). *Report for the Reflection Group.*

Commission (1995b). *Interim report from the Commission to the European Council on the effects on the Policies of the European Union of enlargement to the associated countries of central and eastern Europe,* 6 December.

Commission (1996a). *Communication on the European defence industry,* 26 January.

Commission (1996b). Opinion: *Reinforcing Political Union and preparing for enlargement,* 28 February.

Constitutional Review Group (1996). *Report,* Stationery Office, Dublin, May.

Council (1995). *Report on the functioning of the Treaty on European Union,* 5 April.

Cox, Michael (1995). *US Foreign Policy after the Cold War: Superpower Without a Mission?,* Chatham House Papers, RIIA/Cassell, London.

Denmark (1995). *Basis For Negotiations: Open Europe — The 1996 Intergovernmental Conference,* Danish Government, 11 December.

Deutsch, Karl W (1957). Political Community and the North Atlantic Area, Princeton, NJ.

De Vestel, Pierre (1995), *Defence Markets and Industries in Europe: Time for Political Decisions?,* Chaillot Paper 21, Institute for Security Studies, WEU, Paris.

Dochas (The Irish Association of Non-Governmental Development Organisations) (1996). *Irish Development NGO Perspectives on the EU Presidency: July–December 1996,* Dublin.

European Council (1996a). Progress report on the Intergovernmental Conference, from the Italian Presidency of the Council to the European Council at Florence, 21–22 June.

European Council (1996b). Presidency Conclusions, Florence European Council, 21–22 June.

European Parliament (1995a). *Bourlanges/Martin Report on the functioning of the European Union,* May.

European Parliament (1995b). *Matutes Report on progress made in implementing the common foreign and security policy,* May.

Experts Group on the CFSP (1995). *La politique extérieure et de sécurité de l'Europe a l'horizon 2000: deuxieme rapport,* Brussels, 28 November.

Fanning, Ronan (1979). "The United States and Irish Participation in NATO: the Debate of 1950", *Irish Studies in International Affairs,* Vol. 1, No. 1.

Federal Trust (1995). *Security of the Union: The Intergovernmental Conference of the European Union,* Federal Trust Papers No. 4, London.

Fianna Fáil (1995). *Our Place in the World: Fianna Fáil on Foreign Affairs,* Dublin, November.

Finland (1994). Finnish Presentation Document to the Partnership for Peace Programme, 9 May.

Finland (1995). *Security in a Changing World: Guidelines for Finland's Security Policy,* Report by the Council of State to the Parliament, 6 June.

Finland (1996). *Finland's Point of Departure and Objectives at the 1996 Intergovernmental Conference,* Report to the Parliament by the Council of State, 27 February.

Finland and Sweden (1996). The IGC and the Security and Defence Dimension — Towards an Enhanced EU Role in Crisis Management, Joint Finnish–Swedish memorandum, 25 April.

Fox, Carol (1995). *European Defence Debate,* (Briefing Paper), the Peace and Neutrality Alliance, Dún Laoghaire.

France and Germany (1995). Franco-German letter to the President of the European Union, Baden-Baden, 6 December.

France and Germany (1996). Common Foreign and Security Policy Guidelines, Franco-German seminar of Ministers of Foreign Affairs, Freiburg in Breisgau, 27 February.

Freedman, Lawrence (1995). "Bosnia: Does Peace Support Make Any Sense?", *NATO Review,* Vol. 43, No. 6, November.

Gambles, Ian (ed.) (1995). *A Lasting Peace in Central Europe?,* Chaillot Paper 20, Institute for Security Studies, WEU, Paris.

Gow, James and Christopher Dandeker (1995). "Peace-Support Operations: The Problem of Legitimation", *The World Today,* Vol. 51, Nos. 8–9, August–September.

Grant, Robert P. (1996). "France's New Relationship with NATO", *Survival,* Vol. 38, No. 1 (Spring).

Greece (1995). Conclusions of the Interministerial Committee concerning Greece's position on the Intergovernmental Conference of 1996, 31 May.

Greece (1996). *For a Democratic European Union with Political and Social Content,* Greece's Contribution to the Intergovernmental Conference, March.

Hardeman, Hilde and Florence Benoit-Rohmer (1994). "The Pact on Stability in Europe", *Helsinki Monitor,* Vol. 5, No. 4.

Hjelm-Wallen, Lena (1995). Speech by the Minister for Foreign Affairs of Sweden at the Latvian Foreign Affairs Society, 13 July.

Holbrooke, Richard (1995). "America, a European Power", *Foreign Affairs,* Vol. 74, No. 2, March/April.

Howe, Geoffrey (1996). "Bearing More of the Burden: In Search of a European Foreign and Security Policy", *The World Today,* Vol. 52, No. 1 (January).

Hurd, Douglas (1994). "Developing the Common Foreign and Security Policy", *International Affairs,* Vol. 70, No. 3 (July).

Hurd, Douglas (1995). "The Common Foreign and Security Policy: The Question of Majority Voting", *Die Suddeutsche Zeitung,* 17 June.

Institute of European Affairs (IEA) (1995). *1996 Intergovernmental Conference: Issues, Options, Implications,* Dublin.

International Institute of Strategic Studies (IISS) (1995). *Strategic Survey 1994/95,* London.

Ireland (1970). *Membership of the European Communities: Implications for Ireland,* Dublin.

Ireland (1996). *Challenges and Opportunities Abroad,* White Paper on Foreign Policy, Department of Foreign Affairs, Dublin.

Irish Business and Employers Confederation (IBEC) (1995). *Ireland, the European Union and Economic Integration: A Business Perspective,* May.

Jakobsen, Peter Viggo (1995). "Multilateralism Matters, But How? The Impact of Multilateralism on Great Power Policy towards the Break-up of Yugoslavia", *Cooperation and Conflict,* Vol. 30, No. 4 (December).

Janning, Josef (1996). "A German Europe or a European Germany? On the debate over Germany's Foreign Policy", *International Affairs,* Vol. 72, No. 1 (January).

Kamp, Karl-Heinz (1995). "Germany and the Future of Nuclear Weapons in Europe", *Security Dialogue,* Vol. 26, Number 3 (September).

Keatinge, Patrick (1995). *Towards a Safer Europe. Small State Security Policies and the European Union: Implications for Ireland,* Institute of European Affairs, Dublin.

Kooijmans, Peter (1995). "The OSCE: A problem child with growth disorders", *Helsinki Monitor,* Vol. 6, No. 4.

Lightburn, David (1996). "NATO and the Challenge of Multifunctional Peacekeeping", *NATO Review,* Vol. 44, No. 1 (March).

Luxembourg (1995). Aide-mémoire du Gouvernement luxembourgeois sur la Conférence Intergouvernementale de 1996, Luxembourg, 30 June.

MccGwire, Michael (1994). "Is There a Future for Nuclear Weapons?", *International Affairs,* Vol. 70, No. 2 (April).

Macdonald, Oliver (1995). "International Peacekeeping — The Irish Experience", *An Cosantóir,* October.

Maguire, John and Joe Noonan (1992). *Maastricht and Ireland: Ireland's Neutrality and the Future of Europe,* People First/Meitheal, Cork.

Malone, David (1995). "A Future for UN Peacekeeping?", paper presented at the Royal Irish Academy, Dublin, 2 November.

Marsh, Michael (1992). *Irish Public Opinion on Neutrality and European Union,* Occasional Paper 1, Institute of European Affairs, Dublin.

Martin, Laurence and John Roper (eds.) (1995). *Towards a Common Defence Policy,* Institute for Security Studies, WEU, Paris.

Meiers, Franz-Josef (1995). "Germany: The Reluctant Power", *Survival,* Vol. 37, No. 3 (Autumn).

Muller, Harald and Lars van Dassen (1995). "From Cacophony to Joint Action: Successes and Shortcomings of European Non-proliferation Policy", paper presented to the Second Pan-European Conference on International Relations, Paris, 13–16 September.

NATO (1995). *Study on NATO Enlargement,* September.

Netherlands (1995a). *Common Foreign, Security and Defence Policy: Towards Stronger External Action by the European Union,* Government of the Netherlands, 30 March.

Netherlands (1995b). Institutional Reform of the European Union, Government of the Netherlands, 12 July.

Neuhold, Hanspeter (1995). *Austria Still between East and West?,* Austrian Institute for International Affairs, Laxenburg, July.

Nolan, J. E. (ed.) (1994). *Global Engagement: Cooperation and Security in the 21st Century,* Brookings Institution, Washington DC.

Norrback, Ole (1995). "Security in Europe — With or Without NATO?", speech by the Finnish Minister for European Affairs and Foreign Trade, 6 November.

O'Carroll, Donal (1995). "The Defence Forces and the Inter-Governmental Conference of 1996", *An Cosantóir Review.*

O'Neill, Robert (1995). "Britain and the future of nuclear weapons", *International Affairs,* Vol. 71, No. 4, (October).

Petersen, Nikolaj (1993). *"Game, Set, and Match": Denmark and the European Union after Edinburgh,* Instituut for Statskundskab, Aarhus, September.

Petersen, Nikolaj (1994). *Danish Security Policy after the Cold War: Adaptation and Innovation,* Instituut for Statskundskab, Aarhus, February.

Plesch, Dan (1995). "Sowing the Seeds of War", *European Brief,* October.

Portillo, Michael (1995). "1996: Substance and Symbolism", speech by the British Secretary of State for Defence, WEU Assembly, 5 December.

Portugal (1996). *Portugal and the Inter-Governmental Conference for the Revision of the Treaty on European Union,* March.

Quinlan, Michael (1993). "The future of nuclear weapons: policy for western possessors", *International Affairs,* Vol. 69, No. 3, (July).

Reflection Group (1995). *Report,* 5 December.

Rifkind, Malcolm (1996). "Common Foreign and Security Policy", speech by the British Foreign Secretary, Paris, 5 March.

Roberts, Adam (1995–96). "From San Francisco to Sarajevo: The UN and the Use of Force", *Survival,* Vol. 37, No. 4 (Winter).

Rogers, Paul (1996). *Sub-strategic Trident: A Slow Burning Fuse,* London Defence Studies, 34, London.

Rogov, Sergey (1995). "This Dangerous Crisis Over Arms Control", *European Brief,* October.

Rummel, Reinhardt (1996). *Common Foreign and Security Policy and Conflict Prevention,* Saferworld and International Alert, London.

Salmon, Trevor C. (1989). *Unneutral Ireland: An Ambivalent and Unique Security Policy,* Clarendon Press, Oxford.

Schussel, Wolfgang (1995). Speech by the German Vice-Chancellor and Minister for Foreign Affairs, 11 June.

Scott, Dermot (1996). *Ireland and the IGC,* Institute of European Affairs, Dublin.

Simpson, John (1995). "The Birth of a New Era? The 1995 NPT Conference and the Politics of Nuclear Disarmament", *Security Dialogue,* Vol. 26, No. 3 (September).

Sinnott, Richard (1995). *Knowledge of the European Community in Irish Public Opinion,* Occasional Paper 5, Institute of European Affairs, Dublin.

SNU (Danish Commission on Security and Disarmament) (1995). *Danish and European Security* (Summary in English), Copenhagen, May.

Spring, Dick (1995). Remarks by the Tánaiste and Minister for Foreign Affairs, WEU Council of Ministers, Madrid, 14 November.

Stark, Hans (1995). *L'Union européenne et le conflit en ex-Yugoslavie,* CFSP Forum 3/95, Institut fur Europaische Politik, Bonn.

Sweden (1995). *The EU Intergovernmental Conference 1996,* Government Report, 30 November.

Swedish Parliamentary Defence Commission (1995). *Sweden in Europe and the World: Conclusions of a Report on Security Policy,* Spring.

Trans European Policy Association (TEPSA) (1994–96). *Revision of Maastricht: Implementation and Proposals for Reform. A Survey of National Views, Periodical Bulletins,* Istituto Affari Internazionali (IAI)/ TEPSA.

UK (1995). Memorandum on the United Kingdom Government's Approach to the Treatment of European Defence Issues at the 1996 Intergovernmental Conference, March.

UK (1996). *A Partnership of Nations,* United Kingdom White Paper on the Intergovernmental Conference, March.

US and EU (1995). *The New Transatlantic Agenda,* 3 December.

van Eekelen, Willem (1995). *The Security Agenda for 1996: Background and Proposals,* CEPS Paper No. 64, Centre for European Policy Studies, Brussels.

Wessels, Wolfgang (1995). "How to Mix Transformation and Integration: Strategies, Options and Scenarios", in Barbara Lippert and Heinrich Schneider (eds.), *Monitoring Association and Beyond: The European Union and the Visgrad States,* Bonn.

WEU (1992). Petersberg Declaration, WEU Council of Ministers, 19 June.

WEU (1995a). Contribution to the European Union Intergovernmental Conference of 1996, WEU Council of Ministers, Madrid, 14 November.

WEU (1995b). European security: a common concept of the 27 WEU countries, WEU Council of Ministers, Madrid, 14 November.

Williams, Nick (1996). "Partnership for Peace: Permanent Fixture or Declining Asset?", *Survival,* (Spring).

Witney, Nicholas K. J. (1994–95). "British Nuclear Policy after the Cold War", *Survival,* Vol. 36, No. 4 (Winter).

Yost, David S. (1994–95). "Nuclear Debates in France", *Survival,* Vol. 36, No. 4 (Winter).

Zelikow, Philip (1996). "The Masque of Institutions", *Survival,* Vol. 38, No. 1 (Spring).

◌ APPENDICES

◼ APPENDIX I

THE NATURE OF SECURITY POLICY

A persistent concern in current debates about security policy is the meaning to be ascribed to the term itself. The concept of security, it is widely argued, should not be restricted to the classical threat of military intervention by another state. Given the increasing interdependence of Europe, and indeed the world, in the late twentieth century, the sources of insecurity can be found in almost all forms of social activity, and within states as well as between them. A global or continental free market economy may create wealth in the long term, but leaves winners and losers during the operational life of democratic governments. Societies may feel vulnerable to threats of economic penetration, to the negative effects of transnational ecological damage, or to a loss of cultural identity deriving from more intensive contacts with outsiders.

Viewed in this light, there is arguably a "security dimension" to most sectors of public policy; an important part of security policy as such may well be to ensure that narrowly conceived sectoral policies do not have broader negative effects. However, it is where these varied sources of insecurity threaten political stability, either within the state or between states, that the security policies of governments assume a more clearly defined shape. The overall goal of security is related to particular perceptions of threat; the policy response may involve a mix of different instruments, ranging from persuasion to coercion. The classical form of security policy, where military threats are countered by the threat or actual use of force — defence policy — thus lies at the hard end of a broad policy spectrum.

So far as the operational definition of security is concerned — that is, the definition adopted by governments and international agencies — the primary focus is on measures to promote stability and avoid, or at least mitigate, the effects of political violence. That is not to deny that insecurity has wider connotations and deeper roots, but in the first instance security policy is the business of governments, and the international institutions they work through.

Security policy is also arguably still primarily a matter of international politics, notwithstanding the internal sources of many conflicts and the increasing influence of non-governmental groups, often operating on a transnational basis. A fundamental characteristic of international politics — the absence of a common sovereign in the international arena — hampers attempts by governments to act collectively, towards a common purpose defined by common values. Thus the historical verdict on efforts to create an effective system of collective security is not encouraging; neither the League of Nations nor its successor, the United Nations, fulfilled expectations in this respect. The idea that "aggressive and unlawful use of force by any nation will be met with the combined force of all other nations" (Claude, 1964, p. 224) is simple, but demanding. It requires unconditional deference to a central authority, a very high degree of trust and stability in the relationships of the participants, and strong centralised instruments of enforcement.

These conditions clearly do not exist, even with the disappearance of the Cold War. The unprecedented pace of change in most areas of human activity, if nothing else, would seem to preclude the early achievement of genuine collective security; to the uncertainties of change must be added the persistence of traditional political rivalries even in co-operative ventures.

Three approaches: prevention, protection and crisis management
If universal collective security remains an ideal to be aspired to, what then does actual security amount to? At this point, a semantic caution is in order. The terminology used merely to describe the content of security policy is imprecise; different national and institutional variants abound, and it is necessary to start with a very general categorisation. Three broad functional approaches can be identified — prevention, protection and crisis management. In practice, of course, national and ideological rivalries often obscure these functional categories, but their principal characteristics, summarised here, nevertheless provide an important initial insight into the nature of international security policy today.

The first broad approach, prevention, emphasises measures to prevent potential conflicts arising or developing to the point where they cannot be resolved peacefully through routine procedures. Prevention implies policies of reassurance, confidence-building and inclusiveness. The policy instruments to be employed tend to be those of persuasion rather than coercion: political and economic assistance, the development of an international rule of law, an institutionalisation of mediation and arbitration procedures, and more generally an international culture of openness. There may be misunderstandings and even opposed interests in the short term, but it is assumed there is no inevitable basis for lasting enmities, and a common interest in ensuring they do not emerge. In the long term, its hoped that the patient pursuit of preventive measures may serve to establish some of the basic prerequisites for a more ambitious collective security system. Over time, the interests and even the identities of contending groups may become compatible. A political difficulty in implementing this approach is that its long-term and often seemingly altruistic goals may have little appeal to donor electorates, and less to their finance ministries.

The second approach, protection, is also essentially a long-term strategy. It is based, however, on the assumption that the eventual success of preventive security cannot be guaranteed. Just in case, therefore, provision must be made to deal with military threats of a traditional kind. Given the increasing costs of military policy, collective defence measures may be agreed among groups of like-minded states. Military alliances are sometimes attributed a preventive function, in so far as the very existence of an alliance may deter potential adversaries. Indeed, in the second half of the twentieth century the mutual deterrence role of the major alliances in Europe was arguably more pronounced than defence in the classical sense. However, if there was an element of prevention in Cold War deterrence, it was in a context quite different from that of the ultimate harmony assumed in the overall preventive approach. It was based on a relatively high level of tension between clearly defined and highly-armed opponents, and relied on a capacity for coercion. The term "protection" is used here to cover both deterrence and defence as such. It can be seen as a policy of insurance against the failure of the overall strategy of prevention.

These two approaches to security policy embody long-term strategies, posited on potential conflicts, and involving considerable commitment and expenditure projected into the indeterminate future. Crisis management, on the other hand, concerns immediate responses to actual challenges. The goal is to bring collective resources to bear on settling disputes, if possible, but if not, on containing them and mitigating their negative effects. An important feature of crisis management is that it may involve almost the whole spectrum of policy instruments available to states and international organisations. Exhortation, mediation, economic inducements or sanctions, humanitarian relief, peacekeeping or peace enforcement measures, including threats of further military intervention — 'all necessary means' in the parlance of UN resolutions — all of this is grist to the mill of crisis management.

There are two related difficulties in this aspect of security policy. The first is one of political judgement, in finding agreement on the appropriate mix of measures in particular circumstances, especially in deciding to cross the threshold of the use of force. The recourse to instruments of "hard security" often cuts across attempts to deal with crises through the means of "soft security", such as mediation. The second problem is that of commitment, the willingness to mobilise and apply adequate resources; here, too, the commitment of force, with all its inherent risks, is a particularly difficult decision.

It is important to note that in practice these broad approaches are not mutually exclusive. Although prevention and protection envisage contrasting long-term possibilities, governments usually pursue both strategies simultaneously. The critical question is that of the weight accorded to each. Furthermore, the limitations of any form of social order ensure that crises will arise somewhere, sometime, and the gradual incrementalism of either prevention or protective policies will have to be complemented by the emergency measures of crisis management. The present European system shows a balance of prevention and crisis management, with protection in the background as an insurance policy of last resort. It is far from being a collective security system, but may be described as a co-operative security regime. This is a much looser arrangement, based on a minimum of common values, and with an uncertain division of labour amongst its member states and international institutions.

APPENDIX II

SECURITY INSTITUTIONS: BASIC FACTS

UNO (UNITED NATIONS ORGANISATION)
Founded in 1945 on the basis of the UN charter, the UN is the world's principal intergovernmental organisation, and its almost universal membership makes it an important source of international law.

The Security Council is the UN's most important executive agency, and sits in permanent session. It has 15 members, five of which are permanent members with veto powers (China, France, Russia, United Kingdom and United States). All member states are represented in the General Assembly, and the organisation is served by a Secretariat headed by the Secretary General.

The UN's primary objective is the maintenance of international peace, though during the Cold War persistent disagreement in the Security Council led to increasing emphasis on development and other functional issues. The role of the Security Council has been more prominent since the late 1980s, with a corresponding increase in demands for UN peacekeeping.

CSCE (CONFERENCE ON SECURITY AND COOPERATION IN EUROPE)
OSCE (ORGANISATION FOR SECURITY AND COOPERATION IN EUROPE)
Launched in 1972 and based on the Helsinki Final Act of 1975, the CSCE was the most inclusive multilateral forum for security dialogue in Europe during the Cold War. It included all the members of both NATO and the Warsaw Pact, as well as non-alliance states, with the exception of Albania.

In 1990, following the Paris Charter, the CSCE started a phase of increasing expansion of membership and institutionalisation. It now has 53 members, including the United States and Canada, though Serbia (rump Yugoslavia) is temporarily suspended. In 1992 the post of Secretary General was created. Its Secretariat and its main political centre are in Vienna, with ancillary offices in Prague and Warsaw. The CSCE's High Commissioner for National Minorities is based in the Hague. Summit meetings generally take place every two years, the most recent being in Budapest in December 1994. The CSCE was re-named OSCE (Organisation for Security and Cooperation in Europe) at this meeting.

The CSCE/OSCE is a major source of guidelines on the conduct of inter-state relations and the democratic process, as well as human and minority rights. It is involved in the verification of arms control agreements, conflict prevention and crisis management.

NATO (NORTH ATLANTIC TREATY ORGANISATION)

NATO was founded in 1949 on the basis of the North Atlantic (or Washington) Treaty, as a military alliance to counter the perceived threat of the Soviet Union. Its legal base includes mutual assistance guarantees (Article 5).

NATO currently has sixteen members including the United States and Canada as well as European states. Its highest political authority, the North Atlantic Council, decides policy on the basis of consensus, and is served by a Secretariat headed by a Secretary General based in Brussels. The North Atlantic Assembly is NATO's inter-parliamentary forum. NATO also has a complex integrated military command, with its main headquarters at SHAPE (Supreme Headquarters Allied Powers Europe) at Mons in Belgium. France and Spain do not participate fully in the military structures.

NACC (NORTH ATLANTIC COOPERATION COUNCIL)

In December 1991 NACC (often pronounced "nak-see") was established as a consultative forum to include NATO members and their former adversaries. It now has 38 members.

PFP (PARTNERSHIP FOR PEACE)

IN January 1994, the NATO Summit meeting in Brussels inaugurated the Partnership for Peace programme, whereby individual non-NATO states agree their own measures of military cooperation with the alliance. On 5 October 1994 Armenia became the twenty-third signatory of the PFP Framework Document.

WEU (WESTERN EUROPEAN UNION)

The WEU's origins lie in the Brussels Treaty of 1948, signed by France, the United Kingdom and the Benelux countries, primarily as a military alliance (before the establishment of NATO). Under the Paris Agreement of 1954, or "modified Brussels Treaty", Germany and Italy joined the WEU, as the organisation was then known.

Overshadowed by NATO during the Cold War, the WEU now has a dual role as the European element within NATO and potential defence element of the European Union (EU). IT has a Secretariat in Brussels, under a Secretary General. Ministerial meetings are held twice a year, and the WEU Assembly (based in Paris and comprising members' delegates to the Parliamentary Assembly of the Council of Europe) also meets twice a year.

The WEU now has ten full members (i.e. those in both NATO and the EU), three associate members (i.e. those in NATO but outside the EU), ten associate partners (i.e. countries outside NATO and the EU but potential members of one or both), and five observers (i.e. EU members which are not full members of the WEU).

OTHER INSTITUTIONS WITH SECURITY FUNCTIONS

EU (EUROPEAN UNION)
The EU came into force in November 1993, following the implementation of the Treaty on European Union, or Maastricht Treaty, agreed in December 1991 by the member states of the European Community (itself based on the European Economic Community which was established in 1957 by the six member states of the European Coal and Steel Community).

Article J of the Maastricht Treaty establishes a Common Foreign and Security Policy (CFSP), which acknowledges the role of the WEU. From January 1995 the EU has 15 members, and further enlargement is envisaged.

COUNCIL OF EUROPE
Established in 1949, the Council of Europe upholds the principles of parliamentary democracy, and is the major European promoter of human rights. It now has 32 members.

■ APPENDIX III

CONTRIBUTORS TO THE IMPLEMENTATION FORCE (IFOR)

NATO Member States	PFP States	Other States
Belgium	Austria	Egypt
Canada	Czech Republic	Jordan
Denmark	Estonia	Malaysia
France	Finland	Morocco
Germany	Hungary	
Greece	Latvia	
Iceland	Lithuania	
Italy	Poland	
Luxembourg	Romania	
Netherlands	Russia	
Norway	Sweden	
Portugal	Ukraine	
Spain		
Turkey		
United Kingdom		
United States		

Source: NATO

THE WEU FAMILY STRUCTURE

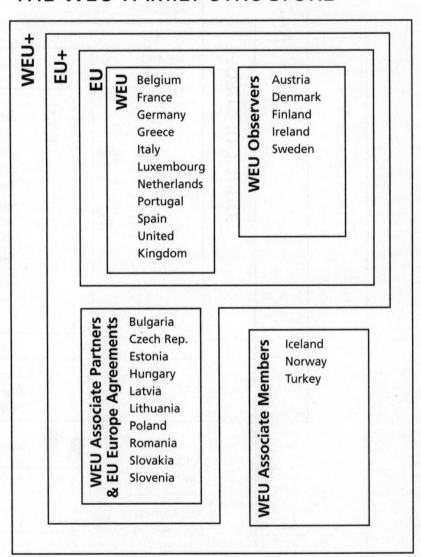

WEU+

EU+

EU

WEU
Belgium
France
Germany
Greece
Italy
Luxembourg
Netherlands
Portugal
Spain
United Kingdom

WEU Observers
Austria
Denmark
Finland
Ireland
Sweden

WEU Associate Partners & EU Europe Agreements
Bulgaria
Czech Rep.
Estonia
Hungary
Latvia
Lithuania
Poland
Romania
Slovakia
Slovenia

WEU Associate Members
Iceland
Norway
Turkey

Source: Adapted from *NATO Review*, Vol. 43, No. 6 November 1995

THE EUROPEAN SECURITY STRUCTURE

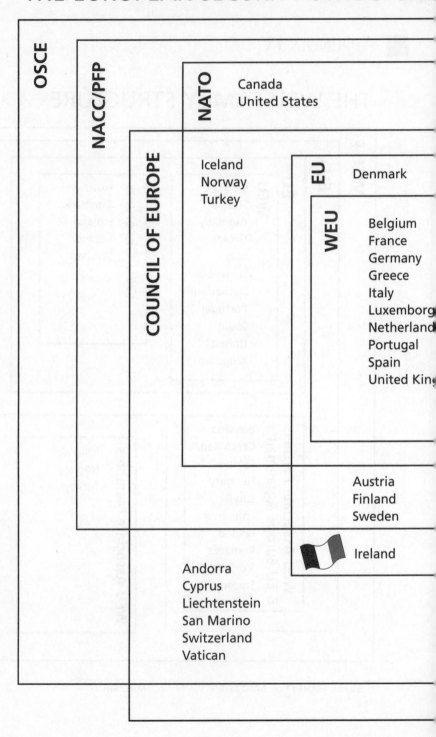

OSCE

NACC/PFP

NATO
Canada
United States

COUNCIL OF EUROPE
Iceland
Norway
Turkey

EU
Denmark

WEU
Belgium
France
Germany
Greece
Italy
Luxemborg
Netherland
Portugal
Spain
United King

Austria
Finland
Sweden

Ireland

Andorra
Cyprus
Liechtenstein
San Marino
Switzerland
Vatican

Albania	Armenia
Bulgaria	Azerbaijan
Czech Republic	Belarus
Estonia	Georgia
Hungary	Kazakhstan
Latvia	Kyrgyzstan
Lithuania	Tajikistan[3]
Malta	Turkmenistan
Moldova	Uzbekistan
Poland	
Romania	
Russia	
Slovakia	
Slovenia	
Ukraine	

Bosnia-Herzegovina
Croatia
Fed. Rep. of Yugoslavia
(Serbia - Montenegro)[1]
Japan [2]
Monaco
FYROM[2]

1 Suspended from activities
2 Observer status
3 Not in PFP

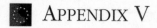 APPENDIX V

TREATY ON EUROPEAN UNION, ARTICLE J.4, AND DECLARATION ON WESTERN EUROPEAN UNION (EXTRACTS)

TEU, ARTICLE J.4

1. The common foreign and security policy shall include all questions related to the security of the Union, including the eventual framing of a common defence policy, which might in time lead to a common defence.

2. The Union requests the Western European Union (WEU), which is an integral part of the development of the Union, to elaborate and implement decisions and actions of the Union which have defence implications. The Council shall, in agreement with the institutions of the WEU, adopt the necessary practical arrangements.

3. Issues having defence implications dealt with under this Article shall not be subject to the procedures set out in Article J.3. [i.e. qualified majority voting]

4. The policy of the Union in accordance with this Article shall not prejudice the specific character of the security and defence policy of certain Member States and shall respect the obligations of certain Member States under the North Atlantic Treaty and be compatible with the common security and defence policy established within that framework.

5. The provisions of this article shall not prevent the development of closer cooperation between two or more Member States on a bilateral level, in the framework of the WEU and the Atlantic Alliance, provided such cooperation does not run counter to or impede that provided for in this Title.

6. With a view to furthering the objective of this Treaty, and having in view the date of 1998 in the context of Article XII of the Brussels Treaty, the provisions of this Article may be revised as provided for in Article N(2) on the basis of a report to be presented in 1996 by the Council to the European Council, which shall include an evaluation of the progress made and the experience gained until then.

DECLARATION ON WESTERN EUROPEAN UNION

The Conference [i.e. of EC Governments] notes the following declaration.

I. DECLARATION

by Belgium, Germany, Spain, France, Italy, Luxembourg, the Netherlands, Portugal and the United Kingdom of Great Britain and Northern Ireland, which are members of the Western European Union and also members of the European Union

on

THE ROLE OF THE WESTERN EUROPEAN UNION AND ITS RELATIONS WITH THE EUROPEAN UNION AND WITH THE ATLANTIC ALLIANCE

INTRODUCTION

1. WEU Member States agree on the need to develop a genuine European security and defence identity and a greater European responsibility on defence matters. This identity will be pursued through a gradual process involving successive phases. WEU will form an integral part of the process of the development of the European Union and will enhance its contribution to solidarity within the Atlantic Alliance. WEU Member States agree to strengthen the role of WEU, in the longer term perspective of a common defence policy within the European Union which might in time lead to a common defence, compatible with that of the Atlantic Alliance.

2. WEU will be developed as a defence component of the European Union and as a means to strengthen the European pillar of the Atlantic Alliance. To this end, it will formulate common European defence policy and carry forward its concrete implementation through the further development of its own operational role.

WEU Member States take note of Article J.4 relating to common foreign and security of the Treaty on European Union....

II. DECLARATION

by Belgium, Germany, Spain, France, Italy, Luxembourg, the Netherlands, Portugal and the United Kingdom of Great Britain and Northern Ireland which are members of the Western European Union

The Member States of WEU welcome the development of the European security and defence identity. They are determined, taking into account the role of WEU as the defence component of the European Union and as the means to strengthen the European pillar of the Atlantic Alliance, to put the

relationship between WEU and the other European States on a new basis for the sake of stability and security in Europe. In this spirit, they propose the following:

States which are members of the European Union are invited to accede to WEU on conditions to be agreed in accordance with Article XI of the modified Brussels Treaty, or to be observers if they so wish. Simultaneously, other European Member States of NATO are invited to become associate members of WEU in a way which will give them the possibility of participating fully in the activities of WEU.'

Appendix VI

Commitments to collective defence and crisis management

A. Collective defence: mutual security guarantees (NATO and WEU)

North Atlantic Treaty
Washington D.C. April 4, 1949

Article 5

The Parties agree that an armed attack against one or more of them in Europe or North America shall be considered an attack against them all and consequently they agree that, if such an armed attack occurs, each of them, in exercise of the right of individual or collective self-defence recognised by Article 51 of the Charter of the United Nations, will assist the Party or Parties so attacked by taking forthwith, individually and in concert with other parties, such action as it deems necessary, including the use of armed force, to restore and maintain the security of the North Atlantic area.

Any such armed attack and all measures taken as result thereof shall immediately be reported to the Security Council. Such measures shall be determined when the Security Council has taken the measures necessary to restore and maintain international peace and security.

Treaty of Economic, Social and Cultural Collaboration and Collective Self-Defence, signed at Brussels on March 17, 1948, as amended by 'Protocol Modifying and Completing the Brussels Treaty', signed at Paris on October 23, 1954

Article V

If any of the High Contracting Parties should be the object of an armed attack in Europe, the other High Contracting Parties will, in accordance with the provisions of Article 51 of the Charter of the United Nations, afford the party so attacked all military and other aid and assistance in their power.

B. Crisis management: the "Petersberg tasks"

Petersberg Declaration (Extracts)

II. ON STRENGTHENING WEU'S OPERATIONAL ROLE

4. Apart from contributing to the common defence in accordance with Article 5 of the Washington Treaty and Article V of the modified Brussels Treaty respectively, military units of WEU member states, acting under the authority of WEU, could be employed for:

— humanitarian and rescue tasks;
— peacekeeping tasks;
— tasks of combat forces in crisis management, including peacemaking.

Western European Union
Council of Ministers
Bonn, 19 June 1992

 Appendix VII

Member States of the European Union

	Population (millions)	GDP per head ($)	Troop contribution to crisis management*			
			UN	IFOR Bosnia/ Croatia	Total	No. of troops per 100,000 population
Austria	7.9	22,110	874	286	1,160	14.68
Belgium	10.0	20,880	824	346	1,170	11.70
Denmark	5.1	25,930	160	801	961	18.84
Finland	5.1	22,980	987	373	1,360	26.67
France	57.3	22,300	510	7,957	8,467	14.78
Germany	80.5	22,920	112	3,997	4,109	5.10
Greece	10.4	7,180	18	236	254	2.44
Ireland	3.5	12,100	753	—	753	21.51
Italy	57.8	20,510	82	2,266	2,348	4.06
Luxembourg	0.4	35,260	—	22	22	5.50
Netherlands	15.1	20,590	100	2,092	2,192	14.52
Portugal	9.8	7,450	401	959	1,360	13.88
Spain	39.1	14,020	48	1,785	1,833	4.69
Sweden	8.7	26,780	167	838	1,005	11.55
United Kingdom	57.7	17,760	416	10,482	10,898	18.88

*As of end of May 1996 for UN and July for IFOR Bosnia/Croatia. These figures do not include contributions of civilian police and military personnel assigned to OSCE missions or the European Community Monitor Mission (ECMM) in the former Yugoslavia. The total national contributions may therefore be understated in some cases. For example, during its term as President of the EU Council (July–December 1996) Ireland contributed 79 military personnel to the ECMM.

Sources: The Economist Pocket Europe, 1994
United Nations
NATO

Appendix VIII

Guidelines Adopted at the Franco-German Seminar of Ministers of Foreign Affairs, Freiburg im Breisgau, 27 February 1996

The task of the intergovernmental conference is to strengthen and develop the efficiency of the common foreign and security policy, as established by the Treaty on European Union, so that it can take full account of the European Union's common interest. The envisaged reforms of the CFSP must strengthen its efficacy, consistency, visibility, continuity and solidarity. To this end, at the intergovernmental conference the two ministers of foreign affairs will actively support the following concrete improvements:

1. Greater efficacy

The EU's capacity for action in the external relations and security sphere must be strengthened above all through more efficient decision-making and implementation procedures.

The European Council's power to set guidelines must be strengthened, with the aim of increasing the EU's capacity for action.

The decision-making procedures provided for in the Treaty must be applied and developed with the aim of facilitating the taking of decisions in order to avoid the inflexibility resulting from the need for unanimity.

To this end, the following approaches, which can to an extent be combined, may be considered:

— distinguishing between political decisions of principle and implementing decisions;

— reference in the Treaty to the principle of constructive abstention for the CFSP;

— taking decisions by qualified majority at the implementation stage.

In particular, as regards the implementation of such decisions, no member State can be forced against its will to commit its forces to military and police actions. These member States will not, however, be able to prevent others from implementing measures which have been decided on.

2. Greater consistency

The Council, member States and Commission must make a greater effort to apply the obligation for consistency already stipulated in the Treaty in the interests of an efficacious and credible foreign and security policy. The member States and Commission must actively and unreservedly support the EU's actions once these have been decided on, in a spirit of reciprocal loyalty and solidarity. This means in particular that the Commission must be bound by the Council decision to the same extent as the member States. A procedure will be established to ensure that the Commission draws up in due time the proposals necessitated by Council decisions relating to the CFSP.

In order to ensure the achievement of this consistency, a Forecasting and Analysis Unit must be created. The member States, Commission and WEU Secretariat should make available to this unit, attached to the Council Secretariat, the appropriate staffing resources and give it access to their information. This unit's task is to pool the experience and knowledge of its members and prepare for action.

3. Greater visibility and continuity

The institutions must be adapted so as to allow the European Union to have a clearer identity in its external relations, speak with one voice and enjoy the necessary continuity and visibility.

A new post contributing to greater visibility and consistency for the CFSP should be created.

The above proposals would ensure greater continuity.

4. Greater solidarity, particularly in security and defence matters

In order to strengthen European solidarity, it is vital to continue developing Europe's security and defence identity by achieving the objective outlined by the Treaty on European Union with respect to defence policy. In this context, an important role falls to WEU, both as the Atlantic Alliance's European pillar and the European Union's defence component. Concretely, we envisage the following improvements:

— A political solidarity clause for all member States should be written into the TEU. This solidarity also involves, of course, taking account of each member State's legitimate interests.

— Entrusting the European Council with the task of drawing up the general policy guidelines in the defence and security sphere, on the basis of which WEU, at the request of the European Union, will, on the latter's behalf, be able to carry out actions, including those with respect to the Petersberg tasks.

— The objectives corresponding to the tasks set out in the Petersberg declaration should be written into the TEU.

— Asserting the European Union's role in determining the common European defence policy.

— The European capacity for action must exist even when all the partners cannot contribute military to an operation. The other States' solidarity should in such a case be expressed by political support, where appropriate.

— Our objective remains WEU's eventual inclusion in the European Union. The IGC should produce clear and specific commitments with this in view. To this end, WEU–EU institutional convergence will be enhanced.

Solidarity must be expressed through the modalities for financing the expenditure on operations in the CFSP framework, which should, as a general rule, be met from the Community budget, in accordance with budgetary procedure and respecting the Council's primacy in foreign policy.

A European armaments policy should be developed on the basis of the existing Franco-German initiatives in the framework of the European Union and WEU, with as its goal the strengthening, improvement and rationalisation of European cooperation and the establishment of a European armament agency.

THE BENELUX APPROACH TO THE IGC

MEMORANDUM OF BELGIUM, LUXEMBOURG AND THE NETHERLANDS FOR THE IGC

Introduction

European integration has played a fundamental role in building peace, prosperity and welfare in Europe. The governments of Belgium, the Netherlands and Luxembourg are determined to safeguard the irreversibility of these achievements. To this end, they consider it essential that the process of European integration continue along the path successfully taken hitherto: close co-operation between states that voluntarily pool their sovereignty by transferring powers to common institutions.

Profound changes have taken place in Europe since 1989. The need for further integration has in no way diminished. The EU's responsibility to contribute to European security and stability makes further expansion necessary. And if an enlarged and more heterogeneous European Union is to occupy its rightful future place in the world — the place that is expected of it — there will have to be, as well as deepening and widening, room for differentiation.

It is with this conviction that the three governments will be taking part in the forthcoming IGC and put forward the following proposals to their EU partners.

The Union's external policy

2.4 Coherence of policy

The Union lacks unity in its external affairs. The three countries attach great importance to the coherence of all the Union's external activities given its single institutional framework. In order to ensure the unity of external representation, they endorse the need for the Commission to play a stronger role. It is also necessary to redefine the rules concerning the activities of the Commission and the Council and relations between the two.

Common foreign and security policy

If the European Union is to pursue a credible foreign and security policy both in Europe and throughout the world, the CFSP will have to be strengthened. This is necessary because it is at present clearly ineffective not only as regards formulation and decision-making, but also at the level of implementation.

Formulation of the CFSP

The formulation of a real foreign policy which is forward-looking and enables initiatives to be taken demands adequate instruments at three levels:

— The Commission, which should make full use of its existing right of initiative.

— A Research and Planning Unit should be set up, with participants from the Member States, the Commission, and possibly the WEU Secretariat. This will make it easier for the Member States to exchange and analyse information. Such a pooling of knowledge could strengthen the Union's ability to set common political goals with a view to preparing joint actions. This unit could be headed by a high-ranking official, to be appointed by the Council of Ministers in consultation with the Commission. This Unit could serve the Council and the Commission in an advisory capacity.

— In the field of CFSP, the European Union must be capable of acting quickly and consistently. The capacity of the Member States to conduct consultations between the meetings of the Political Committee must be strengthened by means of a group permanently stationed in Brussels whose activities are conducted in the framework that currently exists to undertake preparations for the Council.

Decision-making in the field of CFSP

The unanimity requirement often paralyses decision-making. Alternatives must be considered. These will have to take account of essential national interests.

Possible alternatives to the principle of unanimity are as follows:

— decision-making by "partial consensus" or by a strengthened qualified majority;

— decision-making by a qualified majority for sectors of the CFSP as yet unspecified; and

— decision-making by qualified majority on proposals made by the Commission.

Implementation of the CFSP

The implementation of the Union's decisions requires the joint deployment of the human and material resources at the disposal of the Union and its Member States. This joint deployment must be entrusted to the Commission or the Presidency on a case-by-case basis:

— The Commission will have to implement joint actions that have to be carried out in the field, or joint actions that are closely connected with the activities of the first pillar.

— The Council and the Commission could designate special representatives charged with implementing specific CFSP decisions. These representatives would report to the Council on their assignments.

— The Presidency — acting in conjunction with the strengthened CFSP Secretariat or with the Commission and the aforementioned special representatives — would implement decisions that mainly require démarches, definitions of positions, diplomatic negotiations, and political dialogue.

Improved implementation also makes it necessary for funding via the Community budget to become the rule. Account must be taken here of the specific nature of the CFSP. There must be agreement between the Council and the European Parliament to allow for flexible budget management.

2.5 Defence: Western European Union/European Union

The scope offered by the Intergovernmental Conference for the European Union to give shape to its own defence identity should be exploited to the full. The mandate for the EU to do so is already enshrined in the Maastricht Treaty. The interweaving of foreign, security and defence policies calls for the development of a Union defence policy. This is essential if the EU is to pursue an external policy that is effective and credible. The WEU's contribution to the IGC provides an excellent basis for negotiations in the IGC.

Real integration of foreign, security and defence policies will only be achieved once the WEU has been incorporated into the second pillar of the EU. This process of integration must be a gradual one. The 1996 IGC could take a decision to do so in principle and work out the time frame for full integration.

Pending the merger of the WEU with the European Union, the three countries favour speedy and very far-reaching institutional convergence between the two organisations in such a way as to enable the Council of the European Union to instruct the WEU to implement the military implications of resolutions taken by the Council within the framework of a Common Foreign and Security Policy.

The second pillar of the EU Treaty should also incorporate the Petersberg tasks and collective defence, on the understanding that implementation of the latter will remain the responsibility of the Atlantic Alliance. In this area the European Union will have to forge specific links with NATO. A strong Atlantic Alliance and a continued US military presence in Europe form the bedrock of a common security and defence policy. At the same time, the European contribution to security and defence in Europe and elsewhere needs to be given greater emphasis as a way of strengthening the European pillar of NATO. The rapid development of the CJTF concept within NATO is essential in order to enable European joint actions with military implications to be undertaken. Such actions must be arrived at transparently and they must complement operations carried out with other allies.

The deployment of armed forces will continue to fall within the competence of individual Member States. The decision-making process to be worked out by the IGC must ensure that no state can be obliged to take part in a military operation, although states that do not wish to participate must not be allowed to prevent others from doing so, nor may they undermine the financial solidarity required for any joint action.

Finally, the three countries feel that the time is ripe for closer European cooperation in matters concerning the arms industry.

Appendix X

The Finnish–Swedish proposal on crisis management

The IGC and the Security and Defence dimension — towards an enhanced EU role in crisis management

Introduction

The following proposal for an IGC action on the security and defence dimension of the European Union is submitted by Finland and Sweden as a contribution using the conceptual groundwork offered in the Reflection Group's Report and the WEU Contribution to the European Union Intergovernmental Conference 1996.

The proposal is based on the need for the European Union to enhance its role and capabilities in conflict management. This requires an appropriate role also in those aspects of conflict management where military organisations are used (military crisis management; Petersberg tasks).

The Union could have a more active security role even under the existing TEU provisions on the EU–WEU relationship. However, an EU role in military crisis management would be both politically and in practice more credible with a reinforced linkage established between the Union and the WEU and with the competence of the Union in this area spelled out in the amended TEU. At the same time, it is not necessary for the Union itself to perform military tasks.

It is also understood that defining and asserting an enhanced crisis management role for the Union would be the most realistic way forward in the area of security and defence policy at the IGC, while respecting the integrity of the WEU.

The enhancement of the role of the Union in crisis management is consistent with the need for regional arrangements to assume a greater responsibility in this area. The proposal is made with due account taken to the primary responsibility of the UN Security Council for international peace and security under the Charter as well as to the necessity to have a UN or an OSCE mandate for peacekeeping and crisis management.

THE EU'S CAPACITY TO ACT IN CRISIS MANAGEMENT

The proposal to provide the European Union with a capacity to act in military crisis management, including the underlying considerations and the steps and decisions needed, is spelled out below.

1. The European Union will have to be able to respond to the real needs of common and comprehensive security in Europe. Through developing its security role and taking IGC decisions in the CFSP area, the Union will reassert its leading position in the political and economic arena and, as a new step, assume the necessary role in military aspects of conflict management.

2. The European Union needs a capacity to act in military crisis management and, therefore, an appropriate competence for taking relevant decisions.

3. The arrangement will have to provide for participation by the EU member-states in joint peacekeeping and crisis management operations, which would be conducted by the WEU, on the basis of equal opportunity for all and full contribution by the willing.

4. Consideration of the Union's role in, and adoption of a common policy line on, military crisis management will take place in the context of the CFSP. Decisions on issues having defence implications will be taken by unanimity in accordance with TEU/J4(3).

5. An enhanced competence for the European Union in conflict management will be created through the revision of TEU/J/4(1) by including humanitarian and rescue operations, peacekeeping and crisis management (Petersberg tasks) into the scope of CFSP as membership tasks. This measure will not in any way prejudice the possibility for the WEU to undertake independent action.

6. Operationalisation of the European Union's competence in military crisis management will take place through the revision of TEU/J.4 (2) by establishing a reinforced institutional link between the Union and the WEU. Preparations for and decisions on carrying out a common crisis management action by the WEU in accordance with TEU/J4(2) will be undertaken on the basis of full equality between all the EU member-states.

7. The outline of a model determining empowerment, implementation and the generation of capability for joint operations is presented below (8).

8. The TEU/J.4 (2) will have to be revised in order to establish a reinforced link between the EU and the WEU regarding the implementation of decisions on military crisis management adopted by the EU within the scope of CFSP (empowerment). All the contributing EU member-states will participate on an equal footing in planning and decision making related to operations enacted by the EU. It is expected that a declaration by the WEU will be adopted to this end (implementation). The EU member-states are encouraged to provide information of their forces available for such EU enacted and WEU conducted operations. No capability will be created within the EU for planning, organising or using military resources (capability).

9. In joint military crisis management, the member-states of the Union will engage resources which are under national and/or common (alliance) authority and jurisdiction for operations decided upon by the Union and implemented by the WEU. When taking such decisions, appropriate consultation will be needed with other international institutions (NATO). Voluntary decisions on committing and contributing forces will take place in accordance with the respective constitutional (e.g. parliamentary approval) and institutional rules (including CJTF).

10. Development of the Union's security and defence dimension will be based on the equal rights and combined interests of the member-states. Mutual reinforcement of the will and capability of all the members will upgrade the role of the Union in conflict management.

11. Steps towards an enhanced competence in the security and defence dimension of the Union will respect the specific character of the defence solutions of the members and will not affect their status as states pursuing independent or common defence. It is understood that cooperation in military crisis management is separable from collective defence commitments.

12. The revised definition of the EU–WEU relationship will be adopted by the IGC. The decision will not prejudice further development of the security and defence dimension of the Union as stipulated in the TEU nor will it be linked with any particular future step. The decision shall not prejudice any future decisions on the CFSP called for by the enlargement of the Union. An enhanced role for the EU in the area of conflict management will strengthen the common security of the members and contribute to co-operative security in Europe as a whole.

Memorandum
25 April 1996
Finland, Sweden

EUROPE 1996

ICELAND
Reykjavik

☐ EU MEMBER STATES

▓ POTENTIAL ACCESSION STATES

▓ OTHERS

IRELAND
• Dublin

UNITED
KINGDOM

London •

F

PORTUGAL

SPAIN
• Madrid

Lisbon

The boundaries shown on this map are not to be taken
as constituting any political claim.

■ GLOSSARY

CDP	Common Defence Policy
CFE	Convention Forces in Europe Treaty
CFSP	Common Foreign and Security Policy
CIS	Commonwealth of Independent States
CJTF	Combined Joint Task Forces
CSBM	Confidence and Security Building Measure
CSCE	Conference on Security and Cooperation in Europe (since December 1994 called OSCE)
EC	European Community
ECMM	European Community Monitor Mission (in former Yugoslavia)
EDC	European Defence Community
EMU	Economic and Monetary Union
EP	European Parliament
EPC	European Political Cooperation
ESP	European Stability Pact
EU	European Union
FAWEU	Forces Answerable to Western European Union
FYROM	Former Yugoslav Republic of Macedonia
IAEA	International Atomic Energy Agency
ICJ	International Court of Justice
IEPG	Independent European Programme Group
IFOR	Implementation Force (in Bosnia)
IGC	Intergovernmental Conference
NACC	North Atlantic Cooperation Council
NPT	Nuclear Non-Proliferation Treaty
PFP	Partnership for Peace
OSCE	Organisation for Security and Cooperation in Europe (formerly CSCE)
SEA	Single European Act
SHAPE	Supreme Headquarters Allied Powers Europe
TEU	Treaty on European Union (Maastricht Treaty)
UN	United Nations
UNHCR	United Nations High Commissioner for Refugees
UNOSOM	United Nations Operations in Somalia
UNPROFOR	United Nations Protection Force
UNSC	United Nations Security Council
WEAG	Western European Armaments Group
WEU	Western European Union
WTO	Warsaw Treaty Organisation

CHRONOLOGY OF THE NEW SECURITY ENVIRONMENT IN EUROPE

1989

19 January	CSCE agrees to negotiate CFE treaty (Vienna)
5 April	Political reform agreed in Poland
2 May	Hungary dismantles "iron curtain" on Austrian border
29–30 May	NATO Summit (Brussels)
3 June	Repression in China (Tiananmen)
16–19 July	Austria applies to join EC
17 July	EC Commission to coordinate economic aspects of east-west relations
Sept–October	Exodus of East Germans via Hungary and Prague
18 October	Political crisis in East Germany: Honecker ousted
9–10 November	Berlin wall opened
28 November	"Velvet revolution" in Czechoslovakia
2–3 December	Bush-Gorbachev Summit (Malta)
11 December	Revolution in Bulgaria
22 December	Revolution in Romania

1990

January	USSR: conflict in Azerbaijan worsens
22 January	End of one party rule in Yugoslavia
12–14 February	"Open skies" conference (Ottawa): agreement on "Two Plus Four" negotiations on Germany
11 March	Lithuanian parliament votes for independence from USSR
30 March	Estonia seeks gradual secession from USSR
28 April	Special European Council (Dublin) endorses German unification
4 May	Latvia seeks secession from USSR
25 June	EC European Council (Dublin) agrees to convene IGC on Political Union
16 July	Kohl-Gorbachev agreement on German unification
2 August	Iraq invades Kuwait: Gulf crisis starts
4 September	WEU agrees guidelines on Gulf crisis
3 October	Germany united
19–21 November	CSCE Summit (Paris): Paris Charter and CFE Treaty
29 November	UNSC Resolution 678 authorises "all necessary means" in the Gulf

15 December — EC European Council (Rome) opens IGCs on EMU and Political Union

1991

January	Crisis in Baltic states
16–17 January	Second Gulf war starts: air strikes against Iraq
24 February	Land battle in Gulf war starts
25 February	Dissolution of Warsaw Pact announced (implemented 1 July)
28 February	Gulf war ends; Kuwait liberated
March	Yugoslav federal crisis worsens
8 April	EC special European Council (Luxembourg): "humanitarian intervention" to protect Kurds in northern Iraq
May	Violence increases in Croatia
6–7 June	NATO foreign ministers (Copenhagen) agree new role for NATO
25 June	Slovenia and Croatia declare independence
28–29 June	EC European Council (Luxembourg): Troika attempts mediation in Yugoslav civil war
1 July	Sweden applies to join EC
18 July	Yugoslav federal army withdraws from Slovenia, concentrates on Croatia
30–31 July	USA-USSR sign START Treaty reducing strategic nuclear weapons
19–21 August	Abortive coup in USSR: Gorbachev restored but discredited
27 August	EC states recognise Baltic states
29 August	Supreme Soviet suspends Communist Party
7 September	EC Conference on Yugoslavia (the Hague)
19 September	WEU declines peacekeeping intervention in Yugoslavia
7–8 November	NATO Summit (Rome) approves New Strategic Concept
17 November	Fall of Vukovar (Croatia)
1 December	Ukraine votes for independence
8 December	Leaders of Russia, Belorussia and Ukraine agree CIS to replace USSR
9–10 December	EC European Council (Maastricht) agrees Treaty on European Union
17 December	EC states compromise on recognition of Croatia and Slovenia
20 December	Inaugural meeting of NACC (North Atlantic Cooperation Council)
25 December	USSR formally voted out of existence

1992

2–15 January	Effective ceasefire in Croatia
15 January	EC states recognise Slovenia, Croatia
30 January	First Summit of UN Security Council members
7 February	Treaty on European Union signed
21 February	UNPROFOR (UN force in Croatia) agreed
28 February	CSCE grows to 48 members
1 March	Referendum in Bosnia endorses independence
18 March	Finland applies to join EC
24 March	CSCE grows to 51 members
4 April	EC states recognise Bosnia: Bosnian war begins
5 April	Conservative government returned in UK elections
2 June	Referendum in Denmark rejects Maastricht Treaty
4 June	NATO ready to support peacekeeping
3–13 June	UN Environment Summit (Rio)
18 June	Referendum in Ireland accepts Maastricht Treaty
19 June	WEU: Petersberg Declaration
9–10 July	CSCE Summit (Helsinki)
10 July	NATO–WEU cooperation on sanctions enforcement in Adriatic
July–August	Bosnia: refugee crisis, detention camps exposed
23 August	Currency crisis begins
26–28 August	UN/EC conference on ex-Yugoslavia
16 September	Currency crisis splits EMS: UK quits
20 September	Referendum in France accepts Maastricht Treaty
22 September	UN General Assembly votes to exclude "rump Yugoslavia" (Serbia and Montenegro)
3 November	USA presidential elections: Clinton defeats Bush
9 November	US-led interim UN intervention in Somalia (UNITAF)
11–12 December	EC European Council (Edinburgh): Denmark's opt-outs, including "defence"

1993

1 January	EC Single Market
	"Velvet divorce" between Czech and Slovak republics
3 January	USA and Russia sign START II Treaty
February	EC enlargement negotiations with Austria, Finland, Sweden begin
12 March	North Korea announces withdrawal from Nuclear Non-proliferation Treaty
28 March	French parliamentary elections: the Right "cohabits" with Mitterrand
5 April	Norway joins EC enlargement negotiations

6 April	WEU patrols Danube on sanction enforcement
8 April	Macedonia joins UN as "FYROM"
20 April	Germany to contribute to UN intervention in Somalia (UNOSOM II)
18 May	Referendum in Denmark accepts Maastricht Treaty
4 June	UN Security Council authorises force to defend "safe areas" in Bosnia
14–25 June	UN World Conference on Human Rights (Vienna)
21–22 June	EC European Council (Copenhagen): opening to the east
29 June	Dail debates Ireland's participation in UNOSOM II
23 July	UK parliament accepts Maastricht Treaty
31 August	Israeli–PLO agreement on Gaza/Jericho
3 October	USA reverses policy on UNOSOM II
4 October	Crisis in Russia: Yeltsin versus Parliament
12 October	German Constitutional Court accepts Maastricht Treaty
1 November	European Union begins
10–11 December	EU European Council (Brussels) agrees first "joint actions" under CFSP, including European Stability Pact
12 December	Elections in Russia: the "Zhirinovsky factor"
15 December	GATT: Uruguay Round agreed

1994

10–11 January	NATO Summit (Brussels): Partnership for Peace (PFP) launch
4 February	UNOSOM II mandates scaled down
9 February	UN–NATO "ultimatum" on Sarajevo: Russian involvement increases
28 February	NATO's first use of force
15 March	EU enlargement negotiations end
7 April	Conflict in Rwanda worsens
10–23 April	NATO strikes during siege of Gorazde
9 May	WEU: "enlargement" (Associate Partners): Finland and Sweden join PFP
26–27 May	European Stability Pact negotiations launched (Paris)
8 June	Partial truce in Bosnia: siege of Sarajevo lifted
12 June	Referendum in Austria accepts EU membership Referendum in Switzerland rejects participation in UN peacekeeping
18 June	France intervenes in Rwanda
24–25 June	EU European Council (Corfu): further enlargement, relations with Russia
July–August	Refugee crisis in Rwanda

31 August	Russian troops leave Germany and Baltic states
	Northern Ireland: IRA ceasefire
5–13 September	UN world conference on population and development (Cairo)
19 September	USA intervenes in Haiti
23 September	UN sanctions on Serbia ease
7 October	Crisis in the Gulf: Iraq backs down
16 October	Referendum in Finland accepts EU membership
	Elections in Germany return Kohl government
8 November	USA mid-term elections: Democrats lose control of Congress
11 November	USA "withdraws" from embargo on Bosnia: divisions among international community increase
13 November	Referendum in Sweden accepts EU membership
14 November	WEU ministers discuss common defence policy (Noordwijk)
mid-November	Tensions between Greece and Turkey on territorial limits
19 November	British–French agreement on joint air command
22 November	NATO strikes fail to lift siege of Bihac
28 November	Referendum in Norway rejects EU membership
1 December	NATO foreign ministers meet on enlargement, Bosnia
5–6 December	CSCE Summit (Budapest)
9–10 December	EU European Council (Essen)
12 December	Russia coerces Chechnya
24 December	Ceasefire in Bosnia
24–26 December	Algerian fundamentalists hijack Air France plane

1995

1 January	CSCE becomes OSCE: EU membership now fifteen
24 January	EU criticism of Russian coercion in Chechnya hardens
7 March	Bosnia agrees military cooperation wlth Croatia
20–21 March	EU Stability Pact agreed (Paris)
17 April	NPT Review Conference begins (New York)
1 May	Croatian army recovers western Slavonia
7 May	Jacques Chirac President of France
8–11 May	VE-50 commemorations: USA–Russian summit (Moscow)
11 May	Nuclear Non-Proliferation Treaty extended indefinitely
15 May	WEU Council of Ministers (Lisbon)
25 May	NATO limited air strike on Pale
26 May–18 June	Bosnian-Serbs hold UN hostages: France, UK to reinforce military capabilities
2 June	EU Reflection Group to prepare IGC

13 June	France announces resumption of nuclear testing
16–17 June	G7 summit (Halifax)
26–27 June	European Council (Cannes)
30 June	Bundestag approves air deployment in Bosnia
1 July	Carl Bildt replaces David Owen as EU mediator
11 July	Bosnian-Serbs take UN "safe area" (Srebrenica)
21 July	UNPROFOR contributors' conference (London)
3–6 August	Croatian army recovers Krajina
16 August	Chinese nuclear test: terrorist bomb in Paris
28 August	Bomb in Sarajevo kills 37
30 August–	
1 September	NATO starts major air strikes
5–14 September	NATO air strikes resumed: Bosnian-Serbs lose territory
5 September	France's first nuclear test in new series
10 September	EU foreign ministers divided on French tests
mid-September–	
mid-October	Shuttle diplomacy on Bosnia
18–19 September	OSCE seminar on security model (Vienna)
22–23 September	Informal EU summit (Spain)
1 October	France's second nuclear test
11–12 October	General ceasefire in Bosnia
22–23 October	Special summit to commemorate UN 50
27 October	France's third nuclear test
1 November	Bosnian peace talks start (Dayton, Ohio)
4 November	Israeli premier, Yitzhak Rabin, assassinated
14 November	WEU Council of Ministers (Madrid)
21 November	Dayton Agreement
21 November	France's fourth nuclear test
27–28 November	EU–Mediterranean Conference (Barcelona)
3 December	EU–USA Transatlantic Declaration (Madrid)
5 December	France to increase participation in NATO
5 December	Reflection Group report on the EU IGC
8 December	Bosnian Peace Implementation Conference (London)
14 December	Dayton Agreement signed in Paris
15–16 December	European Council (Madrid)
17 December	Parliamentary elections in Russia
20 December	IFOR replaces UNPROFOR in Bosnia
27 December	France's fifth nuclear test

1996

9–17 January	Chechen rebels provoke hostage crisis
25 January	Russian membership of Council of Europe approved

27 January	France's sixth and last nuclear test
30 January	Tension between Greece and Turkey on territorial limits
8–18 February	Bosnia: tension re war crimes, Mostar
9 February	Northern Ireland: IRA ends ceasefire
23 February	President Chirac announces defence policy reforms
late February	Hamas bombs threaten Arab–Israeli peace process
29 February– 1 March	EU–ASEAN summit (Bangkok)
13 March	Middle East "peacemakers' summit", Egypt
13–24 March	China pressures Taiwan
19 March	Reintegration of Sarajevo
25 March	France, UK, USA sign South Pacific Nuclear Free Zone Treaty
26 March	Irish White Paper on foreign policy
29 March	EU Intergovernmental Conference (IGC) opens in Turin
11–27 April	Israel mounts "Operation Grapes of Wrath" in southern Lebanon
18 April	Massacre at UNIFIL post at Qana
21 April	G7 summit on nuclear safety (Moscow)
25 April	Finnish–Swedish initiative on crisis management (IGC) Andorra becomes 55th member of OSCE
3 May	Agreement on landmines (UN, Geneva)
7 May	WEU Council of Ministers (Birmingham)
27 May	Chechnya ceasefire agreed
31 May	Benjamin Netanyahu (Likud) wins Israeli election CFE review agreed
3 June	NATO foreign ministers agree reforms (Berlin)
10 June	Slovenia-EU Europe Agreement
10 June	Formal negotiations open in Northern Ireland
13–14 June	Bosnia implementation conference, Florence
15 June	IRA bomb in Manchester
16 June	First round of Russian presidential election
21–22 June	European Council (Florence)
25 June	19 US soldiers killed in Saudi Arabia
27–29 June	G7 summit, Lyons
30 June	Elections in Mostar
1 July	Irish Presidency of EU begins
3 July	Yeltsin elected President of Russia Chechnya ceasefire breaks down
8 July	International Court of Justice ruling on nuclear weapons
25 July	Coup in Burundi
29 July	China ends nuclear tests
11 August	Tension in Cyprus

14 August	Draft CTBT
22 August	Renewed ceasefire in Chechnya
27 August	OSCE postpones municipal elections in Bosnia
31 August	Iraq attacks Kurdish enclave

● INDEX